I first heard Mark Ongl   n
twenty years ago. We were se   a
Conference of the United M   e
of the more challenging subj   l
a deep desire to find a way   s

MW00425342

redeeming and reconciling lo.. ..... persons locked in various kinds of sin and
brokenness—especially in the area of sexuality. He spoke with grace and resolve.
He always speaks with grace and resolve.

Into the Light: Healing Sexuality in Today's Church is the product of nearly
twenty years of Mark's journey to minister grace and truth in our culture's most
difficult conversation. He is, at heart, a person deeply in love with Jesus and in love
with the people Jesus loves. He writes as a pastor sharing out of his own experience
and study. He speaks with the authority of one who has dared to name sin while
announcing grace in the midst of deep and caring relationships. His words are
direct and simple to understand so that the energy of the reader can be spent
discerning how they might be applied in their lives and contexts.

In a culture and a church that seems to be lost when it comes to God's best for
the human sexual experience, *Into the Light* is a ray of hope. God's Word is true. The
Holy Spirit is working. God's grace is real. Jesus is who he said he is—and does what
he says he will do. And in these pages, Mark gives practical and hopeful advice
about how the average pastor and follower of Jesus can be a part of what God is
doing in his church and our world.

Jeff Greenway
Lead Pastor, Reynoldsburg United Methodist Church
Former President, Asbury Theological Seminary

This book bears the stamp of Mark Ongley's blessed gift of balancing genuine
compassion for the sexually broken, a biblical conviction about the susceptibility of
our sexuality to profound sinfulness, and the courage to address this delicate topic
with candor and clarity that can lead to genuine healing and hope.

Eric Leonard
Park United Methodist Church
North East, Pennsylvania

Standing firmly with one foot in the Wesleyan tradition and another in frontline
ministry, Mark Ongley has a heart for the hurting and the lost. His new book
successfully cuts through the confusion of contemporary culture in order to offer
the church a distinctly "Jesus way" to think about the difficulties surrounding
conversations of sexuality and sexual behaviors and, more important, to minister
to those wrestling with those issues. This book is a gift to all who take seriously
ministry to the hurting in our broken world.

Keith H. Mcilwain
Pastor of Slippery Rock United Methodist Church
Slippery Rock, Pennsylvania

In today's society where the abuse, misuse, and misunderstanding of human sexuality often leads to inner-brokenness, shame, and disillusionment, it is vital that we forge an ethos and personal belief about sexuality that is congruent with our faith and Christian core values. In this masterfully written work, Dr. Mark Ongley candidly discusses the pertinent and sometimes controversial issues of sexuality from a biblical perspective that is relevant and highly informative. Mark's treatment of perhaps the most precious gift given to humanity is balanced, thorough, truthful, loving, and healing. *Into The Light* is a must-read for Christians and non-Christians alike.

Benjamin Franklin Jr.
Senior Pastor, Inner Healing Ministries Church
Adjunct Professor, Ashland Theological Seminary Ashland
Faculty Member, The McCreary Institute for African American Religious
Studies Cleveland, Ohio

I have observed the excellent fruit of Mark Ongley's ministry in the lives of those he has counseled. This much-needed book offers hope for healing the sexual brokenness that stalks every segment of society and the church.

Steve Cordle
Author of *The Church in Many Houses*
Founding and Senior Pastor, Crossroads Church
Pittsburgh, Pennsylvania

Dr. Mark Ongley skillfully and carefully uncovers the sexuality elephant in the middle of our churches. While many would focus myopically on a particular dysfunction or sin, Dr. Ongley demonstrates that the challenges facing the church are more complex. Using Scripture, personal anecdotes, and his years of experience as a healer and counselor, Dr. Ongley encourages readers to walk with God on the path to recovery and wholeness. Those fatigued by the often-vitriolic responses to the changing perceptions of sexuality in our society will find in Dr. Ongley a pastoral heart and voice.

John Byron
Professor of New Testament
Ashland Theological Seminary

Mark Ongley has wrestled with the issues of human sexuality in his ministry, in counseling, and now in written form. *Into the Light* is a must-read for us in the church, a work for us to discern and pray over. We live in time when the church is being bombarded by so many views. Mark helps us focus in on the view of God. I highly recommend opening our hearts to his work and letting God use this to keep us focused in our ministry and the work of the church in an ever-changing world.

Rod Smith
Chippewa United Methodist Church
Beaver Falls, Pennsylvania

When it comes to addressing issues of sexuality the postmodern church has been silent, and part of the end result of this silence has been that "Everyone does what is right in their own eyes." A direct result of this silence is that it has provided a breeding ground for sexual sin and sexual abuse. *Into the Light: Healing Sexuality in Today's Church* dares to bring the issues of sexuality and sexual abuse to the forefront of the discussions that often start around the issue of homosexuality. While homosexuality has often been the scapegoat of any discussion on sexuality, Mark uses it as an entry point to discuss the real issues of sexual abuse and the need for healing. Mark provides the reader with enough information on the causes of sexual immorality and explains how the structures of inner healing may be used to bring healing and restoration. I fully endorse this book as a resource to equip anyone who is interested in sitting down at the table and beginning to discuss solutions for reversing the silence and bringing light to the issue of sexual abuse.

Thomas W. Gilmore
Coordinator of Education
Ashland Theological Seminary, Cleveland Campus

Dr. Ongley brings his many years of experience ministering to wounded men and women to bear on an issue that needs to be brought into the light—sexual brokenness in its multiple forms. Acknowledging the emotive, even divisive nature of this topic, he lovingly invites the reader into a thoughtful conversation rather than a debate. He offers healing to the abused, insight to the befuddled, and wisdom to those who would love to tackle this difficult issue in the church together. This book feels like a means of grace and provides a vision of wholeness and holiness for all God's children.

Paul W. Chilcote
Professor of Historical Theology and Wesleyan Studies
Ashland Theological Seminary

The topic of homosexuality and the church has been studied and debated so much recently, one might suspect there is little left to be said and that the discussion, where it stands today, has proverbially "generated more heat than light." Pastor Mark Ongley's book, *Into the Light,* significantly moves the topic forward by firmly situating the issue of homosexuality within the totality of the church's teaching on all sexual matters. Deftly using the metaphor of the church addressing homosexuality as a dysfunctional family might address alcoholism in its midst with enabling and scapegoating, Pastor Ongley examines human sexuality by building a thorough, logical structure for explicating the Christian theology of sex that succeeds in being both compassionate and faithful to Holy Scripture. Readers of *Into the Light* will be enlightened by the biblical wisdom and inspired by the personal experiences recounted. The author has a pastor's heart and a gift for using evocative images to relay complex ideas. Reading this book will be blessing for the laity and pastors.

Eric Ash
Mt. Olive Lutheran Church, Missouri Synod

Mark Ongley has a pastor's heart for healing the brokenhearted, especially those who are sexually broken. His deepest desire in this marvelous book is to equip churches to minister with integrity to people with sexual brokenness. He calls us to address these serious issues with authority and hope. Given the relative inattentiveness of the church to these issues today, this book is a must-read for every pastor serving people today.

Michael Mahoney
St. Paul Catholic Church and Gates Ministry
New Bern, North Carolina

The issues of sexual trauma and recovery have long been ignored by the church at large and remain steeped in darkness. As such, could there be a better title for Mark Ongley's thorough and balanced work than *Into the Light*?

I first met Mark Ongley more than ten years ago when he was a student in the doctoral class (Impact of Sexual Trauma and Recovery) that I was guest teaching at Ashland Seminary.

Even then Mark's insight, thoughtfulness, and inquisitiveness stood out. Since that time we have presented at conferences together, held weekend retreats, and always without exception I have seen God use him to bring reason and compassion into this arena so misunderstood by the church at large. I have used his materials often with my own clients in their recovery. Their comments tell me they felt "understood, validated, and not judged." Most of all his words offered hope for healing and change. If you are struggling in any of these areas, this book can set you on the right path and quite possibly get the church itself back on track to become the refuge of recovery it was designed to be. I do not feel I am being dramatic or overstating its impact when I say this book can change your life.

It is not just a book to read but is laid out like a workbook. It's designed to bring into awareness new levels of insight—for one to ponder, pray over—and then suggests concrete steps to take next.

I am both blessed and humbled to say that over the years Mark's and my relationship has developed in to a deep and lasting friendship. There are few I admire more in my field or to whom I turn to for advice, prayer, and encouragement along the way.

With some small measure of pride I can truly say: the student has surpassed the teacher.

Victoria Kepler Didato, MA, LPC, LSW, DAPA
Director Child Sexual Abuse Institute of Ohio
Author, *Treatment Issues for Sexual Abuse Survivors and Offenders*
and *One in Four*

INTO THE
Light

HEALING
SEXUALITY
IN TODAY'S
CHURCH

Mark Ongley

 Seedbed

Printed in the United States of America

Paperback ISBN: 978-1-62824-315-4
Mobi ISBN: 978-1-62824-316-1
ePub ISBN: 978-1-62824-317-8
uPDF ISBN: 978-1-62824-318-5

Library of Congress Control Number: 2016945298

Cover design by Strange Last Name
Page design by PerfecType, Nashville, Tennessee

SEEDBED PUBLISHING
Franklin, Tennessee
Seedbed.com

To Lauri.
Thank you for chasing dreams with me.

CONTENTS

FOREWORD

It was June 2015, the second day of a four-day seminar I was leading on emotional healing. There were, as often is the case, more than one hundred people in the room—pastors, physicians, counselors, and caregivers wanting to learn more about Christ-centered counseling and emotional healing. I was teaching on the nature and cause of dysfunctional behaviors in a person's life. I had taught this four-day seminar on emotional healing at least fifty times before, and at least fifty times before I heard the same question that was asked that day.

"Terry, what is your position on homosexuality?" The question, sooner or later, always comes. The person asking seldom, if ever, is wanting to learn something about the topic of homosexuality. It is, instead, a litmus test, an effort to see if I stand where they do on this increasingly controversial topic. The majority of people asking that question are looking for the one-sentence sound bite that will determine whether they will be open to anything else I might have to say on emotional healing, or write me off as a heretic.

Each time the question is asked the tension and anxiety level in the room immediately increases. Some people are anticipating a potential disagreement and debate, possibly even an argument. That makes them nervous. Others are feeling uncomfortable that this may open the discussion up to the broader, and I might add, more important conversation about sexual abuse and dysfunction. Most people want to keep a lid on that emotional tsunami. Eye contact often ceases and people lower their heads, hoping it will all pass quickly and not get personal. Yet the topic of sexuality is always personal, invariably emotionally charged, and desperately needs to be brought out of the closet and into open discussion, especially in the church.

I met Mark Ongley in the fall of 2001. He was taking a doctoral course I was teaching, one of several students wanting to learn more about ministry, leadership, and the transforming power of Christ. As I often do, I spent some time praying over the men and women in the class, asking the Lord to shape a word that was specifically for them.

I didn't know Mark well. Yet I sensed that the Lord was about to do a deep work in his life, and that he would soon be moving into some unknown, yet very important territory for ministry. And so I said out loud what I sensed the Lord was speaking in my heart. "Mark, I am not sure if this fits or not. You decide. But I sense the Lord telling me that you have been a preacher and a teacher. Now you are a healer."

Mark soon switched tracks on his doctoral program and began to study in the formational counseling program I developed. The curriculum focuses on the intersection of Christian counseling, spiritual direction, and emotional healing. For four years Mark made this the focal point of his education. Simultaneously, the Lord was opening Mark to a new and very much unanticipated specialty: ministering to men and women wounded and abused by sexual brokenness. Much like Jesus, people began to seek Mark out "by night," looking for someone who would tenderly and confidentially position them for the transforming touch of Jesus Christ.

Soon, because of his anointing, gifting, and increased understanding of sexual brokenness, Mark became a sought-after caregiver and teacher around the issues of sexual understanding and health. This book, *Into the Light: Healing Sexuality in Today's Church,* represents the depth and breadth of Mark's ministry around this topic.

This book is, in truth, a perfect reflection of the DNA of Mark Ongley. Mark treats the topic of sexuality with:

- **Gentleness.** There is no pushing or shoving found in these pages. Instead, the reader is invited into a loving conversation around a controversial subject.
- **Compassion.** This book is written from the perspective of a wounded healer. There is a deep empathy toward the reader's own story, a subjective engagement that welcomes the reader to walk with Jesus on a journey of understanding and transformation.
- **Clarity.** The topic of sexuality is huge, complex, and multifaceted, and most certainly not without emotional engagement. Yet with that being said, the reader will find a well-marked path with the wisdom of a gifted and trustworthy guide and simple-yet-profound illustrations that open the reader to new levels of understanding.
- **Research.** Mark has written a book that includes some of the best available research on the topic of sexuality. He has integrated insights from theologians, practitioners, behavioral scientists, and wounded healers. This book is far from myopic, instead pulling together divergent disciplines into a well-developed resource.
- **Biblical Insight.** *Into the Light* is rooted and grounded in the Word. It is biblical in the very best sense, opening the reader to a full-orbed understanding of what Scripture presents about this topic of sexuality. It is faithful to the teachings of the Bible, all the while inviting the reader into a grace-filled encounter with Christ.
- **Transformational Principles.** This book, so much like Mark Ongley, will sneak up on the reader in ways that bring deep and lasting change. It will position the reader for transformational engagements with the Lord—many subtle, others quite revolutionary.

This resource is a treasure, in the way it is written and in the content it contains. It holds value for the person on a journey to wholeness as well as for any caregiver wanting to help people encounter the healing power and freedom available through Jesus Christ. I could not recommend it more!

Terry Wardle
Professor of Practical Theology
Ashland Theological Seminary

ACKNOWLEDGMENTS

From everyone to whom much has been given, much will be required . . ." (Luke 12:48). Each time I happen upon this verse, I sigh. So very much has been given to me! God has blessed me with a rich heritage, a wonderful upbringing by godly parents, and a thorough education. It is difficult to imagine myself writing a book without these distinct advantages afforded to me by the grace of God.

A trail of teachers shaped, instructed, and encouraged me, but Stephen Hemenway was the one who inspired me to be a writer. And without the teaching, training, and mentoring of Terry Wardle, I would have so very much less to write about. His mark upon my life is indelible.

Ashes to Life Ministries, the church I am so privileged to pastor, has been gracious and supportive when writing deadlines have swamped my schedule. And over the years numerous friends have prayed much for this book to be written: Wayne Ten Roberts, Vicky Didato, and Don Blystone especially stand out. Heather Escontrias and Eric Leonard read over parts of the book, offering advice and encouragement.

Getting the attention of a publisher was like trying to flag down an airliner. They never circled back for a second look. How very grateful I am God booked my flight with Seedbed Publishing. From takeoff to landing, Andrew Miller and his team have graciously guided me through the process, lavishing encouragement all along the way.

As for the many victims of sexual abuse that God has led my way, how grateful I am that they allowed me into the delicate memories of their past. Their stories have changed me and have brought an edgy realism to this book. Their names, however, have been changed for privacy's sake.

My family is my treasure. Thank you, Lauri, for sharing your life and love. Thanks also to Sarah and Ruth for helping me to not take myself so seriously!

Yes, much will be required from one so richly blessed. Who is equal to paying such a debt? But thanks be to God. Where sin abounds, his grace much more abounds!

INTRODUCTION

Shame keeps people in the closet. And yet true healing for our deepest issues is found most readily when our sorrows and scars come out into the light.

When my daughters were ages eight and three, we were inside the house playing hide-and-seek. I counted out loud as they ran to hide. The younger one kept saying, "Sarah! Sarah!" And I could hear the exasperation of the older one: "Stop following me, Ruth! Find your own place to hide!" Despite the loud countdown, their chatter made their hiding place quite obvious.

Walking into the bedroom, I played dumb. "Where are those girls? I thought they came into this bedroom!"

The youngest cried out, "We're in the closet!"

"Ruthie, be quiet!" soon followed.

Eventually they both came out to warm hugs from Dad.

I think that is a wonderful picture of each of us. We have things hidden in our closet that we hope to God no one ever finds. And yet there's still a small part of us that calls out, "I'm here in the closet!" We want to be found, accepted, and embraced, no matter what the closet holds. Few of us will step out, however, unless we know the Father's arms will fully welcome us.

And isn't this also true of the church? Parading about in our Sunday best, few would guess what clutters the closets within us. Some of our stuff, no doubt, has spilled out in proper places. But the darkest corners within usually hide our sexual secrets and sorrows. Few would even dare crack open their door within the local church.

Statistics tell us church closets are little different than those found elsewhere. Diana Russell's landmark work on incest found the prevalence among religious families differed little from secular ones, with only Jewish families faring slightly better.[1] Thus when you look around the pews on a Sunday morning, you can safely assume that incest of one form or another has happened in about 10 percent of the homes. Likely 30 percent or more of the women seated on a Sunday have been sexually abused. And with the advent of Internet porn and social media, the number of those involved with porn, emotional adultery, and sexual addiction is continuing to grow.

But again, the *last* place many would open their closet door is among God's people. We can barely talk about the subject of sex unless, of course, we are arguing or fretting about homosexuality.

Hence, the purpose of this book is to serve as a key and a flashlight to begin calling forth the little children who long to be embraced. Whether the context is a Sunday school class, Bible study, women's group, or men's breakfast, the purpose is to begin a biblically grounded and theologically informed discussion of this beautiful gift of sexuality. Discussion questions close each chapter to help move the conversation in a profitable and wholesome direction.

The layout of the book may seem strange. Typically a book on a subject such as this begins with a theological section and ends with a practical application of the principles. But that simply won't work with closet cleaning. The issues of sexuality are so delicate and, for some, so painful that a group can't launch into a thirteen-week discussion of sexual brokenness without having some time to stick their heads out of the closet to catch some fresh air.

And so what you will find are three-week cycles: principles, theology, and applications. This cycle gradually moves you through the material. The principles ought to become part of the language and DNA of your church. Elephants and Scapegoats; the Box, Path, and Circus; and talking of one's monkeys can become the frame-work for a safe discussion on all things sexual. Cycle by cycle, you will also establish a theology of sexuality that will bring balance to thorny issues such as homosexuality. Practical suggestions for how to help people process the delicate issues of abuse, addiction, aversion, adultery, and same-sex attraction will provide a way of welcoming people to crack open the doors of shame and to slowly step out into the light.

As for homosexuality, some of you may have already flipped to that chapter to see where I stand. After all, when we speak of coming out of the closet, we typically call to mind yet another singer, actor, or athlete who has identified themselves as gay or lesbian. While special attention is given to that subject at the end of the book, I have refused to make it a dominant theme because there are so many other sexual issues in the closet besides same-sex attraction. In fact, it is our fixation upon that one issue that has so fractured and fissured our culture and church. The truth is, however, we all have some brokenness to own.

So, yes, I hold to the traditional view of same-sex attraction and you will find a reasoned explanation as to why I hold that view. The chapters on theology build a case for God's design being hetero-sexual, monogamous, and covenantal. But homosexuality is not the only issue for which we need to develop a theology of sexuality. Christian couples are bringing pornography into their bedrooms to create more zing. Is that okay? Several of my counselees have defended their frequenting of nudist colonies. Does the Garden of Eden really give them a pass on this? The fictional series *Fifty Shades of Grey* has attempted to normalize the Bondage Dominance Submission Masochism (BDSM) movement to the degree that one counselee asked me, "Where does the Bible even address this?" And, believe it or not, polygamy is making a comeback. When the Supreme Court struck down the Defense of Marriage Act, which defined marriage as being between one man and one woman, pro-polygamists began taking their issue to the courts. For all of these reasons and more, we need a warm and robust theology to guide us in this increasingly disoriented and sex-crazed culture.

So if you believe differently on this one issue of homosexuality, don't discard this book. There is *so much more* for us to consider about the pervasive brokenness within each congregation. We desperately need to broaden the conversation!

As you begin to work through this material, a word of caution: because closet matters are so delicate, they sometimes create a lot of pain when brought into the light. Yes, this book provides some details on how to minister to those with deep brokenness, but you should already have in mind people with expertise who can step in if necessary. Is there a faith-based counselor who can be called upon? What resources might be in your area? Included at the end of this book is a list of print resources that contains possible places to turn.

As mentioned earlier, I have counseled someone involved in BDSM. No, this isn't a person who parades in Goth makeup and leather pants. In fact, she might be sitting beside you this Sunday in church!

Even though being tied up and mildly tortured may seem twisted, she finds that her BDSM sessions meet some very deep longings in her heart. Stripping off her clothes and allowing them to tie her to the table has actually made her feel more comfortable with her body. And those who participate with her have become her closest friends. They value and affirm her more than anyone in her church ever has. As an example, for her birthday they threw an amazing party. The church folks? Not even a card.

She feels trapped, however. If she turns from this activity, as she knows God wants her to do, who will help her bear the loss? Who will provide the care, affirmation, and support that is lavished upon her by her BDSM friends? She has already reached out to several Christians, asking that they simply walk with her through this time and prayerfully encourage her as she attempts to get free. They have pretty much shrugged their shoulders, saying, "I have no idea how to help you. Find a counselor!"

The suffering of sexual brokenness is best endured when people know our story and share the painful journey toward healing. But before we start the storytelling, we need to know it is safe to come out of the closet. My prayer is that this book will equip the church to be the loving arms of the Father, welcoming his children into his healing light.

INTO THE
Light

The Bare Essentials

CHAPTER 1

PRINCIPLE:
The Elephant and the Scapegoat

Can it get any worse? Local congregations and entire denominations are fracturing over the issue of homosexuality. Anger abounds. A seismic shift in popular opinion has recently shaken the cultural landscape as the Supreme Court has ruled that states can no longer ban gay marriage. Stinging testimonies of gays and lesbians wounded by the church spur some to cry out, "Injustice!" And those who hold to the traditional view of homosexuality are increasingly seen as hand-wringing relics from a Puritanical past, clinging to a misinformed view of sexuality.

Yes, I believe it can get worse—but it can also eventually get better. That is my hope. The path forward begins by learning to aim at the true enemy. At present, it seems we are aiming at one another and shooting our wounded. A look at World War II history will illustrate what I mean.

Not-So-Friendly Fire

D-Day, Battle of the Bulge, Pearl Harbor, Midway, Iwo Jima, Nagasaki, and Hiroshima—for many of us as Americans, there are images and emotions attached to each of these World War II references. And yet that worldwide war had another front just as desperate and difficult. Chiang Kai-shek, commander of the Nationalist Army of China, was continually faced with a dilemma. Should he focus his resources on defeating the cancerous Communist forces led by Mao Zedong? Or should he actually join the efforts of Mao's Red Army in defeating the marauding masses of the Japanese invaders? Seeing Communism as the greater long-term threat, he spent most of his efforts fighting his fellow Chinese. In the end, this led to disaster and exile.

Mao's efforts, however, won over the hearts of the people as he tore into the Japanese while at the same time exchanging blows with Chiang's forces. As the people sided with Mao, Communism took over the land. The Nationalist government had to leave the mainland and fortify the island of Taiwan, where to this day it has remained isolated and ineffective. And while Americans are more at one ideologically with Chiang and the Nationalists, we have come to realize Chiang's choice destined him to defeat, exile, and great ruin. Focusing efforts on the wrong foe was calamitous. The lesson for us? Choosing war with the wrong party can lead to disaster and division.

Denominational church families have been doing much the same as we have debated the issue of homosexuality for forty years. We have had a war waging among us that is repulsive to the younger generation and is sapping the life out of the church in general. In my own corner of the kingdom, this caustic debate dominates center stage within the United Methodist Church. Despite the many admirable accomplishments and pronouncements at our legislative assemblies, the eye-catching headlines flashed by the media are always related to the war of words over homosexuality. Could it be, like Chiang Kai-shek, we have become locked in battle with the wrong ideological foe? And are we also heading for disaster and division?

David Kinnaman and Gabe Lyons served the kingdom well by publishing *unChristian: What a New Generation Really Thinks about Christianity . . . and Why It Matters.* Since the 1990s, church leaders have bemoaned the fact that young adults are *staying away* from church in droves. Kinnaman, president of the Barna Group, set about the task of discovering why. What are the perceptions this generation has of the church—the very church in which many of them have been raised? While the entire study is instructive, one finding should rock our world: the number-one perception of this unchurched generation is that the church is "anti-homosexual."[1]

For those of us who love the church and know all of the work we have done to help the poor and alleviate suffering, that one finding is shocking. Anti-homosexual? That's the foremost impression the church has made? Of course there are many reasons for this perception, which go far beyond the bounds of any one denomination. Doubtless at the top of the list are the cantankerous and disgusting protests staged by Westboro Baptist Church that cry out that God hates homosexuals. We could also include the pronouncements by high-profile figures that HIV is a punishment from God, or that Hurricane Katrina was an act of God's wrath because of homosexuality. But certainly the broader contribution to this distorted image are the denominational clashes of ideological titans who wrangle over position statements, posture with disruptive protests, and celebrate over vote tallies.

We who are Evangelicals are quick to quote Jude 3, declaring that we are contending "for the faith that was once for all entrusted to the saints." Our Social Justice brothers and sisters are equally convinced they are proclaiming "release to the captives . . . to let the oppressed go free" (Luke 4:18). Back and forth we wrangle and wrestle while a common foe devastates the cultural landscape.

Finding our way out of the mess we're in will become clearer when we retrace our steps on the path we've tread, discovering who this common foe actually is. Allow me to illustrate with a parable.

Tough Times for the Tifflebaums

Once upon a time there lived a family in great distress called the Tifflebaums. Not the distress that follows a crisis, but the type that accompanies the ongoing agitation of having an alcoholic parent. Lex Tifflebaum had made countless resolutions and sundry half-hearted attempts, but continued to fall into mindless stupors that complicated life for all in the Tifflebaum house.

For the onlooker, it might appear that no one paid for Lex's lapses quite like his wife, Tiffany. When Lex was smashed he often became abusive, but Tiffany made sure his outrage and antics were confined to the bedroom—not that it kept it from the kids, really. All three knew well the weekly scenario. It had played out more times than they could even begin to count. Returning home well after supper, Dad's shouting would begin at the door. Mom would walk him to the bedroom, shushing him all the way. The door would close softly, but the shouting would soon begin full force. The kids had learned to comfort each other, leaning mostly on Biff, the oldest brother. He had taken upon himself the role of parent—finding the snacks, making sure homework got done, turning up the TV to drown out the racket, and making sure everyone stayed in line until the bickering subsided and Mom was able to return. Rarely did they talk about Dad or his issue with the bottle. There was an unofficial "no-talk rule." Actually there was a "no-feel rule" as well; they could not express themselves in any manner. On the rare occasion when the kids spoke up, Tiffany was quick to relate the latest promise from their dad that this would not happen again.

Money was tight for the Tifflebaums. Frequently Lex would miss work or arrive late, but Tiffany did her best to cover for him, calling in to report he was "sick" or out for a doctor visit. Nonetheless, she could not keep him from losing job after job, with the household income usually sliding downhill. As the kids grew older, Tiffany took on work outside the home, handing chores over to the eldest. Biff rose to the occasion, taking charge of his younger siblings and even consoling his mom from time to time. Though barely twelve, he was the little man of the house.

As time went on, and Lex's lapses continued to take them lower, the younger kids also found their way of dealing with life in the Tifflebaum house. The youngest was Marsha, who felt lost in the shuffle. She began to retreat into video games, TV dramas, and Internet chats. Friends were few and she rarely saw them face-to-face. And certainly she would never have anyone over to the house.

Teddy, the middle child, feeling quite left out, sought for attention by a different route. Though in the end it would bring much pain, he knew his mom would rescue him. Sometimes his behavior at school forced her to leave work early to meet him in the principal's office. Whether it was fights with the kids or spats with the teachers, a regular cycle began to unfold month by month. Teddy's grades began to tank as year by year he barely squeaked by. In seventh grade, to Tiffany's horror, a plastic baggie of marijuana was found in his backpack. While she tried to put the best face on the discovery by making him promise to never use any drugs ever again, the rest of the family would not let it slide.

Marsha emerged from her shell long enough to scorch him with scolding. *Didn't he realize Mom had enough trouble without him adding to her stress?* Dad piped in with a stiff warning of painful punishment should it ever happen again. But no one was more belligerent than Biff; he was irate. Had Teddy only heeded his warnings and followed his example, this would never have happened. Punishment was most certainly called for, and if Mom and Dad did not oblige, he would be happy to step in. *If the baggie had been discovered at the school, what shame he would have brought on the family! They had plenty of problems without him stirring up such trouble.*

While in other families such a scene may have been sufficient to correct the straying one, this was not the case with Teddy Tifflebaum. His grades sank lower and he began running with the wrong crowd. When Teddy's best buddy was arrested for vandalism, brother Biff sounded the alarm. Something needed to be done! It was just a matter of time before Teddy would find himself with a record.

While Tiffany assured the family that Teddy had promised to try harder, Dad sided with Biff. Boot camp for bad boys might be an option, or maybe a counselor could straighten him out. The latter was more convenient, and so became the agreed-upon course of action.

The counselor was quick to see what is likely already plain to you, the reader. The real problem in the family was Lex, not Teddy. The unreformed alcoholic dad, whose behavior had been enabled by the rescuing mom, had set in motion dynamics typical for this kind of dysfunctional family. With no one providing parental care, Biff was forced to grow up early and to take on that role. And as is typical for the youngest child, Marsha was lost in the morass and found dysfunctional ways of escaping the pain. Then arose the "scapegoat," as is usually the case. Finding little nurturing coming his way, Teddy decided painful attention was better than none at all, and so began to get in trouble.

At this point, Biff assumed the role of hero, seeing the misbehavior in black-and-white terms. He was quick to channel the family anger toward the wayward sibling, calling for swift action to save the day. And yet all this time the "elephant in the room," that is, the alcoholic dad, was spared the consequences of his errant behavior.

Unpacking the Parable

Organizations, corporations, and yes, even denominations, can adopt similar patterns of relating. Robert Kuyper once identified this dynamic within his own denomination, stating that the "scapegoat" for decades has been homosexuality. Like Biff, the eldest child, Evangelicals have taken up the role of hero and enforcer. Seeing the issue in black-and-white terms, they have largely blamed the Scapegoat for the problems in the denominational family and culture at large. While certainly meaning well, they have unwittingly wounded scores of believers who either struggle with same-sex attraction or love someone who does. Those from the Social Justice arm of the church have worn the mantle of the rescuing mother. Having long believed that homosexuals have been treated unjustly, they have rushed to their defense with fervor. Casting the issue as a civil rights matter, they have advocated vigorously for the ordination and marriage of homosexuals within the church.[2]

But what is the "elephant in the room"? What is the alcoholic dad in this scenario? It is the runaway Sexual Revolution that the church in general has never known how to handle. While self-avowed and practicing homosexuals have received the brunt of prophetic pronouncements and pulpit-pounding, little has been done to address the other more prominent problems that have resulted from the Sexual Revolution: sexual abuse, sexual addiction, adultery, and sexual aversion. In fact, the church generally has found it very difficult to talk about sexuality in any terms at all other than, "Just say 'No!'" And in this way we have been very *unbiblical*. While we have splashed barrels of ink on pages about the six passages of Scripture addressing the practice of homosexuality, precious little has been done to discuss the amazing wealth and breadth of wisdom the Bible shares concerning God's creation of us as sexual beings.

Our inability to discuss sexuality is a *cultural* inhibition, not a biblical one. The Scriptures are very forthright in describing God's design for our sexuality and in addressing the brokenness that results when his design is ignored. The deviant dalliances of David, Solomon, Samson, and others are not glossed over. And even the issue of withholding sexual intimacy from a spouse is candidly addressed by Paul.

In his excellent book *The Meaning of Sex,* ethicist Dennis Hollinger traces the history of the church's view of sexuality down through the centuries. The roots of our inhibitions stretch back to the influence Greek philosophy exerted upon the ancient worldview. For Plato, the material world was essentially evil and obscured the "ideal world" beyond this life. This general theme led to asceticism, which seeped into Christian spiritual practice and eventually translated into a view of sexual pleasure as something detrimental to one's spiritual life. Intercourse was encouraged only for the purpose of procreation and was otherwise to be avoided. Ironically, the only Christian tradition that was able to strip itself free of asceticism was that of the Puritans. Yes, the Puritans! Other than that brief parenthesis in history, God's people have looked dimly upon sexual pleasure and have found addressing issues of sexuality complicated and somewhat embarrassing.[3]

And so in Western culture, Christians have been tight-lipped on all things sexual for quite some time. And as secular culture has become incredibly flippant and indiscreet in speaking of sexuality, the church, by and large, still cannot bring the discussion to the table without being cutesy or condemnatory. To their credit, seminaries are now calling for classes on sexuality to be taught. Not long ago I had the privilege of teaching one such class as an adjunct professor at Ashland Theological Seminary. But we Protestants are about forty years late in responding to this revolution that has ripped our culture apart.

Of course, there are important questions to address regarding the Scapegoat of homosexuality. Realistically, the church at large is years away from reaching a consensus on this controversial subject. But can we not, as the body of Christ, learn to hold this one issue in tension as we join our efforts to rein in the rampaging Elephant and minister to those wounded and limping in its wake? Yes, that is asking a lot from both sides. And perhaps it is too late to hope that two sides, so bitterly divided and heavily invested, could agree to disagree and allow the other to practice their convictions. The final chapter of this book will consider if this is even possible without dividing congregations and denominational assets.

However, as the parable portrays, perspective is the missing element. We are fixated on the wrong issue. What about human trafficking, healing of sexual abuse, and ministry to the sexually addicted and sexually averse? These neglected matters affect perhaps 70 percent of our culture. Believers from the Evangelical and Social Justice camps and all other kingdom folks are needed to address these issues. And as the body comes together to bring healing, grace, justice, and freedom, we will live out before our culture the love of the Savior.

This is not to ignore or dismiss the pain of the Lesbian Gay Bisexual Transgender (LGBT) community and their sympathizers. For many of them, their deepest wounds have been caused by church people. In fact, Andrew Marin has found that gays and lesbians are more likely to have been wounded by the church than to have been sexually abused.[4] Generally speaking, Evangelicals have treated this one behavior as more abhorrent than any other sin. And we have been slow to speak up when injustices have occurred within the church and culture for fear that our intervention might be interpreted as approval of homosexual behavior. Certainly these wrongs need to be righted and everyone should be able to unite to address these injustices.

But there are other issues! Masses of people carry pain they feel no freedom to voice within the local church. More than 30 percent of women and nearly 20 percent of men live lives marred and crippled by sexual abuse. Who will speak for them? And as stated earlier, Internet access to porn and social media sites has accelerated sexual addiction, adultery, and use of porn. Will the church do more than shame people into accountability groups? And the greatest silence is among those in marriages jolted by sexual aversion. No one in the church seems willing to even bring up this delicate issue.

Every tradition within the universal church is needed to rope in the Elephant. The prophetic courage of the social activists can call our nation to account. Evangelicals can be tapped for their zeal for the lost and hurting. Those from the Holiness and Incarnational traditions can contribute with their wisdom regarding proper boundaries in holy living. And the charismatics have much to teach us about the workings of the Spirit to bring healing to the broken. We could cooperate on these issues that are prevalent and, in some cases, largely unaddressed. We could if we weren't so distracted.

Everyone is apparently too busy to cooperate on the larger issues of sexuality. Churches have committee meetings, Bible studies, prayer breakfasts, potlucks, ladies' meetings, bake sales, rummage sales . . . pretty important stuff. And it seems local church leaders like to paddle their own canoes rather than get on board with others to attack Elephants. However, churches obviously find plenty of time, money, and newsprint to spar over homosexual concerns. When it comes to *that* issue, the zeal seems almost inexhaustible.

As a young man, I spent a year in Taiwan as a short-term missionary. It was a remarkable year of immersion in Chinese culture, learning new ways of thinking from an incredibly generous people. Even at that time, more than forty years after Chiang Kai-shek and the Nationalists escaped the mainland to set up their government in exile, there were still a few isolated voices calling for the retaking of the homeland. Most knew, however, that such a plan was foolhardy and wildly unrealistic. The Nationalists had long ago made the mistake of warring against ideological countrymen instead of uniting to oppose the greater menace of Japanese Imperialism. It was far too late to change course.

More than forty years have passed since the Western church began sparring over homosexuality, ignoring the Elephant issues assaulting our culture. Is it too late to untie the boxing gloves and join forces against the dominant sexual issues that confront us?

It is never too late to begin doing the right thing. An Elephant needs to be corralled. Some of us need to stop our crusades either for or against the Scapegoat. The time has come for the church to be equipped to address issues of sexuality intelligently and to minister to the sexually broken effectively. That is certainly the aim of this book. As you read its content and discuss it with others, you will gain some guiding principles to keep you out of the ditches of the ideological debate. A sound theology of sexuality will be presented to provide some guardrails for our discussion. And you will hopefully get a glimpse of how the Elephant has jostled and jolted its victims, including those attracted to the same sex.

And so the first principle to fully embed within our thinking is that of the Elephant and the Scapegoat. We can no longer afford to ignore the Elephant in the room and continue to fuss and fume about the Scapegoat issue of homosexuality. Are you ready to move forward? Then the next step is to understand God's good design of our sexuality as described in the story of creation.

But first, consider if God would have you pray the following prayer:

Lord Jesus Christ, great head of the church, what a mess we have made! Forgive us for making a Scapegoat of one issue while ignoring our own sexual issues. Help us as a local church, and help me as a member of your body, to learn to talk about sexual matters in ways that please you. May we be a part of the solution to rein in the Elephant, and may we not cause further division over this Scapegoat. Fill us with your holy love for people wherever they stand on any of these issues. In your glorious name I pray, amen.

Discussion Questions

1. Were you surprised to learn of the number-one perception of unchurched millennials? Why or why not?
2. In what ways have you observed or experienced the family dynamics of the Tifflebaum family?
3. What prevents people from holding the Scapegoat issue of homosexuality in tension so that we can combine efforts on the Elephant issues?
4. Andrew Marin stated that it is more likely a gay or lesbian has been wounded by Christians than that they have been sexually abused. How have we wounded people who are attracted to the same sex?
5. What about this chapter makes you angry?
6. What about this chapter gives you hope?
7. How can we as a group keep from making homosexuality a Scapegoat issue?

CHAPTER 2

THEOLOGY:
Creation and God's Good Design

As mentioned in the previous chapter, Christians in America have found it difficult to talk about sexuality, despite the subject's prevalence in every form of media. While it may be more common to address the subject at home or on the college campus, the subject seems nearly taboo in the local church. But our tied tongues reflect our American church culture, and not the teachings of the Scriptures. The hesitancy runs deep within our ecclesiastical DNA.

My Grandpa Van Guilder made his living trading cattle and selling timber in a rural western Pennsylvania town. Down the hill from his house stood the local church where he had served as Sunday school superintendent for more than twenty years. Without a doubt, his faith was central to his life. In his waning years, he continued to serve his Lord by handing out evangelistic tracts to everyone he met at the nursing home where he stayed. He and I had an agreement that we would pray for each other every day, although I am sure he must have kept his end of the bargain better than I.

One day as a teenager my parents and I paid him a visit at the nursing home. On the way, my mother cautioned me, "Don't tell Grandpa that your cousin Debbie is pregnant."

"Okay," I responded. "Why?"

"Well, if you tell him that Debbie is pregnant, he will think about how people get pregnant, and that won't be good."

"Okay," I replied. But still curious, I asked, "Why?"

"Uh, well, he *just will*. So just don't bring it up!"

As odd as that interchange may sound, it provides an example of the difficulty with which Grandpa Van Guilder's generation spoke of the subject, at least within the circles of family and church. Apparently the next generation loosened up a bit, as my parents could at least bring the matter into conversation. But when the Sexual Revolution of the '60s erupted in our country, the church overall was clearly caught flat-footed and irrelevant by its inability to comfortably articulate the Bible's balanced message regarding sexuality.

Back in the mid-'80s while in seminary, I was part of a singles fellowship at a nearby church. Mary Fischer, an Australian who had spent several years in China as a missionary, brought a unique cultural perspective to our group. One evening she stated, "You Americans have little idea where you are heading. From all I've seen in the breakdown of the family and the jettison of biblical values, your culture is racing toward a very sickening and frightening future." The comment captured my imagination as I wondered where it was she thought we were heading.

While the problems plaguing our culture are multitudinous and multilayered, certainly the pervasive obsession with sex and the widening mass of abuse victims left in its wake are indicative of a maddening and turbulent trend. Statistics alone tell a disturbing story. Though studies vary, estimates show anywhere from 20 to 40 percent of all children are sexually abused before the age of eighteen, and the rate is increasing significantly each decade.[1] One landmark study of 930 randomly selected women found 16 percent had been victims of incest.[2] But every digit in the accumulated stats represents someone whose longing for love and intimacy was shattered by another's selfish crossing of boundaries. The distorted messages from Hollywood and the porn industry have muddied the waters even further. Victims often wonder what "normal" sex is supposed to look like. So how do we navigate our way out of this mess? The starting point is studying carefully God's good design as set forth in the Scriptures.

Several years ago I was privileged to share in an extended conversation with Calvin Miller. As an author, artist, church pioneer, and seminary professor, Miller impressed my colleagues and me with his deep reflections and broad knowledge of church history. Midway through the day I asked him, "Can you think of any time in church history where God's people handled well the subject of sexuality?" Pausing to stroke his beard a bit, he simply replied, "I don't think so." Wow.

And so it seems today. While our culture bolted out of the gate and raced forward with the Sexual Revolution of the '60s, the church in general sat in the stands either staring at their feet or shouting aloud about the sinfulness of our runaway culture. Rarely has a church in our culture mirrored the balance and beauty found in the Scripture regarding sexuality.

And that is the amazing thing about Scripture. You find incredible frankness when it comes to sex, but also a Spirit-inspired balance. The Bible presents instruction, observation, and inspiration, but never obsession with sexuality. This is a tremendous affirmation of God's authorship when you consider how sexually saturated were the cultures of ancient times. When Bible heroes such as Samson, David, or Solomon strayed from the sexual laws of God, there was no glossing over or excusing of their behavior. Instead we observe the destructive consequences of their actions and the abiding grace of our God. The matter-of-fact teachings of Paul to the "sexual sin city" of Corinth provided guidance with clarity and balance. This stands in stark contrast with most Bible-preaching pulpits of our own time. One study found only 43 percent of mainline church attendees could remember ever hearing a sermon about marriage and sexuality.[3] When was the last time your pastor addressed clearly the positive teachings of Scripture about healthy sexual relations between a husband and wife? It just doesn't seem as though that's fitting fare for stained glass and padded pews. The hesitancy, however, is cultural and not biblical. A quick reading of 1 Corinthians 7 makes this plain. The passage admonishes husbands and wives to "not deprive one another" (v. 5) sexually and was written to be read, of all places, in church on Sunday morning. Whew! Hopefully the toddlers were in the nursery with the curtains closed and door shut!

God's Design and Purpose

Even when they are young, our children try to make sense of the world. Once while on a walk with my fourth-grade daughter, she asked, "Why did God make sumac?" She had been learning about ecosystems and food chains, and was wondering where these odd little trees fit into God's plan. As for sumacs, I'm not sure I had a very good answer for her. But I am sure that God's good design for our sexuality has a definite purpose. Four purposes, actually.

The two creation accounts of Genesis provide many clues that human sexuality is, in fact, purposefully designed. Chapter 1 sets out for us the step-by-step, day-by-day creative acts of God. As heavens and earth, sea and land, vegetation and animal life are created, God's continual comment was that all he saw was good. The crowning act of creation was the forming and shaping of man and woman in his image. Though God's attributes can be seen in all of nature, humans alone were created to reflect his character and nature: "in the image of God he created them; male and female he created them" (Gen. 1:27). Man and woman *together* reflect his image. This has nothing to do with God having body parts. Though throughout Scripture God is predominantly depicted as masculine, the truth of the matter is that he possesses all that is good and positive about masculinity and femininity. And as for us, we together, as male and female, reflect who God is. Our complementarity and equality are in view here, and the scene is beautiful.

Dan Allender, in his book *Sabbath,* spent time speaking of the beauty of the triune God. In his careful description, he cited a study that was done to determine what constitutes a beautiful face. Symmetry alone does not suffice for good looks. In other words, beauty is "a relationship between harmony and distinctiveness."[4] Attractiveness is enhanced as there is variation in the overall symmetry. And so it is with the face of God as we see it reflected in the male and female created in his image. There is certainly sameness, as Adam noted that she "is bone of my bones and flesh of my flesh" (Gen. 2:23). That is to say, "Hey, she's just like me!" But there is also a significant variation in the symmetry—there is the inherent beauty of man and woman in their wonderful complementarity. And so we see the first purpose in creating us as male and female is to reflect the image of God.

This same passage states plainly the second purpose: reproduction. After creating them male and female, he said to them, "Be fruitful and multiply, and fill the earth and subdue it" (Gen. 1:28). Of all the commands issued by God, this is the one where we have truly outdone ourselves in obeying him!

The third and fourth purposes flow out of the second creation account in Genesis 2. More details emerge regarding the creation of these two beings as God shaped Adam from the dust of the earth and later forms Eve using Adam's rib. Of all the work God did in creating the world, it is only into humankind that he breathed "the breath of life." And so when Adam received the breath of God, "the man became a living being" (Gen. 2:7). This one distinct act separates us from all other created beings. The very life of God was imparted by his breath.

Once Adam's tour of the garden was complete, the first gift God gave him was a job. Tending and caring for the garden occupied his time and energy, and as Adam punched the time clock day after day, God observed the first thing in the world which he could not claim was good. "It is not good for the man to be alone" (Gen. 2:18 NIV). And so what was his next course of action? If you are guessing it's the fashioning of a partner, you are wrong. The next act of God was to give Adam *another* job. Naming all of the creatures crawling, flying, and prancing around the garden was no small task, and not without its difficulties. Imagine stumbling upon deer, some with antlers and some without. Then later cattle with horns and some without. Anyone would have been confused. Adam would have also noticed the same species of birds, the males with brighter colors than the female partners. Further observation of the creatures caring for their young might have prompted him to begin classifying some of those animals as mommas, others as poppas.

God was already convinced Adam's aloneness was not good. Taking on the second job helped Adam draw the same conclusion. After weeks of naming pairs of poppas and mommas, he could have well been asking, "Where's my mate? Why don't I have a partner?" And so a "suitable" helper was made—bone of his bones, flesh of his flesh. And once the formalities of introductions were behind them, they became one flesh.

Becoming one flesh was God's answer to addressing this aloneness. Connection with another person is an intrinsic need we all have. This dynamic is borne out through an understanding of bonding. As life begins, we first bond with our mothers. By God's design, a chemical called oxytocin is released in the brain of both the mother and her infant during breastfeeding, thus creating a bond between mother and child. Likewise, bonds begin to form between a couple as they first fall in love and begin listening to each other's voices, holding hands, caressing, and embracing. And again, it is oxytocin that gives us that sense of closeness with another. But as a couple reaches climax in sexual intercourse, the release of oxytocin spikes, developing new neural pathways that provide that "one flesh" feeling. This one-flesh bond that addresses that inner loneliness is the third purpose in God's design for our sexuality. Simply put, it is union with another.

The fourth purpose in God's design is to know another. Genesis 4:1 states it plainly: "Now the man knew his wife Eve, and she conceived and bore Cain . . ." Far from being a euphemism, the use of the word "know" in this verse is a very literal translation of the Hebrew word for sexual intercourse. And by God's design, that is the chief purpose of the sexual act—to intimately know and be known. It was Adam's aloneness that prompted God's creation of Eve. And so it is that the sexual act is far more than a bodily activity to create offspring. Sex is the deepest manner of sharing oneself with another and gaining awareness of one's own self. The following from John Oswalt is full of insight:

> For humans, the sex experience is designed to be the fulfillment of a process of knowing, a process of mutual mastery and mutual submission. Just as the male and female bodies are made for each other, so are the male and female spirits, each supporting and complementing the other. Thus, the enjoyment of sex, as it grows out of a good relationship, cements our knowledge of one another in ways that are ultimately beyond intellectualizing.[5]

Usually in Christian books about sexuality, the author weighs in on the matter of masturbation. Is it always a sin to masturbate? Some have reached their conclusions by pointing to the feelings of guilt so often felt after having stimulated themselves to climax.

Back in the 1980s when I was a seminary student, I heard a professor state that he wondered if those feelings weren't so much about guilt as they were about loneliness. And given God's four purposes for our sexuality, that makes all the sense in the world. It is Adam in the garden all over again, naming animals and wondering, "Where's my partner?" Biologically, it is oxytocin being released to create feelings of attachment, but without another person present with whom to bond. And so the sense of isolation and aloneness is accentuated.

Christians will continue to disagree whether or not masturbation is sinful under any and all circumstances, but we can at least say confidently that it does not fulfill the four purposes for God's design. Stimulating oneself does not reflect the communal love of God's image, it does not create others, it does not bring about union with another, and it does not help us to know another. God's design calls us forth into so much more.

As a Whole or in Parts?

For three months, Tonya had been coming to me for counseling. This dear lady had been sexually abused by five different men beginning at the age of four. The Lord had led us to revisit some of those horrifying memories for the purpose of bringing his healing presence and grace into those places of pain and darkness. As we approached yet another distressing incident from the past, she sighed with pained exasperation. "All he did was touch me there. I was only four years old. Why does it still bother me?"

The answer to that question takes us back to the way we are wired. How we respond to sexual stimuli is far more complicated than what we learned in high school health class. When the church and family remained silent on sexual issues, the school system stepped up to the plate. What most of us observed were diagrams of body parts and an explanation of mechanics. Hand-drawn pictures of breasts, penises, and vaginas brought snickers and side-glances from the class as teachers nervously explained about contraceptives and sexually transmitted diseases.

Add to this the wonderful revelations of biology class. As we learned the classification of the species, there were some amazing surprises. Bats are not birds, but mammals. Dolphins and whales, believe it or not, are part of that family as well. And surprise, surprise—even humans are mammals! Yep, we learned that we are ranked right along with the rest of the animal kingdom. And so the underlying message, though subtle, seemed clear. Birds do it. Bees do it. And we're just talking about body parts coming together anyway. What's the big deal?

God's Word is a journey from one garden to another. In the first garden we find a picture of two people whose needs are completely met—body, soul, and spirit. Nakedness was the norm without shame or embarrassment. While intercourse is not specifically mentioned before the fall, one easily assumes it was part of the picture. And immediately following the fall, Adam and Eve cover that which is uniquely theirs, what we today blithely refer to as "private parts."

Our culture has made a science of sexuality. So much emphasis is placed upon body parts and sexual technique, so little upon soul and spirit. But such a fragmented presentation leads many to believe that they can have sex with their bodies without affecting their souls or spirits. In actuality, however, such demarcations were foreign to the people of God in Old Testament times. Before the influence of Greek thought, the Hebrews never understood human life in terms of body, soul, and spirit. In fact, the Hebrew language didn't even have a word for "body." As Ken Blue pointed out, "The word which comes closest to denoting what we call 'body' is *basar*, but it refers to the total life of a person."[6] And so biblically speaking, your body is *you*. Your private parts are not parts at all. They are you. The most intimate part of you.

Think for a moment about the sign of God's covenant with Abraham. Why did he choose circumcision? If the sign had to be a scar, why on the penis? Why not on the forehead or the arm where it could be seen more readily? As God made his covenant with his good friend Abraham, the sign was to be on the most personal part of his body. To be any more personal, the scar would have to be on his heart—which of course takes place for *us* under the new covenant. But to emphasize how very important and personal this covenant was, God chose this part of Abraham's body. Is it too far of a stretch to conclude from this that touching on that part of our body should be preceded by covenant? For in actuality, our genitals are the closest outward connection to the deepest part of our being.

Returning to Tonya who was mentioned earlier, this was why she still felt pain when she thought of the abuse that took place as a small child. Yes, all the man did was touch her there. But because of the way God has designed us, she knew somehow this was inappropriate. That man didn't just touch a part of her body. He touched *her*—the most intimate part of her. Even as a child, she knew this was a violation, a crossing of a sacred and personal boundary. And the unresolved pain continued to throb thirty-five years later.

Of Love and Longings

Few books on love and marriage have found a following in the Christian community as has *The Five Love Languages* by Gary Chapman. Each of us has a primary way of expressing and receiving love, which Chapman calls our love language. If you were to read a book about 101 ways to communicate love to your spouse, he believes the 101 would boil down to five basic expressions: speaking words of affirmation, sharing quality time, giving and receiving gifts, doing acts of service, and touching. While each person is fluent in one of these "languages," we must learn to express love in ways that most speak to our spouse. Sexual intimacy is relegated to the language of touch, as Chapman sees it. And yet could it not be that making love encompasses *all* of these languages? Nothing communicates acceptance and affirmation as does undressing with the one you love and being welcomed. As for quality time, when else does a spouse have the other's attention so acutely? At times, lovemaking is an incredible act of service, as Paul intimates in 1 Corinthians 7. And when it comes to gift giving, there is no greater gift other than the giving of one's life as Jesus himself demonstrated. Giving all of oneself in such a way is more than "making love." By God's design, it is speaking love into the other person in every way possible.

Though John Lennon attempted to persuade us otherwise, love isn't all we need. The list of basic human needs varies depending upon what school of thought you've been taught. Love is on nearly everyone's list, but so are other needs and longings. Dr. Anne Halley has identified six basic needs: belonging, love, security, understanding, purpose, and significance. It is perhaps easy to see how belonging, love, and understanding might be found in sexual intimacy, but what about the others?

Those who study family systems narrow the list of needs down to two basic categories: love and structure. As described above, the loving bond of intimacy certainly aims to express love. But where is structure found in God's design? Not in the act of sex, but in the covenant of marriage. While a sexual relationship outside of a marriage covenant may fill one's need for love, the inner need for structure, such as our longing for security and significance, languishes until a covenant provides permanence and exclusivity.

Falling in Love, Falling in Line

Bambi, Thumper, and Flower went to the wise old Owl, seeking an explanation for the unusual behavior of some of their forest buddies. "They are twitterpated," Owl informed them. Twitterpation, or what we call "falling in love," is a state of euphoria that seems to put us on our good behavior as we engage in the courtship dance. If love is ever blind, it is surely so while twitterpated. Not only are we blind to the other's faults, we find ourselves spending inordinate amounts of time, energy, and money developing a relationship with the object of our obsession. It's the fodder for countless love songs on the radio as well as countless hours of anxiety for the parents of those so smitten.

Scientists have demystified the wonderful sensation of romantic love by discovering the euphoria is caused by chemical reactions within the brain. Dr. Michael Liebowitz maintained our brain is triggered by visual cues, such as the shape and form of one we find attractive. Under prolonged exposure, the pleasure centers of our brains become awash in the neurotransmitters dopamine and norepinephrine.[7] Interestingly, this chemical bathing of the brains lasts on average two years, at which time the "falling in love" phase will hopefully have given way to the partners making a choice to love regardless of how they are feeling.[8]

If the setting sun or the twinkling night sky have ever awakened in your heart a prayer of wonder and worship for our awe-inspiring Creator God, should we not also sing his praise for how he has created us as sexual beings and provided for us in the covenant of marriage? Seeing us in our loneliness, he designed us to fall in love for a few years—long enough for us to marry, bond, and solidify our relationship. Then once the covenant has been made and the bond strengthened, we fall out of the "in love" phase and into a commitment which, ideally, should fulfill the longings of our heart. And as wonderful as romantic love is, our deeper longing is to be loved for better or for worse, in sickness and in health, for as long as we live. That's God's amazingly wonderful design.

Summary

God's Word takes us from the Garden of Eden in Genesis to the Garden of Paradise in the book of Revelation. In the first garden a man and woman are brought together, naked and unashamed. In the second garden, according to Jesus, people "will neither marry nor be given in marriage" (Matt. 22:30 NIV). Apparently what's going on in that future garden far outshines anything marital bliss has to offer in this life. But the time spanning between those gardens carries an enormous amount of pain and brokenness, especially in the area of our sexuality. God has not abandoned us, however, and extends his grace.

Given all that we have observed in God's wonderful design for our sexuality, why is it so difficult for us as Christians to talk about it? You may be thinking, *Because it's so personal.* And indeed it is! That is precisely how God designed our sexuality—to be a personal and intimate way of knowing another. In fact, even secular scientists have noted that humans alone seek privacy when making love.[9] All other creatures care nothing for privacy because for them it is not about knowing another. It is simply about reproducing.

For us, however, it is a very private matter. Certainly it is very inappropriate to speak of your own sex life in public. That would be a violation of privacy and trust with the one you love. But that doesn't mean we can't talk about the topic of sexuality itself in objective terms. In fact, what we as Christians have to say about sexuality should be of great interest to all. God's design deserves broadcasting!

Years after my cousin Debbie had children, we paid another visit to Grandpa Van at the nursing home—my parents, sister, wife, and I. Grandpa had a long-standing struggle with psoriasis on his hands and was prone to overmedicate with hand lotion. "If a little bit is good, more is better," he would reason. And on this occasion, as we walked into the room, he was rubbing his hands together in a vain attempt to make the lotion disappear. "Why so much lotion, Dad?" Mom asked.

"It's for my syphilis," he explained. Knowing how averse he was to all sexual talk, it was no small task to contain our laughter as we bit our lips and looked at each other with amazed amusement. Had he known what he actually had said, I'm not quite sure how he or we would have handled it!

Before many more years passed, Grandpa Van entered his reward in that place where there's no need to speak of sexual intimacy. Doubtless he has received a rich reward for his faithfulness and has entered the garden where the union with God and the bond with his people are so rich and beautiful, thoughts of sex have become lost in the shadowy memories of this earth.

We who have been left behind, however, live in neither of those gardens. Our world has experienced the shattering effects of sin and rebellion, and God's glorious intentions for our sexuality have been horribly marred. Instead of the deep wonder of sexual fulfillment and the security of the marriage bond, so many have experienced devastating pain and deep loss. A certain blindness has crept in, distorting our perception of all that God has made to be good and holy.

We turn next to a stunning defilement of God's good design. All of God's good purposes for our sexuality are turned on their head as people grasp for what is not rightfully theirs in the sexual abuse of others.

But for now, if the Spirit so leads, join in the following prayer:

Almighty God, Maker of heaven and earth, we stand in awe of how you have designed us. We agree with your Scriptures that we are fearfully and wonderfully made. You saw our deepest need for connection and have shaped us for intimacy. Despite the brokenness of this world, the corruption of our desires, and the manipulation of our culture, we declare that all you have made is good! May we not live in the shadows of shame, hidden in the closet. May we declare the goodness of your sexual design and model healthy intimacy to our children. Enable us, we pray. Amen.

Discussion Questions

1. What are the four purposes of God's design for our sexuality?
2. Would you add any to the list? If so, why?
3. What insights into God's design stood out to you?
4. How would you rate your ability to talk about sexuality on a scale of 1–10? (1= "Uh, I don't even want to answer this question!" 10= "Without blushing, blinking, or smirking!")
5. Humor has been used to communicate truth about God's design of our sexuality. Do you think humor helps the discussion? When might humor not be appropriate?
6. As we consider the topics listed in the Table of Contents, which one are you most anxious to talk about? Why?
7. Which week are you already planning on having the flu so you don't have to be here for the discussion? Any idea why?

CHAPTER 3

APPLICATION:
The Violation of Abuse

If you want to know what God is like, look at Jesus. I'm sure you've heard that many times before. So if you want to know how God would coax someone out of a closet, consider the story of the woman at the well in John 4. True, there's no mention of a closet, but she was certainly a woman with a past who found ways to hide her shame.

The most significant sentence in this passage? "But he had to go through Samaria" (John 4:4). Jesus was on his way to Galilee from Jerusalem, and the shortest route was through Samaria. But few Jews took that route. They wouldn't risk coming within a stone's throw of a Samaritan unless, of course, they were hoping to throw a stone at these despised half-Jews. The extended trip along the east bank of the Jordan was the preferred path for most. But Jesus had to go through Samaria. It had little to do with geography and everything to do with a woman in the closet.

It is commonly believed she came for water in the middle of the day to avoid the catty chatter of the local ladies. Having been married five times before and now living with a man, she had likely suffered unending reproach. Not only did Jesus time his visit for her noon approach, he also sent the clumsy and shortsighted disciples into town to find lunch. Seriously? Does it take twelve guys to find a kosher deli? Not really. But this assured Jesus of a private meeting with this deeply troubled woman who doubtless would have avoided a well crowded with men. As she arrived, he treated her with dignity and respect. He gently acknowledged her sin and piqued her interest in the living water that would completely quench her thirst.

Just as the dumbfounded disciples returned to the well, she headed back to town proclaiming the arrival of who she believed was the Messiah. No doubt they wondered, *Why was he talking with a woman?* As they searched through their sacks of carry-out goodies, Jesus stated he'd already had his meal. *Uh, did he order delivery?* Hardly. His ministry to the woman was part of the Father's will and work, and was as important to him as daily food.

The local church wanting to call forth the captives of the closet may have to travel down paths others refuse to take. Disregarding prevailing prejudices and, perhaps, political correctness, they must offer the living water of forgiveness and healing, washing away the shame that shrouds the hiding ones. And just as Jesus urged his disciples to open their eyes to see the harvest of people coming from the village, I believe God will begin to open your eyes to see the many victims of sexual abuse he longs to call from the closets of the church.

"I've Never Told This to Anyone Before, But ..."

Looking back on the last fifteen years, I am still amazed how God has led people out of the closet and into my care. To be honest, I entered doctoral studies to learn formational counseling not to help abuse victims, but to minister to people with unwanted same-sex attraction. As an Evangelical in the United Methodist Church, I lined up theologically with the traditional view of homosexual behavior—a position I still hold. But in the early '90s, as I became good friends with a gay Christian, my heart began to change. It was no longer enough for believers to defend a theological castle. Churches, I believed, needed to learn to minister to and with people who are attracted to the same sex.

What happened? After my first class on the subject of formational prayer, God began to lead abuse victims to me. Incredible. It was almost as if he was holding them back until the class came to a close, and then he turned them loose. Within a month, I was asked to speak at a nearby church, and God told a senior citizen that he would finally heal her of teenage sexual abuse at the close of the service. And he did! People began to contact me to set up counseling for marital problems, eating disorders, or depression, but within one or two sessions I would hear them admit, "I've never told this to anyone before, but I was sexually abused." Flat-out amazing. In 2006 I was invited to join a team of counselors for the "Come Away with Me" retreats started by Ashland Theological Seminary and now sponsored by Healing Care Ministries. With more than forty retreats behind us, many more victims have since opened up to me.

More doors began to open. Ashland Theological Seminary asked me to teach a class to train ministerial students on issues of sexuality. Then I began offering day-long seminars for pastors and faith-based caregivers, training them to minister to the abused. The stories have multiplied as others are now hearing those very same words: "I've never told this to anyone before, but ..."

The Dynamics and Effects of Abuse[1]

Make no mistake about it. There are men and women in your church who have had their lives deeply affected by abuse. The stats cited in the introduction continue to surface in study after study: one out of every three women and about 16 percent of men. For the mentally or physically handicapped, the numbers are more than 80 percent. Horrendous. You may wonder what has gone wrong in our country, but in my conversations with missionaries, the problem is far worse in other parts of the world.

So how and why does this happen? What are the dynamics involved? Certainly there are many factors that contribute to sexual abuse. One can certainly point to the pornography industry and a culture that is obsessed with beauty and sex appeal. But the main dynamic that drives this troubling and pervasive behavior is power. Not a raging sex drive, but power. It is a means of exerting power over another or a means of escaping a feeling of powerlessness. And so it is that the perpetrators of abuse are always stronger, older, or in a position of authority.

What does it look like? Mic Hunter, in his excellent book *Abused Boys,* provided a comprehensive list of abusive activities that involves far more than contact with genitals. Abuse includes having a child touch someone inappropriately, introducing pornographic materials to them, peeping in on them in the shower, exposing oneself to them, or simply using sexualized talk. In fact, even verbal sexual abuse can be as disturbing as sexual touch given the right circumstances.[2]

When counselees tell me they have never been sexually abused, I believe them. But later on they sometimes recount events that were most definitely instances of abuse that have had an impact. Sometimes their definition of abuse was just not broad enough. For many, however, they have simply refused to give the incident any weight and cannot think of themselves as a victim. Why? In his classic book *The Wounded Heart,* Dan Allender maintained that victims usually experience a confused ambivalence about the event. Somehow there was some pleasure attached to that memory, simply because of the way we are designed and the way abuse often plays out. Sometimes even unwanted sexual touch is pleasurable because of the way we are wired. And perpetrators groom their victims by initiating special activities to build trust with them— activities which meet deep needs for love, appreciation, and connection. Because of these factors, the victims will often lay blame upon themselves, thinking that in some way they must have invited the sexualized touch or activity.

There are sad similarities to the stories of abuse. Those who prey upon children are mostly men. Only rarely is a woman the perpetrator. And the result is a life hampered by a variety of behaviors and inclinations. For some, the trauma of the viola-tion creates a need for safety and self-protection, making them averse not only to sexual intimacy, but also to relational intimacy with the opposite sex. Or the polar opposite can be true. Some victims, driven by a message that they are no longer lovable, become addicted to sex and its false promise of love. In extreme cases one finds eating disorders, self-mutilation, and addic-tions of all sorts. Health issues can surface over time. Increased gynecological problems, delayed puberty, early puberty, and a host of stress-related physical problems can ensue. A number of emotional problems can develop as well: depression, shame, dissociation, self-worth issues, disgust for one's body, self-blame, and self-contempt. Quite often they are bereft of feelings entirely; there is so much pain stuffed in their brain that they simply shut themselves off from any and every emotion.

Now just a word of caution. There's no need to become a diagnostician! Just because you see some of these symptoms does not mean a person has been sexually abused. When all you have is a hammer, everything looks like a nail. And using this list to try to identify abuse victims is irresponsible because there are other issues that can cause each of these symptoms. But having this list might help you to recognize more clearly those who are stepping out of the closet of shame and to help them find the right kind of treatment that will bring lasting change to these symptoms.

The Cracked Windshield

Imagine an insanely vandalized car. Someone has taken a sledgehammer to the trunk and hood. Rocks have shattered headlights and taillights. Doors are missing as a well-equipped numbskull has taken the Jaws of Life to the hinges. Still drivable, right? Uh, not safely or comfortably, but I guess you could get from point A to point B. With this picture in mind, now consider the damage to body and soul described earlier. The vandalized car might be a good illustration for some victims of abuse. They can get through life, but they are presented with some daunting challenges.

Now, let's find another vandal. This one tries to throw a brick through the windshield, but manages only to crack it. No hole, just that spider-webby effect that makes it nearly impossible to see through. Drivable? I guess you could lean out the side and see where you are going, but the challenges have only multiplied.

This additional defacement perhaps illustrates the effect of abuse on the spirit of some victims. Their greatest help in overcoming the trauma of abuse is looking to God for healing. But that view can be horribly obscured. Why? Allender provided a memorable response: "What is the damage of abuse? Simply, *abuse provides the raw data that seems to prove that God is not good*" (italics his).[3] "How can that be?" you might ask. "Can't they see that they are angry with the very One who wants to heal them?" Yeah, that's the point. They can't see. The windshield's been cracked. And guiding them toward healing is akin to running alongside this banged up car, shouting directions to the driver who is behind the wheel, squinting through the messed-up glass.

Windshield Repair

More than once I've heard victims cry out with clenched fists, "Where the hell was God! I was just a little kid! How could he let this happen?" And at this point we all want to step in with our apologetics manuals to address the age-old issue of the sovereignty of God in the midst of a world of evil. That's our temptation. But don't do it! In fact, you might find that they have been there and done that already. Their minds have been on hyperdrive trying to figure out this tangled mess. Applying apologetics will help them about as much as mounting the dented car hood and applying Krazy Glue to the glass. It simply won't work.

Why? Because the real problem for them is the pain in their right brain, not the questions in the left. The answer for them is not systematic theology but biblical lament. You may be drawing a blank at this point because lament is not a common subject in our version of Christianity, but it is as biblical as our need for forgiveness.

Do you remember the story of Amnon and Tamar? Probably not. When publishers were making out the three-year cycle of Sunday school curriculum, that particular story didn't make the cut. (Just a little too edgy.) But 2 Samuel 13 provides all of the lurid details of this story of incest within King David's family. Egged on by his scoundrel of a cousin Jonadab, Amnon plotted to take advantage of his half sister. After he raped Tamar, he heaped on further shame by kicking her out onto the streets. There she began to lament in the customary way, crying out in great emotional turmoil and ripping the sleeves off of her garment. But Absalom, her full-blooded big brother, short-circuited her grieving, telling her, "Be quiet for now, my sister; he is your brother; do not take this

to heart" (2 Sam. 13:20). Huh? How do you not take this to heart?
And why keep it quiet?

Dad wasn't much help either. When David found out, "he
became very angry, but he would not punish his son Amnon,
because he loved him, for he was his firstborn" (2 Sam. 13:21).
What messages did that send to Tamar? You are not loved. You are
not important. Your pain doesn't matter. And, perhaps, Amnon's
reputation and future as the next king were more important than
her vindication and safety. Can you see how devastating this would
be? And note the telling words regarding the victim: "So Tamar
remained, a desolate woman, in her brother Absalom's house"
(2 Sam. 13:20).

Incredibly unjust, right? But that same story in all of its sad
detail has been a pattern in our culture. Victims cry out to parents
or other caregivers about their violation and immediately they are
told a number of things that basically require them to stuff it:

- Don't take this to heart.
- You shouldn't have been alone with that person anyway.
- What did you do to bring this on?
- Just don't go near that person anymore.
- Well, we can't really do anything about it. What will people say?
- Sure, that was wrong. But think of the damage it will do to our
  church (family, organization) if we say anything.

These are the very messages which squelch the grieving process,
increase their powerlessness, and provide fertile ground for all of the
previously mentioned maladies, including their rage toward God.

So if the Krazy Glue of apologetics won't bring clarity to their
view of God, what is the answer? The biggest way to help is found in
the smallest verse in the Bible: "Jesus wept" (John 11:35 NIV). Think
of the context of that verse. In John 11, Jesus had been summoned
by Mary and Martha to heal their brother, Lazarus. By the time he
entered Bethany, however, Lazarus had been dead for four days and

the sisters were well into their grieving. When Jesus met Mary, she and her friends were weeping. Their tears actually triggered his own.

Now he could have taken Absalom's approach: "Do not take this to heart! Hey, dry those tears and blow your nose because I am going to raise him from the dead! Happy days are coming!" But instead he wept with them. He allowed them to grieve. He welcomed their unanswered questions: "If you had been here, [he] would not have died" (vv. 21, 32).

As they watched him weep, the crowd remarked, "See how he loved [Lazarus]!" (v. 36). The truth of the matter? They were seeing how much he loved Mary, Martha, and the rest of them.

Want to know how God reaches out to the broken and desolate ones? Look at Jesus. Want the abused to see God clearly reaching out to them? Let them look at you. Weep with them as Jesus would. As your eyes cloud with tears, their eyes will begin to open to how much God cares.

Whether the abuse took place yesterday, yesteryear, or yester-decade, allow them to grieve. Of course, abuse victims also need safety, so make sure their abusers are kept at a distance. It might also help them if they see you yourself are angry about what has happened to them. But Absalom provided safety and David showed some anger; what Tamar needed and what closet dwellers need is someone to grieve with them.

Denial

Once I had the privilege of counseling George at a retreat—a man in his fifties who had battled sexual addiction all of his life. As is true for many, it began with sexual abuse. His mother, as a single mom, struggled to find a way through life. In order for her to hold a job, her friend, the director of a recreation center, was willing to watch her six-year-old during the days. From the very beginning he assured George that they were going to become special friends who touched each other in special ways. The touch escalated to the point that the man was performing oral sex on George—a practice that continued for the next six years. When George reached puberty, however, the man discarded him and found another young boy.

From that point on, men began approaching and taking advantage of him. He wondered, *Is there a sign above my head that says, "Use me for sex"?* To his surprise, men were willing to pay him money to give him oral sex, and so he dove into a life of prostitution for many years. Such a tragic story.

During one session, as we sat across from each other, he asked, "Why do you think God leads so many abused people to you for counseling? Were you ever sexually abused?"

There was an incident in my life that I had always dismissed. When I was little, an older girl insisted on helping me use the bathroom and wiping me where I usually did not wipe. I said no several times, but she persisted. Compared to George's horrific abuse, I hardly thought that counted and I really had not felt it had affected me much. So I replied, "Not really." He pressed for details, so I related the incident.

"That's abuse!" he cried with his finger in my face. "You need to stop denying it!"

Wow. If an ex-prostitute who had endured such prolonged and insidious abuse so adamantly insisted on this, who was I to continue to stay in denial? And so I have sought God's healing for my own wounding.

How is it that abuse affects some more severely than others? Why did George end up in prostitution and I end up in naive denial? There are a number of factors that determine how deeply the wounding fractures our soul.

Perhaps it is obvious, but the earlier the age, the greater the damage. Some assume that "kids are resilient" and soon get over such violations. Not so. The younger we are the more malleable we are and the deeper the impression left behind. Length and frequency are also important factors. For George, repeated abuse for six years had an incredibly damaging effect. And frequent abuse means one does not have a chance to regain an inner equilibrium before he or she is violated again. Add violence or deviance to the mix and the pain is driven further into the soul. If the offender had a close relationship to the victim, such as a sibling or parental figure, the crippling effect is multiplied and adds to the difficulty of finding healing. These and other factors contribute to the wide variety of outcomes in the aftermath of abuse.[4]

The Gaze That Heals

One of my instructors in the doctoral program has become a good friend and colleague. Victoria Kepler Didato, the founder of the Child Sexual Abuse Institute of Ohio, has done more than anyone I know to bring hope and healing to victims of incest and sexual abuse. Using the biblical story of the poisonous serpents from the wilderness, she addresses the pain of approaching our memories of sexual abuse.

As you may remember, there was an instance in Numbers 21 when the Israelites complained yet again about their trek through the wilderness. This time God chose poisonous serpents as their teaching tool. Soon people were dying from snake bites and crying out to God for forgiveness. Instead of taking the serpents away, the Lord instructed Moses to fashion a bronze replica of the serpents and elevate it so that all could see it. Upon being bitten, if a person would simply look to the bronze serpent, they would be healed.

I'm not a snake person. Not many people are. I don't have pictures of snakes on my walls, never tattooed a red-eyed cobra to my arm, and I don't go searching along river banks to admire copperheads bathing in the sun. There's simply a sickening feeling when I'm gazing at snakes, whether real or photographed. And I'm guessing that to some degree the bronze serpent elicited similar feelings, especially among people who were daily confronted with the real thing lunging at their ankles. But like it or not, you had to look at the bronze replica if you wanted to be healed. And let's face it, it was simply a replica, not the real thing. It was not going to bite.

Didato finds some similarity when it comes to looking back at traumatic memories of abuse. The images we recall are not the real thing. We can't be violated again by simply recalling the memories. But at some point, as God leads us, we may very well have to look once again at those painful images in order to be healed.

Having said that, reading a chapter like this can feel very uncomfortable for someone with abuse in their past. For a few, it can be absolutely troubling. So whether this book is being used in a group-study format or simply being read by a lone individual, know that healing can come as you look back at the trauma as long as you keep in mind a few things.

First, approach such memories with a trained professional. Going back to a traumatic memory carries with it the risk of abreaction. In other words, you might actually begin to experience some of the intense emotion and even the physical pain of the incident being remembered. If not conducted properly, there is a danger of being retraumatized. And so no one should enter this experience alone.

Second, timing is key. God may indeed use this book to identify an issue of abuse, but that does not necessarily mean now is the time to approach the matter. My training in formational prayer stresses the importance of a Spirit-led process. Often there are other matters God wants to address before reaching in to touch a wound of this sort. And so one is wise to find the right resources before heading out on this healing journey.

Third, have courage. The journey can be a rough one, but in God's timing and with trained caregivers, looking back at those painful memories can be absolutely life changing. Many of those who have taken that journey have few regrets. Renewed relationships, better health, greater joy, and emotional stability can be the reward. Some, in fact, have found so much liberation that they are taking the message to others!

Another Woman Returns to the Village

Georgia is a remarkable woman of God. Throughout their forty-eight years of marriage, she and her husband have been active in the ministries of their local church. But one day her inner world began to implode as a memory of abuse crashed through the front door of her life. After several years of seeking healing, however, her life has changed dramatically for the better. Now, like the woman at the well, she has returned to the village to proclaim the news of a liberating Messiah.

It all began as her church, like many others, began to initiate a Safe Sanctuaries program to screen all those who work with children. Right before moving to another church, her pastor dutifully distributed a volunteer application that had been devised to begin the screening process. As Georgia received the form and scanned the questions, her heart was crushed. One simple question turned her world upside down: "Have you ever been sexually abused?" The implication was simple: If you've been sexually abused, then you must not be a safe person to work with kids.

At eleven years of age, Georgia had been raped by her cousins. Compounding the trauma was a big brother who witnessed the event and threatened her that if she didn't do exactly as he said, he would tell their parents what a bad girl she'd been. For nearly fifty years she had experienced many of the symptoms described above. Survival for Georgia meant adopting the "Tough Girl" persona that Dan Allender described in his book. Perfectionism took hold early in life and depression plagued her later years. Like so many others, she had cut herself off almost entirely from both positive and negative feelings. As for her marriage, she was blessed to wed her best friend. But on their wedding night, as he climbed into the shower with her, the pain of the past was triggered and Tough Girl attacked him. Sexual intimacy was nearly nil as she strategized how to avoid him at all costs, even making him wear his clothes to bed.

But then Jesus had to go through Samaria! (Or in this case, her little town in Pennsylvania.) Soon after the new pastor arrived at the church, he received an unnerving call from Georgia. She was irate about the application and this one question in particular. And, she asserted, she had worked with kids all of her life and would never hurt a child! Wow. The pastor said, "Georgia, I don't know what form you are talking about, but it sounds like we need to sit down to talk." And so began her journey of healing as week by week, month by month, they met and studied Allender's *The Wounded Heart* page by page. Life has never been the same since.

For the first time since childhood, Georgia is experiencing joy and her marriage is being radically renewed. With each seminar I have held and each seminary class I have taught, she has given her testimony and answered questions. It has been her way of returning to the village to proclaim how the Living Water is bringing healing to closed-off sections of her soul. And she has announced to other wounded men and women, "Come and see this One who has told me everything that has happened to me and has changed me so dramatically!" (see John 4:29). That is her message and it is summarized in this poem which God helped her write:

"The Moment It Happened"

The moment it happened my soul went into arrest,
The devil cheered: I've claimed another—her life is a mess.
Where was God when this happened to me?
He cried for His child, though His pain she couldn't see.

Maybe it happened one day in the barn's hay,
But wherever it did, you heard someone say,
Listen to me, you've been bad—you must not tell.
The devil's heart soared: you're now locked in my cell.

I've been bad? I'm confused. I don't understand!
I've always told Mommy and she took my hand.
He's right; I've been bad my heart starts to say,
Maybe if I'm quiet it will all go away.

Suddenly ugly, dirty, and cheap,
The feelings of worthlessness now seem to creep
Into every corner of a once innocent life;
I'll just keep smiling, it will mask all the strife.

I'll be good, I'll be perfect, they'll never know,
The pain is still there, it won't cease to flow.
The energy, the drive, it all seems so right
But my heart beats in conflict night after night.

Oh, God!! I need help; give me a trusted earth face,
Someone who can help me find Your amazing grace.

It's time that she accepts My gift of freewill,
To face her pain but will she choose to remain still?
I know that her head has been filled with great lies,
Her heart needs to acknowledge, it must come alive.

My soul that arrested now begins to feel.
My heart once so wounded finally can heal.
For God in His wisdom has kept offering grace,
And now that shines forth in the smile on my face.[5]

Safety at the Closet Door

Of all the sexual subjects that we are so reluctant to talk about, this may well be the most painful. In fact, if you yourself are a victim of past abuse, your heart may be racing. Many questions may come to mind: *Once others read this book, will they suspect this has happened to me? Will I be pressured to go back to memories I have long tried to hide? Why do we even have to bring up this subject?*

Remember once again the Savior's gentle approach with the woman at the well. In a private setting far away from the crowd of clueless men and gawking townsfolk, he simply asked her questions, gradually leading her to the place of brokenness and regret. Out of deep love for this desperate woman, he traveled where few cared to go simply to offer the water that gives life. Firmly and very intentionally, he wooed her out of the closet of sorrow, shame, and rejection.

God will not pull you out of the closet and shame you. But he does invite you to step forward and drink more deeply of that Living Water. Perhaps you've already found the healing that comes with the forgiveness of sins. That, of course, is the most important sip of salvation you will ever take. But having read this chapter, you may have been reminded of the selfish trespasses of others. The list of maladies that attend victims of abuse may have seemed all too familiar. The light seeping through the closet door has your attention and hope is beginning to rise.

Why not leave the confines of the closet? You've become far too comfortable with the smell of old shoes and the safety of colorless clothes that hang as a barrier between you and those who love you most. Will there be pain? Some, of course. As you reach the closet's edge and begin to stand, muscles long-atrophied by hiding and shame will mutter and complain. But as our Savior embraces you, healing will begin to melt away the hurts of your past and restore the strength needed for the future. It will take time, but fresh air will fill your lungs with joy. You will be amazed at the colors you've been missing as the light brings to life the Path of ever-increasing wholeness and holiness that stretches out before you.

And while you are at it, return to the village. Let others know there is a Messiah who has told you everything you have ever done and is setting you free from all that others have done to you. Don't be afraid. There are other thirsty souls peering out through closet doors who also need that Living Water.

Whether or not you are a victim of abuse, consider praying the following prayer:

Gentle Shepherd, thank you for this story of the woman whose thirst was quenched. Thank you that your mission was to meet her at her deepest point of pain and shame. Quench our thirst for greater wholeness while at the same time increasing our hunger to do your will. May we become your welcoming arms at the closet door as you lovingly call others out into your light. In Jesus' name, amen.

Discussion Questions

1. What stood out to you in this chapter?
2. What did you learn about abuse that was new for you?
3. Would you find it easy or difficult to help an abuse victim grieve? Why or why not?
4. What could your church or small group do to let people know there is help for the sexually abused?
5. What resources are available in your community to help someone who has been sexually abused?

The Naked Reality

CHAPTER 4

PRINCIPLE:
The Box, the Path, and the Circus

You don't have to read very far into the story of Jesus before you learn about the Pharisees. They were like the religious police of Jesus' day. It was their job to live out the laws of Jewish life, both those handed down by Moses and the many others that their ancestors had added to the list. More than just live out the laws, they kept a watchful eye upon the people to make sure they toed the line as well. It was all about the Box.

For the Pharisees, the walls of the Box were made up of hundreds of do's and don'ts. Hundreds. What you could and could not do on the Sabbath, what you could and could not eat, how you related to the opposite sex, how you practiced your piety with spiritual disciplines. Hundreds. And the policing involved judging who was in and who was out. While such a mind-set is tedious, there seems to be some payoff for knowing you are in, and being able to say that your neighbor is out!

Another responsibility of Pharisees was to make sure all teaching in the synagogues fit into the Box. So when a new teacher came down the pike, they took time to assess whether truth or heresy was being placed on the table.

Luke 7 tells us about the encounter between Jesus and a Pharisee named Simon. Apparently Simon wanted a closer look at this new teacher and so invited him to dinner. Only God can judge Simon's motives, but his words and actions seemed to indicate Jesus was on trial. As the teacher and his disciples entered the home, they were not greeted in the customary ways. The formal welcome kiss at the door was missing. No feet were washed. And, as strange as the custom may seem to us, no one's head was anointed with oil. Jesus and the other twelve guests simply took their place at the table.

A woman of the city "who was a sinner" entered the dining area as well. The nature of her sin was not explicitly stated, but as the story plays out, it is really not a stretch to say she gained her reputation from *sexual* sin. Given Simon's spiritual OCD, we can well imagine he was a good bit put out when she stepped into the dining room. Perhaps he fretted, "People are going to think she's quite familiar with my place and has beaten a path to my door!" But soon the fretting turned to disgust.

Overcome with sorrow for her sin and sensing the goodness of our Savior, she began to weep at his feet, so much so that she actually bathed his feet with her tears. Now I don't know about you, but when I cry enough to drench a dozen Kleenexes, there's more than just tears involved. There's this stringy mess that starts hanging out of my nose. Jesus' feet, already covered with the dust of the streets, likely became a muddy, slimy mess. On top of that, literally, she began to wipe up the muck with her hair and kiss his feet. (If Simon's spiritual OCD was also actual OCD, he must have been quite freaked out!) Finally, she anointed his feet with a perfumed oil.

The initial shock turned to indignation. Simon concluded, "If this man were a prophet, he would have known who and what kind of woman this is who is touching him—that she is a sinner" (Luke 7:39). But Jesus, far more than just a prophet, read Simon's thoughts from across the table. And so he posed a question.

> "A certain creditor had two debtors; one owed five hundred denarii, and the other fifty. When they could not pay, he canceled the debts for both of them. Now which of them will love him more?" Simon answered, "I suppose the one for whom he canceled the greater debt." And Jesus said to him, "You have judged rightly." (Luke 7:41–43)

With that, Jesus went on to state matters of fact. Simon had not kissed him, washed his feet, or anointed him, largely because he had no love for him. His only thought was to see if Jesus belonged to the Box. The "sinful" woman, on the other hand, had demonstrated a broken and contrite heart. The conclusion? Her many sins had been forgiven. And the implication for Simon? His many sins remained!

Boom! You have just witnessed the implosion of the Pharisee's Box! How could this be? How could that woman be closer to God than Simon? She was not a Box person at all. As far as he was concerned, she didn't even live in the same zip code as the Box! Simon had duct-taped the corners of his Box for years. He knew the do's and don'ts and minded them meticulously. But this woman of the streets was holier? What an outrage! If anything, she was a circus freak!

Taking It a Bit Further

Who's in and who's out? That is a critical question that drives the church's debate regarding gays and lesbians. But it is also an underlying question that shapes how we view *all* relationships within a local church. Who belongs? Who fits in?

The Box is all about position.[1] Are you in? Or are you out? And the walls of the Box are the do's and don'ts that so often become a part of church life:

- *Do* read your Bible.
- *Do* attend church.
- *Don't* drink and especially *don't* get drunk.
- *Don't* cuss, smoke . . . (You get the idea.)

There are many problems with the Box mentality. First of all, let's state the obvious: there's sin inside the Box! Boxed-in people simply don't notice their own sin because it isn't on their list! Workaholism, gossip, manipulation, materialism, slander, and more are often found in the Box. And ready for the big one? Judgmentalism.

Life in the Box actually breeds both judgmentalism and shame. Boxed-in people can't help but notice those not good enough for the Box. "Uh oh. That person goes to the bar. So I guess they're not one of us!" And shame is used to keep people in line.

The church I pastor is called Ashes to Life. Most of those who attend are in recovery from alcohol, heroin, cocaine, or some other kind of substance. We've done all we can to make people feel welcomed and accepted. But when someone relapses, they often feel the weight of shame-laden questions. Can they come back? Do they have to earn people's approval before they return? Will they still be loved? Those are the kind of questions that grow like mold in the dark corners of the Box. Eventually your clothes smell of them! And you expect to be hit with them if you're ever caught outside of the Box.

The Circus is the exact opposite of the Box. Circus folks don't even care about the do's and don'ts. Furthest thing from their minds, really. If it feels good, they're doing it—if they can get away with it. No rules. No limits. Do what you want. After all, it's the Circus! "Yeah, go ahead and laugh at the bearded lady and kick the two-headed dog on your way out of the tent! Who cares?"

What Scripture reveals about spirituality and belonging is that it's a matter of direction, not position. So the question is not, "Are you in the Box?" Instead, it is, "Are you on the Path?" Seems like a subtle difference, but it actually makes *all* the difference. And you don't have to go far to find this in the Scriptures.

The story of the prodigal son is a favorite for many. As I've heard pastors and teachers plumb the depths of this parable, I have been amazed at the many layers of meaning. But the broad structure of the plot clearly communicates these three ways of belonging. The kid brother who took an early inheritance off to a far country basically joined the Circus. Without regard to his father's wishes, he simply went off to do what he wanted to do. Plenty of friends arrived while he had money for one Circus act after another. But when the money dried up and the kid hit bottom, he began to think of home.

Big brother, however, has been camped out in the Box. When the party began for the prodigal, his ire was evident. "Hey, Father dear, you never threw a party for me! I didn't go off and blow your money on wild living. I've stayed put, slaving away here in the fields. I've been doing the do's and avoiding the don'ts. What about me!?"

The Path began with the embrace of the Father and continued on to the party. And if Jesus had written and produced a mini-series instead of a pithy parable, it likely would have gone on to tell of the younger son submitting to the father, working by his side, and enjoying parties and celebrations along the way. The concluding episode, no doubt, would have the elder brother finally breaking out of his self-righteous Box and jumping in on the next line dance.

Can you see how this paradigm of belonging affects church life? When someone in my church relapses back into addiction, my word to them is, "Hey, you are still on the Path. You didn't go back to the Circus. You just stumbled. Let us help you get up and move forward!" And our church is living it out. One lady, after seven months clean from heroin, fell into a bad relationship and relapsed. For months she avoided our people, partly out of shame and partly out of fear that she might try to use us for money. An arrest and jail time were God's way of getting her to detox. But once clean, she was still very anxious about returning. Would we open our arms again? Or would we wag fingers and say, "You should have known better!" The day she walked through the church door, tears were shed as arms embraced her. The worship started and she left the building. Following her out, I found her smoking a cigarette and crying. "Why did I ever leave?" she sobbed. "And why didn't I come back sooner?"

Now in her case, she did go back to the Circus. But no penance was required by the fellowship in order for her to fit back into a box because there is no Box.

God meets us on the Path. He reveals to us the issues he wants to deal with at that point on our journey. And as we move toward the cross, the Path gradually transforms us.

I've been in an accountability group. For most in the group, the issue is staying clean from heroin and alcohol. For me? Speeding. It is practically an addiction, and in the past I have discerned that its roots were some long-held core lies and memories of inferiority. God has brought some healing that has broken its hold on me, but the temptation to push the pedal often comes back.

When I first brought the matter up in the accountability group, one of the guys said, "You're kidding! I have to give that up too?" My response was, "Right now, focus on the heroin. That's your place on the Path. I'm just further down the Path. Obey the traffic laws, of course, but right now God has you focused on heroin."

As we travel the Path together, we pray for each other, study the Scriptures, urge each other further down the Path and, if we stumble, lovingly help each other to our feet.

Does Holiness Come in Boxes?

Back in the early 1990s, I did a brief stint as a youth pastor. The senior pastor was a tremendous administrator and gifted preacher who was nearing retirement. One day he wistfully reflected, "I know the legalism of the past was not good, but at least people lived holier lives!" I guess that depends on your understanding of holiness.

The Box and Path look at holiness from different angles. As God's people, we are set apart from the world as we walk the Path. But the process of God's sanctifying work is to transform us as we travel, restoring the image of God stamped on our being in the garden but marred by the fall. The Path transforms us until the day we see Jesus face-to-face and our bodies are "conformed to the body of his glory" at the end of time (Phil. 3:21).

Once you get the right goggles on, you begin to see the Box, Path, and Circus throughout the New Testament. Paul's letter to the Galatians helps us to understand holiness on the Path. Though the presenting issue was whether or not Gentile believers were required to be circumcised, the deeper issue was the role of the law in the community of believers. The do's and don'ts of the Pharisees were creeping into the life of the church. And so Paul questioned them. Had they been justified by the works of the law (2:16)? Had they received the Holy Spirit through the works of the law (3:2)? Were miracles worked among them through works of the law (3:5)? The answer was the same in all three instances: no! It was through believing what they had heard and putting their faith in the work of Christ. And so Paul concluded the only thing that mattered was "faith working through love" (5:6). In other words, what counts is an active relationship with God on the Path.

As elsewhere, Paul had to guard against the charge of lawlessness. By dismissing the works of the law, was he advocating for the lifestyle of the Circus? Absolutely not! They were not to indulge or gratify the flesh. As the works of the law were ineffective in bringing about righteousness and a Spirit-empowered life, so too the works of the flesh only bring destruction. Those who live their lives at the Circus "will not inherit the kingdom of God" (5:21).

It is not the way of works that brings about the life God desires. Efforts to stay in the Box by working the do's and don'ts profit nothing. And the outworkings of indulging fleshly human desires eventually enslave and devour Circus goers. Both the works of the law and the works of the flesh fall short. Works don't cut it. It's not works at all. Paul told us it is fruit (5:22–23). The fruit of the Spirit is a natural by-product of walking in the Spirit along the Path. Trees don't work and struggle to produce fruit. They are simply positioned in places where sunlight bathes them, rain refreshes them, and good soil nourishes them. That's life on the Path. It is not human effort to obey laws. Nor is it allowing the flesh to rule over us and produce the works of the flesh. It is, as Paul said, *walking* in the Spirit. Hmm . . . that even sounds like a Path, doesn't it?

He went on to say that if we are led by the Spirit we are not subject to the law and will, in fact, fulfill the law as the fruit of love, joy, peace, patience, et al., grows in our lives (Gal. 5:13–14, 22–23). This is the life on the Path. It is being led by the Spirit and positioning ourselves for his life-changing power through various means of grace. And as we stay on the Path, we are gradually transformed into the likeness of Jesus.

Perhaps it is easier for me to see the power of this paradigm because by God's grace we are reaching some pretty rough folks. Most have logged a lot of time in bars and behind bars, so the term "church fights" has a whole new meaning at Ashes to Life. Though our church is small, we go against the grain of the usual demographics. We have more men than women, more tattoos than gray hair, and piercings abound in places more than just ears. My hospital visits take me to the psych unit far more often than to the other floors. Some attendees come from the local halfway house, some from three-quarter-way houses, and a few from the homeless shelter. Want to worship with us? Then arrive early before the coffee pot is drained. And sorry about the cigarette smoke outside the front door.

The language can be a bit rough as well. Gary was active in our discipleship group and also a weekly cell group when he first became involved. God had used his father's death and a rigorous rehab to set him free from thirty-seven years of drinking. At the end of cell-group meetings, when asked how to pray for him, he always said, "Yeah, I need help with my profanity. I just can't seem to stop!" And so week by week we prayed.

One day he walked from his three-quarter-way house to the Family Dollar down the street. Two young men from a Box-type church began to witness to him. (It may have been the church that has the sign saying, "Independent, Fundamental, Bible-Believing, KJV." That's my guess.) With a brief introduction, they began with their questions. Did Gary know that he needed to get saved? Well, yes, that's what he had learned at Ashes to Life. Was he sure if he was actually born again? Well, he thought so. Was he baptized the right way? After all, God would want more than just sprinkling.

"Well, that's not what I'm learning about God."

"Look, you simply need to come to *our* church!"

"F--- you! I go to Ashes to Life!" (Ah, yes! Thank you, Gary, for that advertisement! Not quite how most of us would have worded it.)

So does his language and angry hand gesture mean Gary isn't in the kingdom? Hardly. While he may not fit into the Box of those two men, his feet are firmly on the Path. God has delivered him from alcohol and is in the process of cleaning up his language. He's been set apart for God's sake, and God is making the separation clearer for all to see week by week, month by month, year by year. The Path does that for faithful folks.

Now holiness is certainly about obedience. And one should not be put in a position of spiritual leadership unless they have some degree of maturity and control over obvious sins that cause people to stumble. They should be a good bit further down the Path than the average Joe. But the desire to obey God and to live a holy life, whether a leader or not, flows from a different source depending upon how you understand belonging. The obedience rising up from the Box is driven by fear and obligation. If you don't comply, you are out. You won't belong anymore. But the Path says, "Hey, you already belong. This is who you are, so live it out" (see Ephesians 5:1–2). It is walking in step with the Spirit of Jesus and finding his enabling so that you put to death the works of the flesh because you *want to* out of a holy love for God, not because you *have to* in order to remain in the Box.

Sexual Issues

The Box does crazy things to our perspective when it comes to sexual issues. Oh, it's pretty easy when it comes to judging the Circus types. Those at the Circus are simply indulging their rebellious flesh and are apathetic about lists of sexual prohibitions "as long as no one is getting hurt." But it gets dicey when it comes to judging those who claim to be Christians. Dicey indeed. Because as we noted earlier, there is definitely sin inside the Box, including sexual sin. Therefore Box types have to rationalize why their sexual sin isn't as bad as someone else's.

And so the Box nurtures a valuing system when it comes to sexual sin. Just to illustrate, let's use monetary values. A single man who gazes at porn? Let's say that's a $2 sin. Add masturbation and you are up to $5. Premarital sex in high school? Probably $25. Pre-marital sex with your fiancée while in your twenties, however, takes you back down to around $10. You get the idea?

Now it gets tricky with adultery. A man who cheats on his wife is starting out at $50, but there could be adjustments to that price. If his wife is sexually averse and a terrible nag, I guess we are back down to around $35 on the Box price list. But if she's a real sweetheart, then jack it up to $90!

In our volatile sexual economy, some values have been changing dramatically. The view of homosexual acts from inside the Box used to fetch more than $900 a decade ago, but now it has tumbled to around $150—more or less, depending upon your denomination.

Do you see how crazy this is? As we will discuss more carefully in chapter 7, all sin is equally sinful in the eyes of a holy God. Sexual sins are no more tainted than other transgressions. Without question, they can be more damaging than other sins, but they are not more sinful.

Jesus made this plain in the Sermon on the Mount. The Ten Commandments state clearly that we are not to commit adultery. But Jesus took it deeper. With life on the Path, even if you stop to look at a woman with the intent to lust after her, that is just as sinful. To be sure, my wife would have a preference. If given a choice between the two, I am sure she would rather I look and lust than to actually act it out in adultery. Jesus stated that both are equally sinful. But you can be sure the latter transgression would be a lot more costly on many levels.

Church life on the Path takes some of the acidity out of the discussion of sexual sin. Can you imagine the following conversation? "So you fight temptation to have sex with people of the same sex? Let's pray for each other because I fight temptation to have sex with the opposite sex. Similar struggle, just a different flavor."

No matter what a person's sexual struggle, they are welcome to the fellowship of the Path. How does that sound to you? Well, if you've spent most of your life in the Box, that probably sounds pretty unsettling. In fact, you may have some of the following questions or concerns:

- You're going to have gay and heterosexual couples sharing the same pews?
- Cohabitating couples taking communion with our elderly widows?

- Where do we draw the lines?
- How do we let people know that we believe living in sin is, uh, sinful? It's our job to point this stuff out, isn't it?

We sometimes become confused concerning the role of the church. We are called to be the body of Christ, not the body of John the Baptist. Our role is not to dress in burlap, hoist a placard, and stand on street corners telling people they are going to hell. It is clearly the Holy Spirit's role to convince people of their sin (see John 16:8). Our part is to live out the love of Christ among the last, least, and lost around us. Am I saying that Jesus never took the role of prophet and rebuked people? No, he certainly did. Scorching rebukes, in fact. But those on the receiving end were the Box types of his day—the Pharisees. As a friend of mine once remarked, "He was trying to elevate them to the level of sinner." Sometimes it takes punching holes right through the Box so that people can see their own sin as the light of the truth finally pours in.

Using Shame for Kingdom Work

What?! Using shame for God's work? Yep. Happens all the time in the Box, especially with sexual issues.

Years ago a colleague of mine, while single and serving on staff of a large church, fell for a single lady. Though they didn't "go all the way," they went too far too quickly. Conscience-stricken, he confessed to the lead pastor. The lead pastor brought it to the attention of a regional supervisor. And (get ready to gasp) the regional supervisor made an example of him, sending a letter to all of the pastors of that denomination in that part of the state. Ouch!

More recently, a small denomination sent a message to its entire clergy: *If you ever get caught with sexual misconduct of any kind, you will lose your pastorate.* As that letter hit wastebaskets across the country, I'm guessing vows were made: "I will do anything to keep from getting caught!"

I've heard many more such stories. A lay leader who was pressured into confessing to a congregation on a Sunday morning his use of porn. A counselor who required men to confess to their wives every time they lusted after another woman. An accountability group that penalized members by making them pick up dog poop in the park if they slipped up.

For some reason, even though we certainly don't verbalize it, we have this notion that shame and rejection are good tools to keep people in line. Perhaps they are wielded with all the best of loving intentions. The concern, of course, is containment. Keeping people in the Box. It's about managing behavior so that marriages are not ruined and testimonies are not soiled. But they only drive people deeper into hiding within the church closet.

Am I not concerned about behavior? Of course I am. All sin has a price and sexual sin is particularly damaging. The question, however, is how we best help move people forward on the Path toward greater healing. As we will discover in chapter 7, sexual addiction in particular is driven by shame and fear of abandonment. So to use shame and rejection as "accountability tools" serve only to hinder transparency and drive people further into the clutches of the closet.

Certainly there's a place for warning people about the harm of sexual sin. The first seven chapters of Proverbs are filled with such warnings: "Can one walk on hot coals without scorching the feet? So is he who sleeps with his neighbor's wife; no one who touches her will go unpunished" (Prov. 6:28–29). Once someone has abandoned the Path and run headlong to the Circus, rebuke and correction may be exactly what is needed. Galatians 6:1 advises that we do so humbly and gently. But using shame and fear of rejection only adds fuel to licentious desire and drives people further into hiding.

Healing Power on the Path

Wow. We really have our work cut out for us, don't we? If the church is going to deal intelligently with sexual issues, it means changing the way we view the matter of belonging. That is a difficult shift to make. Even in our recovery church where I refer to the Box, Path, and Circus with blatant redundancy, the traditional church folks among us catch themselves slipping back into that all-too-familiar mind-set. But the effort to be more biblical in how we view church life is well worth it. Grace and love is really what people long for, isn't it?

When God first began leading abuse victims to me, I received a rather bizarre phone call from Tonya, a woman I referred to in chapter 2. "Is this Pastor Mark Ongley?"

"Yes, it is."

"Do you counsel homosexuals?"

"Uh, I can."

"Well, I'm supposed to come to you for counseling, but I don't want to!" she said angrily.

"Hmm, Okay."

That very day God had spoken to her as she drove to work: "Dan Drystone is going to talk with you and you need to do what he says." And sure enough, Dan, who was lay leader of my church, approached her and said, "I know you are in a lesbian relationship, but I think you ought to get counseling from my pastor. He could help you."

She was furious. She didn't want help and certainly not from a pastor!

The first appointment she marched through my office door, planted her hand down on my desk, pointed her finger in my face, and demanded, "Why should I trust you?!" Whew! She plopped down in her chair and began to tell me how church people had so deeply hurt her because of her attraction to women. She finally had found an out-of-the-way church, worshipped faithfully, and began to volunteer her time to do janitorial work. But her mopping was interrupted one day by the pastor who yelled, "Get out of this church and don't you ever come back until you get your act together!" Deeply crushed, she exited and vowed she would never go to church again.

Later in the conversation, wanting me to know about the nature of her relationship with her lover, she snapped at me once again: "And I want you to know that it's not about sex!"

Pausing for a moment, I replied, "I don't suppose it is. My guess is you simply want to be held in the arms of a woman and feel loved."

With that her face flushed red, tears coursed down her cheeks, and she choked out the words, "That's exactly it."

Five different men had sexually abused her, beginning at the age of four. Having grown up in a family of eight children who all shared an overwhelmed and deeply dysfunctional mother, she lacked a proper sense of attachment. These factors fueled a revulsion of men and a longing for feminine touch. We followed the leading of the Spirit from session to session for nearly two years. Eventually, yes, the Holy Spirit convinced her she had to leave her partner, but not without first bringing healing to some of the torturous memories of sexual abuse. Separating from her partner was one of the most difficult things she had ever done—the bond was so tight. No, I didn't drag her through a study of Leviticus, Romans 1, and 1 Corinthians 6. I allowed the Holy Spirit to do the convincing in his own way and in his own timing.

Early on she made the remark, "If you think you're going to convince me to marry some guy through all this counseling, you can forget it! The idea of being in bed with a man makes me want to puke!" I assured her my goal was only to follow the leading of the Holy Spirit and cooperate with what I saw the Father doing in her life. But one day, to her surprise, she found herself enjoying the flirtation of a man at work. Eventually she married and has recently served in Africa as a short-term missionary.

Yes, quite a success story. And no, not everyone I counsel has that kind of success. For many the results of counseling have been far less dazzling. But the point here is not about changing homosexuals into heterosexuals. The issue is pointing people toward the Path, which changes us all from one degree of glory to another.

Five months into the counseling process, I asked her what had been the most helpful thing in her healing journey. Was it technique? A particular prayer practice? A clever insight from psychology or Scripture? I actually expected she would refer to the healing God had brought to the memories of abuse or to the mending of her heart regarding her mother. Quite the contrary. The most healing factor was my love and acceptance. She cited as an example what had happened at the end of that very first session.

Knowing that first appointment was going to be a challenge, I had sought God's direction ahead of time. Very clearly, I heard him say to offer her communion. So at the end of the session I brought out the elements, prayed a blessing over them, and partook from the Lord's Table with her, with both of us drinking from the same chalice. That simple act, she claimed, was one of the most healing moments of her journey. In retrospect, I believe the message to her was that we were both on the Path. There was no Box for her to break through. There was no list of do's and don'ts for her to master before she would be accepted by me or by God. The road ahead would be guided by the Spirit and attended by grace and love.

Helping people exit the closet into God's healing light involves a loving invitation to travel the Path. Shame and judgmentalism are left in the Box where they belong. As a friend of mine who used to minister to transvestites once stated, "I love the hell out of them. Literally, I *love the hell out of them!*" And that's what the apostle Paul said, isn't it? "The only thing that counts is faith working through love" (Gal. 5:6). Sounds like a good strategy for ministry to all people, but especially to the sexually broken hiding in the closets of our churches.

The Box, the Path, and the Circus is the New Testament way of understanding belonging. Ingrain this in your own thinking. Make it a part of the language of your church. You will be surprised how it takes some of the toxicity out of the gay/straight church debate and moves us all toward greater wholeness.

To that end, I invite you to pray the following prayer:

Gracious Lord Jesus, thank you for the power of the cross, which has delivered me from the destruction of a Circus existence. Forgive me for getting too comfortable in the Box of do's and don'ts, for I acknowledge that this is not the life of faith and love. You have issued the simple invitation: "Follow me." And so I place both feet on the Path. Lead me forward. Continue your work of transformation in my life. To you be the glory forever! Amen!

Discussion Questions

1. What grabbed your attention in this chapter?
2. What were some of the do's and don'ts that you remember from the church in your childhood?
3. Do you agree that all sin is equally sinful? Why or why not?
4. Have you ever seen shame used "for the kingdom of God"? Do you think there is ever an appropriate time for God's people to use shame?
5. How would viewing church life this way take some of the toxicity out of the gay/straight debate?
6. What would it take for your church to make this kind of shift in its thinking? Are there practical ways to reinforce the concept of the Path?

CHAPTER 5

THEOLOGY:
The Fall and Open-Eyed Blindness

A few years ago I was pastoring two churches with three worship services averaging a combined attendance of two hundred thirty... *with no staff!* Until staff was hired, I had to pedal furiously to keep up with the traffic. But there were a few moments during each week that were a restful delight. One of those time slots was the Wednesday afternoon Bible study with some wonderful retired ladies of the smaller church. They were genuinely interested in the Scriptures and they served as the spiritual backbone for that little congregation.

One afternoon they invited me to go on a day-long bus trip to see the drama *In the Beginning* at Sight & Sound Theater, a production depicting the creation of the world. With my exacting schedule, there was no way I could spare an entire day on a bus with senior citizens. My response? "Thanks, but no thanks! Rather busy!" I should have noticed the winks and smiles. Thinking I was just being polite and simply couldn't afford the ticket, they pooled their money and bought me one. "Uh, gee, you shouldn't have!"

Actually, it was worth every one of their pennies and every minute of my time. It was an amazing production that had me weeping at the end.

The vast theater was turned into a garden of delight with both live and animated creatures. After man was formed from the dust, God took Adam on a wonder-filled tour of the Garden of Eden. There was such joy in their relationship as Adam kept asking God, "Hey, what's this? Look how beautiful!" When Eve arrived, it simply added to the celebration.

But enter the Serpent, stage right. Doubts were raised as Satan posed his questions and planted his lies. "You will not die; for God knows that when you eat of it your eyes will be opened, and you will be like God, knowing good and evil" (Gen. 3:4–5). Eve and Adam both saw the fruit, believed the lies, and took a bite. Then their eyes were opened to their nakedness. Shame and separation entered the world. And . . . *then we broke for intermission!*

Freshly supplied with soft drinks, roasted almonds, and other concession-stand goodies, the curtain rose to reveal a very different scene. The lighting was dim, the landscape brown and bleak, and the characters aged. The rest of the drama depicted the remainder of Adam's nine hundred thirty years of life. Throughout the performance, he continued to cry out again and again, "God, where are you? I just want to see your face! If only I could see your face again." Wow.

Just as Satan promised, their eyes were opened. Opened to their nakedness but closed to the face of God. And so we live in this time between the Garden of Eden and the Garden of Paradise with an open-eyed blindness to the face of God. It is a season obscured by the three seeds of deception planted by the Serpent regarding who we are (humanity), what God is like (divinity), and what life is all about (nature). The dimness of soul will continue, generation to generation, until we reach that next garden where we will finally see God face-to-face.

The Curse and the Mission

Shame leads to hiding and blame. God began to call out to Adam, "Where are you?" (Gen. 3:9). Eventually Adam and Eve stepped out of hiding. Adam blamed Eve, and Eve blamed the Serpent. Out of shame they had covered themselves up with leaves. Out of mercy, God soon shed blood and covered them with skins. Then came the curses.

Instead of seeing God's face clearly, they would be thrust from the garden. No longer would they walk upright, reaching up to God, and finding their worth in a relationship with him. Both would be cursed with bentness.[1] Man would bend toward his work, finding his worth and value from tilling the ground. Instead of eating freely from any tree, his work would be accompanied with toil and sweat. And the curse of the woman? To be bent in desire toward her husband. Instead of creating with joy as God had done, childbirth would be joined with great pain.

As for the Serpent, a prophetic warning was issued. The offspring of the woman would eventually crush him—what most believe is a reference to the coming Messiah whose death would disarm and defeat him. And with this pronouncement, God began his mission, the preparation of the world for the coming of Jesus Christ. To see Jesus would be to see the Father's face once again. And with his arrival the full restoration of truth would begin in earnest.

Obscured Vision

With the fall came not only an obscuring of the face of God, but a distorted way of viewing the world. The lies planted by Satan were insidious. As stated earlier, there were lies concerning who we are, what God is like, and how life is ordered. Instead of living out their dominion over the created world under the direction of the Creator, Adam and Eve, our representatives in the garden, submitted to the suggestions of a created being and tried to become like God by consuming a piece of created fruit. Instead of receiving from the Tree of Knowledge and the Tree of Life in God's good timing, they tried to grasp equality with him on their own. These lies instilled in the garden continue to distort our vision to this very day. We continue to buy into the suggestions of the Evil One, idolizing and submitting to the created world and seeking to grasp and exploit the very things God would have us simply receive from his hand in his timing.[2] It is a matter greatly affected by what we today call "worldview."

As Old Testament professor John Oswalt has taught for many years, two worldviews were ushered in when our first parents were ushered out of the garden. The pagan worldview dominates the globe and flows directly from the three seeds of doubt planted at the beginning. The other view of the world is God's. It is the truth revealed in the garden, the very truth that he has been restoring through the ongoing revelation of his nature and character.

As the diagram on page 75 makes plain, there are several key differences between these worldviews. First note that in the pagan worldview, humanity, divinity, and nature are all part of the same pie, with the arrows illustrating the porous boundaries between them. The foundational principle here is *continuity*. In this view there is an interconnectedness among the three elements of divinity, humanity, and nature. Clear and distinct boundaries do not exist between these three. Inherent to this view of the world is the means of *manipulation*. People survived in ancient times by attempting to manipulate the cosmos. Continuity and manipulation provide the framework within which the system functions.[3]

The perceived need among people with open-eyed blindness is *security*. How are we going to provide for ourselves? How will we protect ourselves from threats? How will we continue the family line?[4] In this system of thinking, security is obtained by manipulating the deities through acts of idolatry and sexuality.

So how exactly did this play out? Oswalt imagined something like this: Joe Pagan, in preparation for the year ahead, has planted a field with grain. It is absolutely essential for his family's survival that they harvest a healthy crop. On the horizon, however, dark clouds are looming. A little rain would do his field some good, but a gully washer would bring ruin and disaster. Survival and security are on the line. How can he manipulate that storm for favorable results? By appealing to Baal, of course, the god of the storm. And as all his neighbors know, this means going to the stone idol. To you and me, that simply looks like a rock shaped to represent Baal—perhaps even carved by Joe himself! But to Joe, it *is* Baal. Why? Because of the continuity between deity and nature. So sacrifices are made to the stone that is Baal in order to influence the storm,

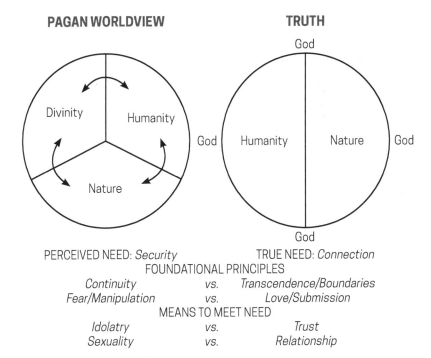

PERCEIVED NEED: *Security*   TRUE NEED: *Connection*

FOUNDATIONAL PRINCIPLES

Continuity	*vs.*	*Transcendence/Boundaries*
Fear/Manipulation	*vs.*	*Love/Submission*

MEANS TO MEET NEED

Idolatry	*vs.*	*Trust*
Sexuality	*vs.*	*Relationship*

which is *also* Baal. If the sacrifices are sufficiently, uh, sacrificial, Baal's arm will be twisted and he will provide a gentle rain. But if not, then famine could well be their fate. See how this open-eyed blindness of continuity and manipulation generates fear?[5]

So what is the truth? As God has revealed himself down through time, we find that a proper worldview is governed by the principle of transcendence. Notice again the diagram. God is set apart from creation because he himself has created it. He alone is God and is totally other. Instead of the continuity imagined by the pagan worldview, there are clear boundaries. God is not a force to manipulate through idolatry in order to gain a sense of security. That's just not how life works. Our greatest need is not security, but relationship and connectedness. Manipulation gets us nowhere. We are designed to relate with a personal being through love and submission, not by grasping and twisting arms.

Corrective Lenses

The Scriptures reveal God's ongoing work of providing corrective lenses for humanity. A proper worldview needed to be shaped, and the Bible relates the mission of God in restoring not only a worldview, but in restoring humanity to himself. And what a story it is! In fact, the Bible is unlike any other work of ancient literature. Written over a period of many centuries by perhaps as many as forty different authors, each from varied walks of life, the Scriptures contain history, poetry, law, prophecy, parables, doctrine, and personal correspondence. And yet despite all of this, within its pages is found this unfolding narrative of the mission of God. From the Garden of Eden to the Garden of Paradise, God is at work bringing restoration to a fallen world.

One way to observe this mission is God's effort to ingrain within his people's thinking that he alone is God and that he is a transcendent being. Early in the account he chose Abram, vowing to bless the nations through his descendants. From the exodus through the exile, from generation to generation, the message was reemphasized: there is no other God, and idolatry is not the means to meet one's needs. And yet it is a lesson God's people had to continue to relearn as they repeatedly relapsed into the pagan practice of sacrificing to idols to appeal to gods and goddesses. The polytheistic worldview of the neighboring nations was incredibly persistent. Following the divine discipline of the seventy-year Babylonian exile, however, idolatry and polytheism were finally set aside. The lenses were nearly in place. The stage was at last set for the coming of the Messiah who, incredibly, would claim that to see him was to see the Father. At this point, monotheism was so firmly entrenched that the leaders cried out, "Blasphemy!" But had the mission of God not been carried out over the centuries, the response of the people would surely have been polytheistic. Instead of beginning to understand God as Trinity, they would have begun the worship of three gods: Father, Son, and Spirit.

Let's rewind a good bit and reconsider the two opposing worldviews. A critical phase in God's mission of reshaping their lenses was the entry of his people into Canaan. This is described in the Torah. While the word *Torah* has a breadth of usage, commonly it refers to the first five books of the Old Testament. Torah literally means "instruction" or "teaching." And so the Law and the narrative of the Torah were meant to serve as the curriculum for the mission of God. The overall aim? To shape their worldview as they entered the Promised Land.

It is commonly said from pulpits and in seminary classrooms that we become like the gods we worship. The Bacchanalian feasts, celebrated in honor of the Roman god of wine, were drunken affairs. Likewise, Greek worship of Aphrodite was steeped in sensuality. In summarizing the demise of the northern kingdom of Israel, the writer of 2 Kings stated, "They followed worthless idols and themselves became worthless" (17:15 NIV).

And so God, in an effort to shape his chosen people, began to reveal himself to them in a variety of ways so that they would become like him. His character is seen in the various names attributed to him. His interaction with his people revealed his principles and the miracles revealed his glorious saving power. And of particular importance for this discussion, the laws handed to Moses were a key instrument in shaping their view of divinity, humanity, and nature. God desired that they know him and reflect his character. This became apparent throughout the laws of Leviticus as he repeatedly stated, "You shall be holy, for I the LORD your God am holy" (Lev. 19:2). His plan to wean them from the practices of their pagan neighbors was clearly the intent of the Law, as he declared, ". . . you shall not do as they do in the land of Canaan" (Lev. 18:3). The laws made clear not only the boundaries of behavior but also their separation as the distinct people of God.

Sex at the Center of the Universe

So what does all this have to do with sexuality? Some of the pagan narratives state that gods and goddesses came about through sex. In fact, the creation of nature and humanity was attributed to the copulation of deities. As you may have read or seen in the movies, myths sometimes include accounts of humans and gods having intercourse with each other. All of this, of course, further illustrates the porous nature of the boundaries between the three realms in the pagan worldview, and it led to the pagan custom of using sex as a means to manipulate the cosmos. And so intercourse with animals and temple prostitutes was practiced in order to ensure the fertility of crops and cattle. Porous boundaries were applied to human relationships as well. Certainly there were marriage covenants, but it was expected that men would have intercourse with prostitutes, relatives, animals, and the wives of neighbors.[6]

The pervasiveness and tantalizing persuasiveness of this sexualized worldview was the very reason God dictated such clear sexual boundaries for his people as they entered the Promised Land. The bulk of these restrictions are found in Leviticus 18 and 20. Have you read them lately? Many of them seem out of sync with our culture. "Do not have sex with your Aunt Millie." *Uh, thanks for the warning, God, but I'm not going there anytime soon!* "No sex with your neighbor's cow." *Yuck! Not tempted with that at all!* But some of the other prohibitions certainly do address the idolatrous and grasping tendencies of our own generation. The specific intent was not to create a comprehensive list to address every sexual activity known to humanity, but to forbid his people from the practices current at that time in Canaan.

More will be said about this in chapter 11 as we take a closer look at these boundaries. For now, simply keep in mind the purpose for laying down the boundaries in the first place. It was all about shaping worldview. Yes, I know the common arguments thrown about which defend the current practice of same-sex marriage. But I promise we'll get to that later.

Idolatrous Submission and Exploitive Grasping

Adam and Eve started a trend. They set a twofold pattern of disobedience: idolatrous submission and exploitive grasping. Instead of ruling over and caring for creation, they *submitted* to a serpent and *grasped* for what was not theirs. And so it is for us. We submit to the created order, bowing down to it in idolatrous fashion to meet our needs. Or at times we exploit it, grasping for what God has put out of bounds—again, to find our value and to meet our aching needs. As did the pagans of old, we want to blur the boundaries of life and grasp for what we want instead of receiving from God in his good timing what we need most. We have resorted to manipulating our way through life to find our identity and fulfill our longings instead of submitting to God and trusting in him.

But didn't God give us the created world, including sex, to meet our needs? Well, yes—within the boundaries that he has set. And there is a God-ordained order to the meeting of needs. Terry Wardle helped to clarify this for me when I heard him say that God is to be the *source* and the created world the *resource*. In other words, God is to be the ultimate source for the fulfillment of my longings, and he has blessed me with a marriage, a family, and friendships as resources to help meet those longings. When we begin to lean into the created world as our main source, idolatry and exploitation follow.

Isn't it obvious how this works out in the expressions of our sexuality? There will always be the temptation to blur the lines or to outright discard the boundaries God has made plain. There's the idolatrous submission to porn and fantasy to meet our need for significance, love, and purpose. Or the exploitive grasping of sexual abuse and seduction that become our means of escaping a sense of powerlessness. And the fruit of our behavior has been quite bitter, hasn't it? Perhaps this is nowhere more apparent than when it comes to imprinting.

The Power of Imprinting

Victoria Kepler Didato, one of my instructors in doctoral studies, made reference to the dynamic of sexual imprinting. Our first sexual experience has an imprinting effect upon us, shaping how we understand sex, our role in sexual intimacy, and ourselves as sexual persons. Now if we consider this dynamic in light of God's design as discussed in chapter 2, it indeed inspires wonder at his creative hand. Those first few years of "twitterpation" are the days of head-over-heels craziness when we are speaking all five love languages. We fall all over ourselves in buying gifts for, spending time with, affirming, caressing, and serving the person we are gaga over. By God's design, it is into such a state of euphoria that we bring the security of the marriage covenant and experience our first moment of sexual climax. And so our very first sexual experience takes place at a time when our partner is going out of his or her way to be loving, caring, sensitive, and tender. At least that's the plan. God's plan, that is.

But how often does that plan play out? Whew. In our culture? Not very often. Instead of trusting God and submitting to his plan, we grasp and exploit in order to get what we want when we want it to fill those deep longings. To be fair, we live in a culture that coaches us to marry about fifteen years after our bodies are ready for sex, and then bombards us with images and messages to get what we want *now*. But what is the result? If the first sexual experience takes place outside of a twitterpated honeymoon, how does that imprint affect us?

In her work with victims of sexual abuse, Didato found the imprint is often the message that sex is something done *to me* instead of done *with me*. How tragic. John Money of Johns Hopkins University maintained that the teen boy who is urged on by his dad or his buddies to say or do anything to get the prom girl to cave in will find himself carrying that imprint into his marriage. He will view his wife as someone to convince and conquer.[7] Can you see how this might affect a marriage?

The sexual imprint is stubborn. It greatly affects one's perceptions of intimacy and is not easily changed. But there is hope. Just as God has been reshaping worldview with his truth, I have witnessed how God can reshape the distortions of his design through Spirit-empowered prayer.

Baal and Sex

Let's revisit the gods and goddesses of ancient times to gain a perspective for the present day. An evolution of sorts took place for Baal. His name dots the text of the Old Testament, and initially he was god of the storm. But with time, perhaps due to the sexual ways in which he was worshipped, he began to represent perverse sexual practices. Scripture, in fact, refers to Israel's unfaithfulness to God as "prostituting" themselves before Baal. And Hosea spells out clearly that such spiritual adultery was rife with sexual forms of worship (Hosea 4:12–14). With that in mind, I believe the story of Gideon is instructive for us.[8]

Yes, you probably think of him as the frightened soldier who twice laid the fleece on the ground, needing a sign from God to bolster his faith. Or you might remember his remarkable transformation as he charged into battle with just a handful of torch-carrying, trumpet-blowing warriors. But the transformation from wimp to warrior was initiated by a challenge from God: "Pull down the altar of Baal that belongs to your father" (Judg. 6:25). Before the empowerment of the Spirit and the change in character, he was called upon to repent from the pagan practices of his family and culture, practices that included sexual acts far from God's design.

The starting point is the same for us, isn't it? To see our way clearly through this time between the gardens requires an adjustment in worldview. The culture around us is blurring sexual boundaries with even some theologians stating that we can basically shelve our Bibles and choose for ourselves where we want to draw the lines.[9] But just as Jesus pointed the religious leaders of his day back to Adam and Eve for answers regarding divorce, so also with us today. The ongoing mission of God has been to focus our eyes more fully upon his original design in the garden, seeing that he is holy, we are made in his image, and sex is simply a created thing to be used as he intended. Sex is not the center of the universe and we are not to submit to it in worship or to grasp for it as the source for meeting our unmet longings. For many of us, the way out of the closet of shame is blocked by a stubborn altar to Baal.

Re-hitching the Horse

The town where I live is blessed with a small and fairly conservative Christian college that makes a good effort to be involved with the community. Pastors are allowed library privileges, thankfully, and may borrow as many as six books at a time. And so while doing research on sexual issues, I took advantage of their resources. At times I wondered if the librarians began to worry about this pastor who kept checking out the books on sex! "Uh oh, here he comes again. Put campus security on alert!"

As I culled through the books, I noticed something similar about all of them, whether written from a secular or a Christian perspective. Not just that a zealous librarian had cut out or blackened the pictures and diagrams, but that both perspectives put the cart before the horse. Here's what I mean.

A theme running through the secular books guided readers toward spicing up their sex lives. *How does one get more spark, zing, and zip? Try this technique or experiment with this position. And if those approaches fail to rekindle the fire, then work on the relationship, because if the relationship is healthy, sexual intercourse will be at its best.*

The Christian books? Pretty much the same. Certainly they added the God element. *Hey, God created us as sexual beings, so this is a good gift from him. Set aside any prudish Puritanical baggage passed down from your parents or imposed by that elderly junior high Sunday school teacher. God wants sex for Christians to be every bit as tantalizing and exciting as it is for those secular folks.* Now there was certainly less talk of techniques and positioning, and I assume there were fewer pictures and diagrams. (Not as many pages were cut out!) Oh, and lest I forget, there was also that final word of advice. *Work on the relationship, because even the experts tell us that sex is best when the relationship is in good shape.*

Hmm . . . Do you notice what is backward? As we noted in chapter 2, God did not make us sexual beings and give us relationships so that we could be sexually fulfilled. Exactly the opposite! He made us relational beings and gave us sex to meet those deep needs for union with another and knowing another. Though it may not seem like it, the difference is huge! If sexual fulfillment is what we are made for, then that feeds into our bent toward unholy sexuality. In other words, if sexual fulfillment is a basic right for human beings, then all the more reason to use power to exploit and manipulate. If God created me for the purpose of sexual release, then all the more reason to bow down to this created world to find that need met.

However, if I am created for relationships, if that truly is my deepest longing, then sexual activity becomes subservient to those relationships. That, then, is the lens through which we view the multiple choices set before us. Exploiting another person for sexual gratification? Leaning into another person to get an emotional buzz? Using pornography for titillating stimulation? Degrading lovemaking by introducing deviation? These and other issues are all put into perspective.

Perhaps this very moment is the time to get the horse back out in front of the cart. Is God calling you to tear down this altar of Baal? Is it time for you to surrender your sexuality to him? Depending upon your level of brokenness, the road ahead could be very difficult. Oh how closet clutter can cling to us! Fully repenting from the addiction of fantasy and porn or the aversion toward intimacy may take much effort, accountability, and counseling. But in pulling down this altar, the Spirit can begin a work of transformation from wimp to warrior, from slave to free.

Consider the following prayer, and if the Spirit so leads, pray it from the heart:

Gracious Creator God, I acknowledge your good design for my sexuality. Despite what Satan has done to distort and destroy this good gift, I acknowledge that what you have made is exceedingly good. You have created us as relational beings and have granted us sexuality so that we might more fully know another and be known ourselves; so that we might gain a sense of belonging, acceptance, and love as we bond with another; and so that we might find significance and purpose by participating in your act of creating life.

I surrender to your purposes for my sexuality as defined in your Word. I renounce the world's message that sexual fulfillment is a right. I refuse to meet my emotional needs through ungodly relationships and improper sexual activities. I will look to you as the source for the fulfillment of my desires and to my spouse alone as the resource you have provided. In Jesus' name, amen.

Discussion Questions

1. In your own words, what are the key differences between the pagan worldview and the worldview of the Bible?
2. What elements of the pagan worldview do you see currently in our culture?
3. What was the greatest "Aha!" moment as you read this chapter?
4. Explain what is meant by putting the cart before the horse.
5. Of all the content in this chapter, what part do you think your local church needs to hear the most?

CHAPTER 6

APPLICATION:
The Idolatry of Fantasy and Adultery

Say all you want about the convenience of Netflix, there's still nothing quite like the big screen. A bucket of butter-drenched popcorn in your lap and a five-dollar soft drink sitting cold and stout in the armrest cup holder, what more could you want? But what we really pay for is the atmosphere. A sound system surrounds you so that it feels as though you are right there on the city street side-by-side with Captain America and the Avengers as they battle the creepy space invaders. And, of course, the big screen itself draws you in. With jarring clarity, you enter the world of drama, especially if you are wearing 3-D glasses!

But eventually the credits roll, the darkness begins to lift, and you reenter the real world. *Oh yeah, that's right. It's just a movie.*

It's not reality! You stand, feel the stiffness in your legs, and begin to shuffle out of the seats, sometimes with your shoes sticking to the cola-coated floor. And even when you step out into the bright sunshine of the parking lot, there's still a feeling that lingers. You might even glance skyward to see if there is some spacecraft shaped like a centipede coasting menacingly toward your town. And if the movie was especially engaging, those feelings may hover over you for the next few days. I can still remember as a kid, with *Jaws* still fresh on my mind, experiencing some anxiety as I walked into Lake Erie the next day. Yeah, *Lake Erie!*

A friend of mine, sharing his story of God's help with his own sexual issues, likened sexual fantasy to the movie theater experience. In the fog of temptation, the fantasy appears so wonderfully real, so very engaging, that true reality seems to be on a different planet. But eventually the lights begin to go back on as it dawns upon you that what your mind was wrapped up in was a mere shadow of reality. And yet . . . that feeling, despite the summoning of reality, still lingers like the smell of popcorn—a fragrance to relish, a taste to long for, but of no nutritional value.

"What Were They Thinking?"

You've seen it happen, haven't you? The high school teacher who loses her job because she seduced a teenage boy. Or the executive who leaves his wife and kids to marry a girl twenty years younger. Perhaps less extreme, you may have had a friend who seemingly was living "the dream" when suddenly he traded it all in for a messy relationship with a coworker. What gives?

A colleague once urged another pastor to admit to his affair and work on his marriage. "If you come clean now, you will save your family and career." Incredibly, the man ignored the advice and lost everything. Everything. And even this week as this chapter is being written, the tremors rippling through the Internet find their epicenter at ashleymadison.com, a site that helps wandering hearts connect for adulterous trysts. After losing all of its intimate data to hackers, more than thirty million people have been exposed for their involvement, including some pastors and Christian leaders. Incredible.

Or, I'm guessing, this subject may hit closer to home. You yourself have experienced this. What started out as connecting on Facebook or chatting on Skype snowballed toward a cascade of bad decisions and an avalanche of personal destruction. So you may have asked yourself, "What was *I* thinking?!"

Wise Words for Dispelling Fantasy

When counseling people dealing with adultery, fantasy, or sexual addiction, I often recommend meditating upon Proverbs 4–7, which contain a father's instructions to his sons regarding wisdom and sexual sobriety. There one finds nuggets of insight and stiff warnings that help keep our feet on the Path. While there is some scholarly debate about exactly which chapters were authored by Solomon, it certainly adds some punch when you realize that the marriage of his mom and dad was the result of their own adulterous affair.

Consider, for example, his admonition concerning faithfulness to one's wife.

> Drink water from your own cistern,
>   flowing water from your own well.
> Should your springs be scattered abroad,
>   streams of water in the streets?
> Let them be for yourself alone,
>   and not for sharing with strangers.
> Let your fountain be blessed,
>   and rejoice in the wife of your youth,
>   a lovely deer, a graceful doe.

May her breasts satisfy you at all times;
>   may you be intoxicated always by her love.
Why should you be intoxicated, my son, by another woman
>   and embrace the bosom of an adulteress? (Prov. 5:15–20)

"Intoxicated." Interesting choice of a word. But adultery is often like getting smashed sip by sip by sip.

No one ever goes out to the bar with a plan to get drunk and then to drive into an oncoming car, killing a young family. That would be insane. So how does it happen? One sip leads to another. Soon sips become guzzles. Judgment eventually is blurred and reaction time is delayed. Despite good intentions or innocent motives, self-control yields to the alcohol and tragedy is the result.

That is a good explanation for the unthinkable consequences of some cases of adultery and fantasy. The first sip is simple flirtation, a testing of the waters. Feels kind of good when the wink is reciprocated, knowing that, hey, someone still finds you attractive and desirable. The next sip is equally sweet. But before too much is consumed, judgment begins to get fuzzy, rationalizations become persuasive, and the element of risk simply adds to the excitement of it all. Once in the driver's seat and grasping the wheel, a person soon finds themselves in a ditch or worse. Young families are destroyed and friendships ruined, careers are lost and honor stained.

How does this happen to begin with? Let's take a deeper look at God's design for us as relational beings to see if we can get a better grasp of the sip-by-sip process of emotional inebriation.

Connection

As we noted in chapter 2, Adam needed a little convincing that it was not good for him to be alone, and so he was sent off to name all of the animals. Observing the pairs of animals and the nurturing of their young may have called forth his own longings for connection with another—a bond of knowing and being known. And so, with the help of his Creator, his own love story began with Eve. The bond between them took effect when the two became one flesh. There is deep treasure to this story, which we will continue to dig for in succeeding chapters. But for now let's take a look at how a bond is formed. There's an unfolding process of connecting with another that is absent from the garden narrative.

Donald Joy has written two books crammed with insight on the wonder of bonding between two people. There he described a twelve-step process for forming a healthy bond. When two people meet and their hearts begin to intertwine, it usually runs the following course:

1. Eye to Body
2. Eye to Eye
3. Voice to Voice
4. Hand to Hand
5. Arm to Shoulder
6. Arm to Waist
7. Face to Face
8. Hand to Head
9. Hand to Body
10. Mouth to Breast
11. Hand to Genital
12. Genital to Genital[1]

We've seen this played out in countless movies, haven't we? Now certainly there are those films where they jump to the twelfth step in a Hollywood minute, but when it is played out in true-to-life form, we see the man's head turn to take a look at the woman who catches his eye. Eventually their eyes lock together as all else in the scene seems to fade. The voice-to-voice phase? That usually takes too long for most movies to portray. But eventually there's a first date where one person takes the risk of grasping the other's hand, an arm goes around the shoulder, lips may meet in the face-to-face encounter....

I need say no more because you know so very well how this all plays out. And you also know how painfully awkward it becomes when one leapfrogs over a few steps, goes for the big kiss, and then realizes the other person was in no way ready for that move. Oops!

And so it is, by God's design, a bond is gradually formed and a covenant is made. Eventually that bond is brought to completion in the twelfth step. Our genitals, which are the closest outward connection to the deepest part of our being, finally join together with the other's and we are fully bonded.

Now back to the matter of adultery. What does it mean to commit adultery? Immediately we think of intercourse with a person who is married to another. But Joy sheds interesting light on the true meaning of this word by having us consider what the word "adulterate" means. If a water source becomes adulterated, a foreign substance has been introduced that has polluted the water. If theology is adulterated, false teaching has somehow crept into its core. And so biblically speaking, adultery is the bonding with another person in such a way that it pollutes our original bond with our spouse.[2]

In the workplace or in your church activities, emotional bonds are formed quite naturally. That is all well and good. But, as Jesus so clearly warned us, once we begin taking the steps toward pair bonding by fixing our eyes on another's body in such a way that we crave and long for that person, we are beginning the adulterating process. Soon lingering eye contact is made, then we can't get enough of hearing that person's laughter, and hands begin to touch in meaningful ways. The further down the steps we go, the more intoxicated we become.

So how do we get ourselves into such a mess? Some are quick to blame unmet needs at home, which is a sad way of taking the blame off of the errant one and placing it on the spouse. Regardless of circumstances at home, we are always responsible for our sinful choices. Having said that, however, unmet needs may contribute to someone's vulnerability to temptation. The following is a pattern

I've observed as I've counseled people over the years. See if this makes sense.

Living Under the Influence

Remember the wise old Owl in chapter 2 teaching Bambi and his forest buddies about twitterpation? There we reminisced a bit about the early days of a relationship when we are head-over-heels with our newly found loved one. Ah yes, the love-is-blind phase of the relationship where we cannot see the faults of the other person and can't stop expressing our love. All five love languages, in fact. Can you remember all five? Well, we spend gobs of quality time; buy gifts we can't afford; go out of our way to serve ("Here, Sweetie, let me get that for you!"); whisper wonderful words of affirmation ("You are just the strongest man I know!"); and, last but certainly not least, physical touch and touch and touch. . . .

But let's remember the other part of that twitterpation phase: it lasts only two to five years! Why? It's just the wisdom of God, frankly. That season of temporary insanity is God's way of binding our hearts together until our lives are joined by covenant. Then we return to our senses. Another few years of twitterpation and we would go broke from the gift buying and lose our jobs from all of the quality time spent affirming, serving, and touching each other. Probably that's part of the rationale behind a little-known law in Deuteronomy 24:5 that forbade men from serving in the army during the first year of marriage so that one could "be happy with the wife whom he has married." Young men were to stay at home to bring happiness to their wives. And it could be God didn't want lovesick boys wielding swords and facing the enemy. Just too risky for everyone involved!

What does all of this have to do with adultery? Once our brains quit producing the chemicals that yield the twitterpation high, we feel as though something's gone wrong in the relationship. Not only that, we are no longer blind to the other's glaring faults and we each go back to speaking our primary love language. According to Gary Chapman, the author of *The Five Love Languages,* hardly ever does someone marry a person with the same love language. Sad, but true. So if the husband's love language is serving and the wife's is quality time, he could be wondering why she doesn't appreciate all the things he does for her while she is getting upset that he's unavailable. Both can become frustrated, empty, and lonely. If communication is lacking, walls can go up and add to the agony all the more.

So unmet needs? Yeah, in some ways that can set us up for adultery. We all need love, and in the years of falling out of the "in love" phase we can begin to experience a time of confusion and adjustment. And so while we are wondering what went south in the marriage, we may run into someone at work, at church, or on Facebook who, wonder of wonders, speaks our love language! And then some of those dynamics begin to churn within us, we start down the twelve steps of bonding, and become twitterpated with yet another person. And the foul and polluting agent of infidelity begins to corrupt our original bond.

Hitting Bottom

People in recovery often speak of "hitting bottom." And when it comes to the intoxicating influence of twitterpation and the magnetic pull of bonding, the further you fall into it, the more likely you will land with a thud. When bonding first begins, there's always a sense of being in control, not letting things get out of hand, simply enjoying some harmless flirtation . . . until you reach that point of no return. Whether the crash occurs as the affair is brought to light, or if it simply surfaces as one loses the twitterpated passion, hitting bottom can be horrifying.

And at its root, you are practicing idolatry. Simply put, you are meeting your needs in ways God has forbidden. You have bowed down to something other than God and submitted yourself to something other than his plan to fill an aching hole inside. He is our Source and he puts people into our lives as appropriate resources for meeting those needs. One of those people is your spouse. But in this age of open-eyed blindness, it is all too common for needs to go unmet and hearts to begin wandering. In fact, psychologist Larry Crabb maintained our needs will never be perfectly met in this world no matter how sweet the marriage. Referencing Jeremiah 2:13, he called them thirsts. Our great sin, as God worded it for Jeremiah, is that we dig out for ourselves broken cisterns for quenching our longings instead of going to him, the Source of living water.[3] By forsaking the Source and attempting to quench our unmet needs in ways not of God, eventually we get burned. Or as Solomon cautioned his sons:

> For the lips of a loose woman drip honey, and her speech is smoother than oil;
> but in the end she is bitter as wormwood, sharp as a two-edged sword. (Prov. 5:3–4)

No matter what the idol, whether it is sexual or not, the lure is tantalizing and the initial experience is scintillating. Okay, maybe more than just the initial experience. It could be an ongoing season of pleasure. But it will end. And it will end badly. Then the horrifying nature of the idol will be revealed.

Ravi Zacharias related the story of Malcolm Muggeridge, a British journalist of the previous century who spent his younger years working in India. Alone one evening, he was standing by the river and noticed a lady on the other side. As was the custom then, she was having her evening bath. Though his initial thought was to not betray his wife, Kitty, he eventually caved into lust, stripped off his clothes, and dove into the river. Driven by a desire to reach her before she could get away, he swam furiously for the other side. But she waited for him. And when he breathlessly emerged from the water he found a toothless grin on a face deformed by leprosy.

"Lecherous woman!" he cried, falling back into the water. But as he swam away, he was pummeled by the truth that it was he himself who had the lecherous heart.[4]

Swimming against the current of God's grace, pursuing loves that are not rightfully ours, and being driven by a sense of entitlement and opportunity, we eventually emerge from the murky waters to see things as they are. The final picture is far from pretty and our waywardness smacks us square in the face. Solomon's warnings to his sons are proven true:

> "But he who commits adultery has no sense; he who does it destroys himself. He will get wounds and dishonor, and his disgrace will not be wiped away. (Prov. 6:32–33)

The Biblical Poster Boys

Well, we can hardly address the matter of adultery without considering some of the examples in the Scriptures. The golden boy in this regard is Joseph; a single man far from home, serving the household of a seductress who daily teased, tempted, and enticed, and yet he steadfastly refused. He insisted he could never disappoint God in such a way. And so he was falsely accused of rape and sent to prison. Years later God rewarded him, but he paid a heavy price for his faithfulness to God.

The other extreme? Samson. Even before he was born, God promised his parents that this child would be a great deliverer for the Israelites. But the guy just couldn't say no to forbidden love! He tried marrying a Philistine woman. That didn't go so well. Another passage tells of his overnighter with a prostitute in Gaza. (Probably wasn't in your Sunday school curriculum!) Then there was Delilah. Have you read that recently? She betrayed him a total of four times! How could he not have seen through her treachery? Unless, of course, he was totally intoxicated.

Somewhere in between the two is David, the one described as the man after God's own heart (see Acts 13:22). So much has been preached and written about his affair with Bathsheba, but let's simply consider how he hit bottom. Having attempted to cover up his deed with murder and deceit, he married Bathsheba and she gave birth to a son. Before long, however, one of the most dramatic personal confrontations in the Bible ensued. The prophet Nathan entered the throne room with a phony complaint about a wealthy man having confiscated a poor man's only sheep, serving it up for supper. King David, the former shepherd boy, took the bait. "The man who has done this deserves to die!" he cried (2 Sam. 12:5). Nathan then thrust his finger in David's face, saying, "You are the man!" (2 Sam. 12:7). He had taken the only "sheep" of Uriah the Hittite and then sent him off to his death. It was David himself who deserved to die!

What follows is the pronouncement of God's judgment. The life of the child would be required, strife and violence would break out within David's family, and eventually his own wives would be ravished by another man close to him.

In light of his outright deceit and rebellion, some have justifiably objected to David's title: "Man after God's Own Heart." How could a man who so horribly abused his power possibly fit such a description? Not only had his adultery polluted the bonds with his wives, the treacherous plot to conceal the deed by arranging for the husband's death likely had not gone unnoticed by the people. No doubt rumors were flying and honor was lost.

Perhaps it was David's humble contrition that revealed a heart tender toward God. Certainly his immediate and remorseful response to Nathan's rebuke was pleasing to God. So obvious was his remorse that before leaving the room, Nathan stated, "Now the LORD has put away your sin; you shall not die" (2 Sam. 12:13). The days preceding the death of his child, David fasted, wept, and interceded for God's mercy for the son. Later David composed Psalm 32, revealing how his hidden crimes had torn apart his soul, spirit, and body. And Psalm 51, his well-known psalm of confession, clearly exposed a heart that had been broken by his outright rebellion against the God who had so greatly blessed him.

Consider two other evidences of David's repentance. The very fact that Psalms 32 and 51 were included in the Psalter says a lot. There's no attempt to put a favorable spin on his sin or to sweep the matter under the carpet. Making his prayers available for a worshipping public to sing in the temple speaks of an unparalleled transparency, doesn't it? Not only that, the genealogy laid out in 1 Chronicles 3 lists four sons born to David and Bathsheba, one of them named after the finger-pointing prophet himself: Nathan! Incredible.

Why bring all of this up? While Joseph was the poster boy for steadfast obedience and Samson for outright rebellion, David provides the example of heartfelt repentance.

Weeping Prophets

Sometimes it takes a prophet to begin true healing, especially for those intoxicated with sexual sin. When it comes to substance abuse, recovery people call it "intervention." And so a person blinded by the stupor of twitterpation needs a voice from the outside to confront with clarity and compassion, speaking the truth of the matter. They need intervention.

And why a weeping prophet? As you may already know, the name tag was first worn by Jeremiah, the one who warned God's people about the coming invaders who would serve to execute God's wrath for their centuries of infidelity toward him. And he was truly God-sent. At times he wanted to stuff the message to keep it from the people. But then within him that message became "something like a burning fire shut up in my bones; I am weary with holding it in, and I cannot" (Jer. 20:9). God was compelling him to speak.

Hear his sorrow concerning the false prophets and priests who were committing spiritual adultery:

My heart is crushed within me, all my bones shake; I have become like a drunkard, like one overcome by wine, because of the LORD and because of his holy words. For the land is full of adulterers; because of the curse the land mourns, and the pastures of the wilderness are dried up. Their course has been evil, and their might is not right. Both prophet and priest are ungodly; even in my house I have found their wickedness, says the LORD. (Jer. 23:9–11)

Then also note his agony for those who would be destroyed by the coming horde of invaders:

For the hurt of my poor people I am hurt, I mourn, and dismay has taken hold of me.

Is there no balm in Gilead? Is there no physician there? Why then has the health of my poor people not been restored?

O that my head were a spring of water, and my eyes a fountain of tears, so that I might weep day and night for the slain of my poor people! O that I had in the desert a traveler's lodging place, that I might leave my people and go away from them! For they are all adulterers, a band of traitors. (Jer. 8:21–9:2)

So it is with God-sent, weeping prophets who must confront adultery. They take no joy in the message they must deliver, they agonize over the destructiveness of sin, and they ache for the wounds that the adulterers will endure. But they are compelled by God to speak.

Once a parishioner of mine disclosed to me a sexual affair. He was a fairly new Christian but had grown much in his love for God and knowledge of his Word. In his loneliness, however, he connected with an old flame through Facebook and soon was drunk with passion. She would often leave her husband and travel from out of state to spend weekends with him.

As his pastor, I had to confront him with his adultery. I loved him—still do. Taking him out to dinner, it seemed, was a good plan. As we talked, he was so excited about the relationship while at the same time fearful of what I would think. The fact that she was married didn't faze him. "Hey, her husband's an addict and treats her abusively! She keeps telling me she's going to leave him." No amount of reasoning could sway him. I assured him I loved him, but made equally sure he understood he was heading for destruction. He soon moved away to be with her. Within a year her marriage came to an end, and he himself fell into much sorrow.

Those intoxicated with the bonds of adultery at times seem so enthralled with the feelings, they can hardly hear what you are saying. The image comes to mind of Lot's family at Sodom's city gate. The angels had already performed an astounding miracle and forcefully urged Lot and his family to flee from the coming destruction. But they hesitated. Whether dazed in disbelief or not wanting to lose their possessions and friendships, we do not know. But the angels seized each one by the hand and led them out of the city, urging them to run for their lives without looking back.

People caught up in these kinds of entanglements seem to glaze over in disbelief when warned. *How can something that feels so wonderful be wrong? Maybe God has led us together! I can't bear the thought of leaving and breaking his/her heart.* Obviously, you can't seize their hands and drag them away from destruction, but you can be God's weeping prophet, urging them to repent without looking back.

Entering Detox

The drug addicts in my church insist the first step to get off of heroin or cocaine is a highly structured detox. Admitting oneself into a hospital detox unit is the preferable option. Or if there is a warrant out on you, turn yourself in to detox behind bars. Some recover to a point where the temptation to return is only feeble and fleeting. Others endure degrees of vulnerability the rest of their lives. But everyone knows that you can't dabble with the drugs or stay in the place of exposure to them. You need to replace the drugs with something else.

"People, places, and things." That's one of many mantras in the recovery community. To stay free from alcohol, one must change the people, places, and things that are associated with drinking. Hence the meetings! You can find an Alcoholics Anonymous meeting on almost any night of the week in large towns and communities. Regular attendance gives a struggler new people to journey with, new places to go to other than the bar, and new opportunities for using their time wisely. Regrouping with your drinking buddies inevitably results in a downhill slide into drunkenness.

So it is with the intoxicating effect of adultery. Once the bonds reach a certain degree of intimacy, it is almost impossible to keep from sliding further down that hill. Detoxing from the relationship is absolutely necessary. A person needs to kindly but firmly cut all ties possible. Obviously, if the person is a coworker, complete avoidance may be impossible. But this is where an accountability partner or group becomes essential.

A friend of mine once pointed out, "Hey, you can't really hold anyone accountable. They will only tell you what they are willing for you to know." Quite true. And so, as discussed in chapter 4, the accountability needs to be free of the shaming tendencies of the Box and infused with the grace that comes from the Path. Otherwise, the person will not feel free to share honestly in every detail. And the support of an accountability partner or group should be used as a guardrail on future encounters with the other person. For example, a simple text message to a friend which says: "Going to be in her office today. Pray. Ask me later how it went."

And as one detoxes from the drug of adultery, they should find ways to cling to God, the Source of living water. They have ended a season where their constant thought has been on the bonds formed with this other person. Repeatedly throughout the day they have checked for texts and e-mail messages, they've lingered on thoughts of their next rendezvous, they've gone to sleep at night with fantasies of more and more and more. They need to learn simple ways of practicing the presence of God instead of "practicing the presence" of this other person. Seeking his strength and nearness moment by moment will help wean them from their obsession.

God in the Details

Returning to the story of David and Bathsheba, I find it instructive to see how God brought good out of their destructive and sinful liaison. Consequences were painfully abundant, however. Incest ensued and eventually murder. David's son Absalom ended up attempting a coup (nearly costing David and Bathsheba their lives), and flaunting his power by publicly sleeping with David's concubines. Much sorrow and loss followed David's infidelity.

But then there was the birth of Solomon. God had promised peace during this child's reign as king, and so David and Bathsheba gave him this name, which is derived from the Hebrew word for "peace" (see 1 Chronicles 22:9). But God had a different name in mind. Sending Nathan as his messenger, he told the proud parents that the child's name should be Jedidiah, which literally means "Beloved of the Lord" (2 Sam. 12:24–25). As time went forward, God's favor and love were demonstrated throughout Solomon's life. Despite his own waywardness, God blessed him more than any other king of Israel. And it was through the line of Solomon, this son of adulterers, that the Messiah would eventually arrive. God's grace truly is amazing, isn't it?

And so with any adulterous fling, God can bring about something good. To be sure, there will be devastating consequences. You will likely walk away a good bit more humble and wiser. But if one repents in the manner that David turned from his sin, God can bring restoration. The bond with your spouse can be renewed and strengthened. And one day he may use your experience of brokenness as a way of helping others.

Finding the Exit

Remember the movie theater? When the credits start to roll and the lights begin to come on, reality gently pulls us back to the real world. "Hey, it was just a movie!"

God may be using this chapter as the finger of Nathan, calling you to examine your own brokenness. Has your heart been wandering? Sip by sip, have you been savoring a bond formed with someone other than your spouse? Until now perhaps you've felt, "Hey, no harm done. It's all innocent fun. Nothing sexual has happened and so it is all good." Is that the truth? Or has it become clear to you now that an alien bond has begun to pollute your marriage because you have dared to live life with the buzz of twitterpation?

And so the movie credits are beginning to roll, the lights are gradually brightening, and it is time to realize that the world of fantasy and adultery are not reality. The sizzle and zing of bonding with another is not what God has intended for you. It is time to stand up, stretch a bit, pick up your trash, and head for the door. Oh yeah, you will be tempted to savor the feeling of that bond as you reach the parking lot. And even as the days roll onward, your hungry heart will be tempted. Sitting at the computer, you will want to stray to sites that lead to destruction. Or lying in bed at night, your mind will want to dredge up again the images of fantasy just to take another sip.

Now is the time to take decisive action. Like David, respond with heartfelt confession and repentance. Become transparent. Recruit your own personal Nathan who will hold your feet to the fire. Kindly, but oh so firmly and completely, sever all ties with the person you have bonded with. And work to repair and strengthen the bonds of intimacy with God and your spouse.

Your sin will likely have consequences. And there will be moments when you are severely tempted to dabble once again with sinful liaisons. But just as God eventually brought about good from David's illicit relationship, he may yet redeem your losses. And so, if God is speaking to you in this present moment, why not step out fully into his healing light? Consider the following prayer as your first step toward renewed faithfulness to God and your spouse:

Gracious Lord God, how can I be a prophet for others when my own heart has wandered into sin? Please forgive me for intentionally bonding with someone who is not my spouse. In the name of Jesus, I renounce that bond. Guide me to people who can graciously hold me accountable as I detox from this relationship. And bring healing to the primary relationships of my life. To you be the honor and glory forever! Amen.

Discussion Questions

1. What did you find most helpful in this chapter?
2. Drunkenness was used as a metaphor for adultery. Do you think this is a fair comparison? Why or why not?
3. Read Proverbs 7:6–23. How does this account support the intoxication metaphor? What else do you notice from these verses, which speak of the dynamics of adultery?
4. When you consider Donald Joy's twelve steps of bonding, how does it apply to the bonding within non-romantic relationships? And how would they be helpful in understanding the process of dating and courtship?
5. What would disqualify someone from being a prophet for a person caught up in adultery?

CYCLE THREE

The Beginnings of Modesty

CHAPTER 7

PRINCIPLE:
All God's Children Got Monkeys

What keeps people in their closets, especially when it comes to sexual sin? I believe it is related to a principle we considered in chapter 4: all sin is equally sinful. Though we know this intellectually, it just doesn't feel that way when you are huddled in the clutches of the closet with your sexual sin. We feel convinced that if people truly knew our particular sin, we would be rejected because surely our sin is worse than others. That is why it is so very important for our churches to fully grasp this principle: "all God's children got monkeys."

Your monkey might be alcoholism or workaholism. It might be a sexual addiction or an inappropriate use of anger. Maybe the monkey is a high need for approval that makes you stumble all over yourself to make a certain person happy. The fact of the matter is that God is at work in all of us no matter how far down the Path you may be. God is still perfecting you.

The Woman Caught in Adultery

My friend Terry Wardle spoke about the nicknames of the Bible. Imagine Simon the Leper, years after being healed, still being called Simon *the Leper*. Or what about Blind Bartimaeus? "Hello! I'm not blind anymore!" Then there's this precious story of the woman caught in adultery. How would you like that as your moniker? But as Wardle went on to say, it was in the midst of their leprosy, blindness, and adultery where they finally met Jesus!

Several things stand out in this tender story found in John 8. Jesus was already teaching in front of a crowd when the scribes and Pharisees arrived and thrust the woman before him and the onlookers. Jesus remained silent before her accusers, writing something on the ground as they ranted. They continued questioning him until he finally said the well-known words, "Let anyone among you who is without sin be the first to throw a stone at her" (v. 7). He continued to write as one by one everyone left. When they were finally alone, he asked, "Woman, where are they? Has no one condemned you?" Then he sent her away with, "Neither do I condemn you. Go your way, and from now on do not sin again" (vv. 10–11).

Did this story really take place? That has always been a lingering question. Nearly all translations have this story in brackets or flagged with footnotes, making clear that this account is not found in many of the most reliable manuscripts. And yet it feels to us as though the story is true. It seems as though it is something Jesus would have done, doesn't it?

Tradition tells us that not everyone has thought so. After describing the trail of manuscripts that do and do not contain this story, William Barclay referred to comments made by Augustine who indicated the story was omitted in the early manuscripts because it came scandalously close to condoning adultery. Early church leaders feared it would encourage believers of weak faith in a permissive pagan culture to slide into immorality. And so Barclay concluded: "In spite of the fact that the early manuscripts do not include it, we may be sure that this is a real story about Jesus, although one so gracious that for long [people] were afraid to tell it."[1]

The accusers left one by one, beginning with the elders. Perhaps they were convinced of their own monkeys either by Jesus' words or by what he was writing in the dirt. One wonders also about the onlookers. What were they thinking? Perhaps those who had gathered to hear him teach also found it difficult to stomach Jesus' inaction toward the adulteress and his seeming softness toward sexual sin.

What is "minor" surgery? You've heard this before, right? There *is* no minor surgery when you are the one under the knife. Minor surgery is when it's the other guy. Our perspective gets a bit skewed when we ourselves are not the one going through the pain. All sin is equally sinful in the eyes of a holy God. And because of this principle, sexual sin is not worse than other types of sin. More damaging? Usually. Worse? Nope. However, there's a tendency to view our monkeys as minor when compared to the sexual sin of another.

At Ashes to Life we have ingrained this principle into our thinking: all God's children got monkeys. We even have a small stuffed chimp on the windowsill of the sanctuary to remind us. All of us have issues and stand in need of grace. Most of our people have a history of substance abuse, and so there's a tendency for some of the "regular folks" to think that "those people" are the ones who really need help while the rest of us have it pretty much together.

How can we get out of this mind-set? Perhaps looking at the birthplace of our monkeys would help us to be more compassionate.

The Nature of Monkey Business

One of my monkeys is people pleasing. For most of my life I have been way too concerned about what others will think of me. As a college student, I began to recognize this issue and resolved to overcome it. The campus ministry I attended emphasized Scripture memory, and so I soon memorized Galatians 1:10: "Am I now seeking human approval, or God's approval? Or am I trying to please people? If I were still pleasing people, I would not be a servant of Christ." Whew! Problem solved, right? Nope.

Can you imagine trying to pastor a church as a people pleaser? No easy task, let me tell you. There are always people who believe the pastor just doesn't get it and needs to do church their way. Or what about preaching? Fearing the opinion of others definitely becomes problematic. Pretty tough to preach repentance when you are used to couching your words so as not to offend someone. My early years behind the pulpit were pretty much spent stationed literally *behind* the pulpit, close to my notes, never stepping out where people could catch a glimpse of me.

Not that I didn't try to be more animated with preaching. In fact, Saturday nights I would practice in the empty sanctuary, pacing back and forth across the platform. You would have thought I was going to be the next T. D. Jakes! And Sunday mornings I would pray Psalm 138:3: "When I called, you answered me; you greatly emboldened me" (NIV). I would step up to the pulpit believing for boldness, but the chains of timidity still kept me bound.

Yes, I prayed to be filled with the Spirit. Yes, people laid hands on me as *they* prayed I'd be filled with the Spirit. I meditated upon Romans 6, 7, and 8. I counted myself dead unto sin and believed God to set me free. But Sunday after Sunday, week by week, I continued to find it difficult to rise above my need for acceptance. Having meditated on the Scriptures and prayed every prayer I knew to pray, I simply began to believe that this was as good as it was going to get. So I continued to preach the victorious Christian life to my people while all the time wondering why it wasn't more evident in my own life.

Freedom finally arrived, however, and I continue to grow in my freedom. In fact, I seem to make people angry with me on a regular basis now! How did God begin this emancipation? Through an understanding of the Structures of Healing.

The Structures of Healing

"The ground is level at the foot of the cross." Ever hear that before? It is a common way to say that we all got monkeys. Some monkeys cause more injury than others, but a monkey is a monkey.

Fifteen years ago, I began reading the New Revised Standard Version of the Bible and I found some interesting variations in how some verses were translated. One that relates to monkeys is Paul's broad blessing to the Thessalonians: "May the God of peace himself sanctify you entirely; and may your spirit and soul and body be kept sound and blameless at the coming of our Lord Jesus Christ" (1 Thess. 5:23). As a prayer for them to be "sound and blameless," this benediction ties together wholeness and holiness in this Spirit-led work of sanctification. And this is supported with Paul's reference to the "God of peace." The Jewish understanding of peace holds much greater depth than our use of the word implies. For us, *peace* typically means a lack of strife, conflict, or animosity. And so when we say that Jesus died so that we might have peace with God, our first thought is, *"Okay, I am no longer in trouble for my sin. God and I are at peace."* But *shalom,* the Hebrew word for peace, encompasses the idea of wholeness and well-being. So it is that when Isaiah described the atoning work of the Messiah, he stated, "But he was wounded for our transgressions, crushed for our iniquities; upon him was the punishment that made us whole [*shalom*], and by his bruises we are healed" (Isa. 53:5). In this well-worn Old Testament prophecy, most translations render it "the punishment that brought us peace" (NIV). While it certainly involves payment for our transgressions, the atoning work of Jesus Christ goes much deeper. It provides healing and wholeness for the soul sickness at the root of our sinful choices.

Terry Wardle, author of numerous books and founder of the Institute of Formational Counseling, pioneered a discipline of Christian counseling that incorporates the best of Christian tradition with the latest findings of psychology regarding the effects of trauma upon the brain. *Healing Care, Healing Prayer,* his textbook for those trained in formational prayer, described the dynamics of inner healing through what he called the Structures of Healing.[2] No other paradigm for inner healing so clearly ties together wholeness and holiness.

At the top of this diagram you find life situations. A simpler term would be "trouble!" These are the situations and circumstances that usually get our attention. Threats of divorce, financial collapse, loss of a job, or conflict with key people all have a way of sounding an alarm that something is wrong with the way we are living. In recovery language they speak of "hitting bottom." But as this diagram illustrates, there are a number of layers below the life situation that are contributing to our problems.

The Structures of Healing

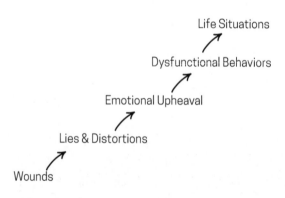

Let's begin at the bottom and work our way up. All of us experience emotional wounding during our lives. There are basically two general types of wounds. The first type of wounds are those things that have happened to us or were done to us. Examples are abuse, betrayals, traumatic events, and shaming. As we often say, kids are impressionable. So the younger we are when these things happen to us, the greater the impact they will wield.

The other type of wounds are deprivations. Each of us are born with core longings. Needs. We were created with a need for love, security, understanding, purpose, significance, and belonging. Growing up in a home where some of these are lacking has an effect on us. And we all grew up in imperfect homes because no one has perfect parents. So at least to some degree, we all have areas of neglect. All of us.

So what happens when we experience wounds of either type? It cracks open the shell of our soul a bit, making us open to distortions. I believe it is the Evil One himself who is quick to plant those suggestions, distorting our understanding of who we are, who God is, how God views us, and what life is like. Psychologists call these cognitive distortions. The Bible simply refers to them as lies.

Lies cause pain. Just imagine if you go through life with a message being played over and over in your head that you are stupid, you will never amount to anything, God doesn't love you, God could never forgive you, sex is dirty, etc. Can you imagine how that would create inner pain and stress? Of course you can because, as I've said, this is how life works. We all have messages like those floating around within us. Now in your left brain—that is, the analytical half of your brain—you can know the actual truth about yourself, God, or life. For example, it may be firmly planted in your mind that God loves you unconditionally. But at the very same time, on an emotional level, you live with a feeling that in reality God is deeply disappointed with you. Day after day, this is how you feel. What do you do with that pain?

Well, like most of us, you have found at least three ways to handle pain: adopt behaviors to kill the pain; avoid the pain; or fill the aching, unmet need. These are dysfunctional behaviors. Again, the Bible is so much simpler. One three-letter word addresses the matter: sin. Yes, anytime we adopt a behavior to kill our pain; avoid our pain; or fill a deep, unmet need *instead of* turning to God, that behavior becomes an idol for us.

These behaviors are myriad. Just think for a moment about the things people do to kill their pain. Right away some obvious addictions come to mind: alcohol, drugs, and sex. But what about some not-so-obvious addictions: work, shopping, hoarding, Facebooking, gaming . . . oh wait, we are getting personal now, aren't we? Now let's state the obvious. There is nothing wrong with work, shopping, saving, social networking, or gaming. And actually, what is wrong with drinking, sex, and prescribed drugs? Nothing, right? But when these or any other activities begin to erode our relationships with God and others, or when they begin to compromise our well-being, then they have likely crossed the line and become dysfunctional and sinful.

And the list goes on and on. In addition to killing pain, there are sinful ways that we avoid pain. These may surprise you. What about perfectionism? Nothing wrong with striving for excellence per se, but some people are perfectionists because every single thing has to be in its place or else they feel stressed and anxious. Manipulation is another biggie. In order to deal with stress, fear of conflict, or loss of control, people will manipulate their way through life using anger, guilt, or shame.

Some of the above behaviors are also related to filling the void of an unmet need. Have an aching for significance? Perhaps that has led to an addiction to work or busyness. Did you grow up in an unstable environment with frequent moves or family fighting? Perhaps that explains the deep need for security that you try to shore up with a number of coping skills. A lack of love? Sex, whether extramarital or not, can be either a pain killer or a need filler. But again, we are talking about excess to the degree that it is compromising Jesus' command to love God, love our neighbor, and the implication that we are to love ourselves.

All sin is equally sinful and all monkeys are equally despicable because they are idolatrous attempts to deal with pain and stress apart from the cross of Christ. And so, keep the drum beating out this message over and over: *All God's children got monkeys! All God's children got monkeys!* And yes, I know, some of you perfectionists are saying, "That's not proper grammar! It should be, 'All *of* God's children *have* monkeys!'" Take it to Jesus, my friend. Your monkey is running loose.

How These Monkeys Dress

People pleasing. Doesn't sound very sinful, does it? Hard to put it on par with smoking crack or having multiple one-night stands. But again, all sin is equally sinful, even if it is not equally damaging and debilitating. But I would argue that people pleasing was, in fact, damaging my life to some degree. It affected my marriage, my ministry, and especially my personal well-being. That monkey, along with its cousin workaholism, were sending me into one burnout after another as I sought to fill my aching need for significance by getting people to like me and to think I was successful for God.

But God has given me much victory over the people pleasing and I am making progress on the workaholism. How? Not just by memorizing verses, meditating, and praying, but by asking the Holy Spirit to reveal and heal the wounds and lies at the root of my idolatrous life. A huge step toward freedom came when God revealed a memory of hunting deer with my dad at age thirteen. Wanting to please my dad, and longing to make the rite of passage of killing my first deer, I blew it. Shot way too low. Dad was more than just a little disappointed. And at that moment I began to believe that if I am a disappointment to my earthly dad, then I must certainly fall short of my heavenly Father's favor. A pattern of behavior became firmly fixed as I tried to ease my self-disgust by getting people to like me. But once God brought healing to the memory and spoke truth to my distorted thinking, I finally made strides in overcoming people pleasing. Seriously. Not only did that long-awaited boldness begin to flow, I actually started offending people without thinking about it. Even from the pulpit. Weird, but kind of cool for a people pleaser.

Not long after this transformation, a church invited me to speak at their Sunday evening healing service, where I spoke on the Structures of Healing. Many remained for prayer, including a lady named Marnie. When I approached her, I asked how God had been speaking to her heart. She replied that she had believed a lie that she was ugly. After conversing a bit, I had her tell God how this lie had affected her life. She cited a number of things, including an incredible lack of confidence in social situations. Eventually I had her renounce this message as a lie and to ask God to reveal the truth. Within a few seconds she was laughing. "What's so funny?" I asked.

"God reminded me of a poster someone has at work. It says, 'God don't make no junk!'"

"Ah, then that is your truth. Any time you are tempted to believe that you are ugly, simply speak out this truth!"

Following our time of prayer, she asked if she could begin counseling with me. Not long after that, we were sitting in my office and she began to tell me about several dysfunctional issues in her life. The most pressing issue seemed to be an uncontrollable urge to flirt with men. Now she was not the stereotypical floozy frequenting the bar scene. Hardly. She was the leader of a popular interdenominational Bible study for women. But her uncontainable flirting had gotten her into very awkward situations, with men even showing up at her door. Try as she might, she could not stop.

As is standard practice with formational counseling, we asked the Spirit to guide us. What lies or wounds might be driving this behavior? Within seconds she gasped. "Oh my gosh, I can't believe what he brought to mind! I've never told anyone this before. When my ex-husband wanted to be intimate with me, he could never get aroused unless I dressed up like a nurse or a school teacher." Can you see how degrading that would be? We grieved her loss and asked God to bring healing to that memory, which he was quick to do.

At the end of the session we both began to connect the dots. Is it obvious to you as well? The pain of not being enough to arouse her husband would be fertile ground for a lie such as, "I am ugly." And what better pain killer than to see the grins and winks of the men she flirted with? The answer was not simply memorizing and repeating, "I am fearfully and wonderfully made" (Ps. 139:14). The healing came as God flooded her wounded memory with grace and spoke those wonderful words: "God don't make no junk!" And, yes, grammatical perfectionists, keep chasing that monkey. God's speaking this language too!

Embraced at the Closet Door

So what does this all have to do with the church closet? That's a fair question. What does this monkey business have to do with helping people to come out of the darkness and into God's healing light? Quite a bit, actually. Shame keeps us in closets, and the impression that church people are uppity moral do-gooders who have it all together simply pushes us back into the far corner of the closet with our backs against the wall, probably with our mom's old wool coat pressing against our face.

Phillip Yancey, in his book *What's So Amazing About Grace?*, began with an account from a friend. In a chance conversation with a prostitute, this friend learned her straits were so dire that she was renting out her two-year-old daughter to men for kinky sex. When he asked why she wouldn't go to a church to find help, she replied, "Why would I ever go there? I was already feeling terrible about myself. They'd just make me feel worse." How tragic, Yancey concluded, that the last, least, and lost who used to flock to Jesus now want nothing to do with his bride.[3]

Perhaps word will get out that not all churches are blind to their monkeys, and that sexual sins are no more leprous than other dysfunctional ways of dealing with pain. It is okay to not be okay. Everyone on the Path has an issue needing God's grace. That's the process of sanctification, a process that continues until we see Jesus face-to-face.

In 2007 a pastor sought me out. The worship leader of his megachurch had approached another man at a city park for sexual favors, only to be arrested by an undercover police officer. His secret activity was now exposed on the local news, shocking his family, jolting the congregation, and costing him both his job as a high school music teacher and his role as worship leader. Not only did my colleague want my opinion on how he was handling the matter, but he asked if I would begin to counsel this man who had been yanked from the closet and thrust into the spotlight.

Bill traveled nearly two hours to meet with me twice monthly. One contributing factor in his addiction to same-sex encounters was the repeated childhood sexual abuse from a man that the family had trusted. As God brought healing to the wounds of abuse, Bill began to find freedom to live above his sexual urges.

He progressed rapidly, in fact. Why? I believe it was because of the love his church showered upon him just outside the closet door.

- A church member found a managerial position for him at a department store.
- The people in his cell group collected money to pay for a lawyer.
- The men of the cell group began meeting with him several times a week for prayer and encouragement.

- The women of the group surrounded his wife and daughter with support.
- The group again pooled together money to buy the daughter back-to-school clothing.
- *Again*, as Christmas arrived, they gave money for the family to buy gifts.
- Incredibly, when the family was off for a week in the summer, the cell group surprised them by building a deck for their house and by landscaping the yard.

Talk about grace that is amazing! Rather than throwing him under the bus for having been caught in such a mess, they embraced him! The love extended to Bill and his family helped them to survive this otherwise crushing experience.

But there's more to that story! A few years after the counseling sessions ended, God led me to move to Beaver Falls, Pennsylvania, just forty minutes from Bill. A ministry to people in recovery developed, which led to the forming of Ashes to Life Ministries. Most of those who now attend our worship services are either homeless, recovering from addictions, or both. And our worship leader every Sunday? Bill!

Did everyone in our church embrace him? Sadly, no. We have not kept Bill's story a secret, nor have we made him wear a scarlet letter. But when a few discovered the nature of Bill's brokenness, they immediately objected—even though Bill has lived free of the behaviors of his past. Apparently those few folks have overlooked the important principle of acknowledging the prevalence of monkeys and that sacred level ground at the foot of the cross.

God can take our messy closets and turn them into a message for the broken! But that transition begins by being embraced and loved by God's people as we come out into the light. How much easier to nestle into that embrace when we know those outside the closet door fully admit that their own monkeys are no better nor worse than those we bring from the closet!

Just because the Circus has left town doesn't mean you are monkey-free. With that in mind, join me in the following prayer:

Lord Jesus Christ, thank you so much for your salvation. Again and again, as I have confessed my sins, you have forgiven and cleansed me.

"Nobody's perfect!" is the mantra of the masses. But I repent of that mind-set! Until I see you face-to-face, may your Holy Spirit always be making me more like you. So I gladly and freely ask you to reveal the monkey that you want to remove from my life at this point on the Path. I will respond with repentance and thanksgiving. And may my desire to live a holy life be an encouragement to those peeking out of the closet. To you be the honor and glory forever! Amen.

Discussion Questions

1. If the prostitute Yancey described walked through your church doors on a Sunday or any other day of the week, how do you think she would feel? Welcomed? Accepted? Loved? Or might there be a few folks who would make her feel judged?

2. Did any lights go on for you as the author described the Structures of Healing? What dots were you able to connect between your wounds, lies, and monkeys?

3. How can we get this message across to your congregation? Does the saying, "All God's children got monkeys," work for you? If not, what would be a better way to package it so that it becomes ingrained in the congregation's thinking?

4. If someone from your congregation or small group was arrested for a sexual indiscretion, how do you think it would respond? What if the transgression was sexual abuse? Would that make a difference in how the congregation would reach out to the person?

5. Given your particular congregation or small group, how does this matter of monkeys affect how it would welcome a gay, lesbian, or transgendered person?

CHAPTER 8

THEOLOGY:
Restoration and Grace

Some traditions place a lot of weight on the value of a person's testimony. Revelation 12:11 indicates that it is a firmly biblical practice, "But they have conquered him by the blood of the Lamb and by the word of their testimony, for they did not cling to life even in the face of death." A friend of mine stated that in the midst of extreme difficulties and temptation, one thing that kept him from caving was the thought that he didn't want to soil the testimony of what God had done in his life.

And testimonies inspire, don't they? We especially like to trot out onto the stage the dramatic stories of miraculous healing. A favorite for many is the story of Don Piper, Baptist pastor and author of *90 Minutes in Heaven*. After the close of a Baptist ministers' conference, Piper's Ford Escort was slammed head-on by a veering eighteen-wheeler with the combined impact of 110 miles per hour and with all the wheels on one side rolling up over the car. The truck then careened into two other vehicles. Paramedics took Piper's vitals, pronounced him dead, logged the time in their records, and then cared for others at the scene. More than an hour later, with traffic backed up for miles in both directions, a fellow pastor walked onto the scene, not knowing who had been involved but asking if he could help. Suddenly he felt the Holy Spirit urge him to pray for the man in the smashed car. The officer on site told him he was wasting his time because the man was dead. But sensing the Spirit's urgent leading, the pastor insisted. Making his way into the wreckage by crawling through the back hatch, the former military medic placed his hand on the neck and felt for a pulse. Nothing. So he laid his hand on a bloodied shoulder and prayed fervently. After much intercession, he felt led to sing "What a Friend We Have in Jesus." Within minutes he could hear Piper singing with him! In disbelief, the EMTs came, checked, and found a pulse! And in the intervening years, many lives have been touched by Piper's testimony.

Most of us Christians believe God can raise the dead simply because the Bible describes such miracles, but we also doubt we will ever see it happen. Piper's testimony, however, certainly supplies a vitamin B shot to the arm of faith. God can do anything![1]

Much less in demand are the testimonies of people like Joni Eareckson Tada. Believers of my generation recognize the name as a talented lady whose life was unalterably changed when a diving accident snapped her spine and left her a paraplegic. Much grace from God has enabled her to endure affliction; a grace that has spilled out onto others through her testimony, teachings, artwork, and example. Though you are more likely to pack the pews with a story like Piper's, Tada's testimony means as much or more for me.

Let me tell you about one of my heroes. Doug has battled sexual addiction all of his adult life. Like most sexual addicts, the roots tap down into his early childhood when, as a toddler, his father began to force sex upon him. In fact, he witnessed other instances of sexual abuse within his family during those years. This continued until he reached the age of twelve. In high school, as his buddies began to look up to him for his knowledge of sex, he formed his identity around sexual prowess. This continued on into college, where his fraternity crowned him "Slut King." While his friends saw sexual freedom, Doug felt enslaved as the insatiable desire for sex continued to rage out of control. Trips to the adult bookstores were near daily occurrences. There he would find anonymous encounters with both men and women. Despite frequent visits, he still craved more.

And yet at this stage of his life he also became a Christian and began to have a vision for what freedom might look like. An uncle took him to church, where Doug saw a young family at worship. The image of the young couple with two innocent kids became fastened to his soul. That was what he wanted! But his current addiction made that goal seem impossible.

The journey began. Year after year he went through countless therapy sessions. Accountability groups and twelve-step programs became a part of his weekly routine, but slip-ups and relapses continued. At age twenty-eight he married and had two children, but his wife had multiple issues of her own and eventually they divorced. Then began twelve years of singleness. Progress toward freedom was slow and costly, but finally he ended up at a seven-day "Come Away with Me" retreat sponsored by Healing Care Ministries.[2] That was a decisive turning point in his recovery, as issues of his identity were addressed and deep healing was found for some of his childhood wounds. Doug continued meeting with a formational counselor for another three years and finally found enough freedom to begin dating and to eventually marry. That is his testimony of a twenty-seven-year hard-fought battle with the deep brokenness of sexual addiction, and it is a story he has told at the seminars and classes I have taught. Yep, he's my hero.

Does God raise the dead? Yes, and Don Piper's testimony is proof. Can God completely and instantly heal sexual addiction or other forms of sexual brokenness? Yes, and there are testimonies out there which also offer proof. But more often than not, the restoration journey is an uphill climb—or as in Doug's case, a trip up Everest requiring a team, grappling hooks, pitons, and safety ropes! But this is the message of restoration and grace.

The Journey Begins

Philippians 2 provides a peek behind the celestial curtain, giving us a glimpse of the Son of God's decision to bring restoration to the created world. The following words, it is commonly thought, were the words of a hymn sung by the early church, encapsulating the theological bedrock for our faith.[3]

> Have this mind among yourselves, which is yours in Christ Jesus, who, though he was in the form of God, did not count equality with God a thing to be grasped ["exploited" NRSV], but emptied himself, by taking the form of a servant, being born in the likeness of men. And being found in human form, he humbled himself by becoming obedient to the point of death, even death on a cross. Therefore God has highly exalted him and bestowed on him the name that is above every name, so that at the name of Jesus every knee should bow, in heaven and on earth and under the earth, and every tongue confess that Jesus Christ is Lord, to the glory of God the Father. (Phil. 2:5–11 ESV)

In chapter 5 we noted the mind-set of Adam and Eve as they rebelled in the garden. Submitting idolatrously to a created serpent and trying to grasp equality with God by taking in the created fruit, they brought upon us all the curses of the fall. That mind-set has continued as all of us have carried out these two acts of disobedience: submitting and grasping. We've submitted to idolatrous practices, seeking to find our needs met by leaning into people and other created things. And we've grasped for that which is not ours to take instead of receiving with an open hand. This twofold disobedience has affected our approach to the created gift of sexuality, hasn't it? We have bowed before the altar of sexual fulfillment, sometimes submitting to sex to fill our souls, and at other times grasping and exploiting to get what we want when we want it.

· But notice that Jesus began the journey of restoration with a decision to exemplify a twofold obedience. First of all, he did not grasp or exploit equality with God. Rather, he emptied himself of the rights and privileges of such an existence and became a part of the created world. Instead of exploiting people, he served. And second, instead of submitting to and bowing down to the created world to find fulfillment, he submitted to the plan of the Father, obeying to the point of shedding his innocent blood. And because he did not grasp for or submit to the created world, he has been exalted! And it is the created order that will now bow down *to him* and confess that he who became last and servant to all is indeed now *Lord* over all! By this the Father has been glorified!

The blood of sheep, goats, and bulls pointed to the atonement that would come from the death of Jesus our Savior. The well-known prophecy from Isaiah 53 reminds us of the full scope of that atonement. Not only were our sins laid upon him, but "upon him was the punishment that made us whole, and by his bruises we are healed" (Isa. 53:5). As the cross was thrust into the time line of history, provision was made for our healing and wholeness. Restoration and grace not only reconciled sinners with a holy God, but began the work of making us whole. And so it is that the collateral damage from the grasping and submitting of sexual brokenness can be brought to Calvary, because wholeness and healing are made available through the blood of Christ.

A Beachhead for God's Mission

Now to illustrate this important event in the overall mission of God, let me default once again to a World War II metaphor. Do you remember any of the details of D-Day? An elaborate plan was devised to establish a beachhead on the shores of Normandy. The logical place to carry out such an invasion would have been Calais, which lay at the narrowest part of the English Channel, and so a ruse was conducted to make it appear such was the strategy in place. But on May 6, 1944, the real plan unfolded as five thousand ships carrying 156,000 soldiers embarked upon the largest sea invasion of its kind.

The landing was the beginning of the end for the Nazis. The key word, however, is *beginning.* Battle after battle was fought as the Allies swept across Europe. Then there was an enormous pushback by the Nazis. Launching their own surprise attack on December 16, they threw 200,000 troops at the weakest point on the Allied line of defense, creating a "bulge" in the battle line. Those six weeks of battle were the bloodiest for the Americans as they sought to liberate Europe. But the bulge did not break and, as we all know, VE Day finally came that next spring with the conquest of Berlin, and the eventual liberation of captives from the death camps.

Bethlehem and Calvary established the beachhead in the mission of God. Though the powers of darkness have now been disarmed, the war wages on. The Father of Lies continues his own pushback. As Martin Luther once penned, Satan "doth seek to work us woe; his craft and power are great," and he is "armed with cruel hate."[4] The war will continue until Christ returns and the kingdom is finally and forever established. Until that time, we carry on that message of restoration and grace, offering healing in this season where we experience the benefits of the kingdom as "already and not yet." That is, the benefits are already available, but not quite yet in all of their fullness.

In chapter 2 we discovered God's good design for our sexuality. There I made the point that our genitals are the closest outward connection to the deepest part of our being. That is why being wounded sexually or having someone withhold from us sexually cuts so deeply. Restoration and grace are available for us in this time between the gardens. As with physical healing, it is an "already-and-not-yet" reality. The testimonies range from the rare instantaneous healing of abuse, addiction, aversion, and same-sex attraction to the more common slow and difficult journey of gradual healing. For some the restoration seems steady and noticeable. Others will testify to God's abundant grace despite limited results. But by far the majority will say it was worth putting their feet on the healing path. Just ask my hero Doug.

Putting Sex in Its Place

The journey of restoration, remember, very much includes God's work of restoring a proper worldview. The realms of deity, humanity, and nature must be placed into proper perspective. The Lord our God is one Lord, transcendent and personal, Creator of all. There are clear boundaries between us and him. Similarly, there are clear boundaries between humanity and nature. Clear boundaries are a part of all of life, including sexual relationships.

The New Testament clarifies our vision regarding the proper place of sex and marriage. Are you sure you want to hear this? Jesus and Paul had some rather stark words to share. It may not be the good news you are looking for. Read ahead at your own risk.

First of all, marriage is optional. Yes, hand-wringing match-makers, not everyone in the kingdom needs to get married. In fact, Jesus and Paul indicated that those who want to serve the kingdom to the fullest might be better off staying single. Marriage is not necessarily God's plan for everyone! Celibacy doesn't require wearing a clerical collar or a nun's habit, and you have just as good of odds at living happily ever after. Imagine that!

This unfolds for us as the Pharisees, of course, again tried to trip up Jesus. A hot-button issue of the day was this: Under what conditions was it proper to file for divorce? One school of thought held that you could divorce your wife for any reason that suited you. The Pharisees cited an injunction from Moses: "Why then did Moses command us to give a certificate of dismissal and to divorce her?" (Matt. 19:7). Jesus had already taught the disciples that their righteousness needed to exceed that of the Pharisees, and his Sermon on the Mount in Matthew 5 illustrated he was raising the bar significantly on what the law required. And so Jesus, adopting a typical form of Jewish interpretation that stated, "The more original, the weightier," pointed them back to the garden and God's design for marriage.[5] "Therefore what God has joined together, let no one separate" (Mark 10:9).

The disciples, a bit startled, stated, "If such is the case of a man with his wife, it is better not to marry" (Matt. 19:10). And, believe it or not, Jesus agreed. "Not everyone can accept this teaching . . ." (Matt. 19:11). And the motive for accepting celibacy, he clarified, was for the sake advancing the kingdom. But he clearly and specifically affirmed, "Let anyone accept this who can" (Matt. 19:12).

Sound crazy? Maybe it does. But the apostle Paul said much the same. Like Jesus, Paul acknowledged that singleness for the kingdom is not for everyone, but that clearly there are advantages for furthering the work of the gospel. "The unmarried man is anxious about the affairs of the Lord, how to please the Lord; but the married man is anxious about the affairs of the world, how to please his wife, and his interests are divided" (1 Cor. 7:32–34). Same goes for women, according to Paul. And get this: Paul was writing this to Corinth, of all places. The sexual sin city of the ancient world!

But Paul had more to say to this new church in sex-saturated Corinth, not just about marriage, but about the very ownership of their bodies. Church members were engaging with prostitutes, for crying out loud. And so Paul addressed this pointedly: uniting with a prostitute makes your body "one flesh" with her. Your bodies don't even belong to you, he wrote. In fact, your bodies are now temples of the Holy Spirit. When you become one flesh with a prostitute, you are joining the sacred with the sacrilegious. He concluded with, "For you were bought with a price; therefore glorify God in your body" (1 Cor. 6:20).

On another occasion Jesus was tested again, only this time by the Sadducees. Their big issue was the resurrection. They did not believe in it and wanted to prove their point with a hypocritical hypothetical: *What if a woman has multiple husbands in this life? If there's really a resurrection, that will present a problem. Whose ring will she wear in the next life?*

Without missing a beat, Jesus said, "those who are considered worthy of a place in that age and in the resurrection from the dead neither marry nor are given in marriage" (Luke 20:35). Wow. There you have it. No marriage in the next life! At least not in the same way that we marry here. The writings of Paul and John, and the words of John the Baptist give us a sneak preview. Jesus is the groom and the church is the bride. What's going on up there will far outdazzle the weddings and honeymoons of this life.

So what's the bottom line here? Is marriage just for the weak and out of control? Is it unspiritual to be married and to enjoy a vibrant sex life with your spouse? Not at all! In fact, the New Testament clearly declares the sacredness of the marital bond and how it foreshadows our final union with Jesus Christ in the Garden of Paradise. But it is not, as John Oswalt put it, "the be-all and end-all of human existence."[6]

So what do you think? Remember, you were forewarned. I said you were reading at your own risk. Give up sex for the kingdom? Your body doesn't even belong to you? No marriage in heaven except some sort of mystical union with Jesus? Okay, these are probably not key themes to be offering at your church's "seeker-sensitive" service. They don't play well with our sex-crazed crowds. In fact, I doubt they were ever an easy sell in any generation. Consider the following from Herbert Hensley Henson (yes, his real name), Anglican bishop of Durham, spoken nearly a century ago:

> The sexual appetite (which is the most insistent and the most important of our bodily desires) presses for satisfaction. . . . So we start with the certainty that sexual indulgence will be popular and that Christianity will be most difficult precisely at that point.[7]

Thanks for the warning, Herbert. And so it is.

Restoration and Grace for Healing

Before we consider the matter of healing for sexual brokenness, think with me again about physical healing. Just as you likely believe God can raise the dead, you also believe God can heal. You've heard the testimonies. Perhaps your own testimony includes an answer to prayer for physical healing. But even though you and I firmly believe in God's power to heal physical illness and to raise the dead, our experience has been that not everyone is healed when we pray.

A few might be healed instantaneously. God has blessed me to be a part of such a prayer session. Others, however, find healing in a progressive fashion. No, I'm not talking about prayer combined with chicken soup and seven days' rest bringing healing to a cold. Rather, I believe most of us have witnessed or personally experienced instances where very clearly God has sped up the healing process for someone through Christ-honoring prayer.

The experience of many, however, has not been instantaneous or progressive healing. Instead, some learned to lean into a sustaining grace that helped them to endure the illness or disease until their bodies righted themselves or else God took them to be with him.

Entire books have been written to lay out a theological framework for a healing ministry along with ways in which to pray for the sick.[8] That is not my purpose here. Simply observe with me the theological principle of the kingdom of God that we are in this season of what many call the "already and not yet." The restoration of all things has begun, but all of the benefits of the atonement will not be experienced this side of heaven.

Jesus taught his disciples how to pray and gave them authority to heal and cast out demons. As the gospel is proclaimed, we are to continue to pray and believe God for the healing of bodies and souls. But in this time between the gardens, some will be healed instantaneously, some progressively, and some when they reach the next garden.

Terry Wardle, my friend and mentor, has been a pioneer in the development of prayer for inner healing. In the previous chapter we walked through the Structures of Healing, which he developed— a grid for understanding how all of us have been wounded and stand in need of grace. Terry's monkey? Workaholism. His books and teaching seminars are punctuated with word after word of his testimony. Agoraphobia, panic attacks, and clinical depression also became the debilitating potholes on his journey. By the grace of God, however, he has experienced an amazing degree of healing. Even his eye color began to change once emotional healing began to flow within him. As dramatic as the change has been, it has also been a long and agonizingly slow process. Those looking for hope with their own brokenness have prodded him with, "Has God completely healed you?" His response has been, "I am healed. I am being healed. One day I will be completely healed."[9]

That's the way of the kingdom between the gardens—"already and not yet." The greatest healing experience for us is the moment we are reconciled to God and our spirits are born again through a prayer of faith. But that is just the beginning. Hope of further healing remains for us in this life and complete restoration in the next.

Healing for Sexual Brokenness

In Revelation 12, as cited at the beginning of this chapter, the martyrs overcome the Evil One through the blood of the Lamb and the word of their testimonies. Testimonies are indeed powerful. They mock the Enemy of our soul and feed our feeble faith. But in our highly polarized culture, testimonies have been used as weapons to attack ideological and theological foes.

As the church of America has debated homosexuality, testimonies have been trotted out to center stage. Hey, I've done it myself! Friends of mine and some of my counselees have found healing to varying degrees. When someone has been dramatically healed to the point of being attracted solely to the opposite sex, out onto center stage they go. If they have a spouse and kids, all the better! And so the crowd chants, "See, they *can* change! They are *not* born that way!"

But the other side of the debate has rightfully done the same. Without question, there are those who prayed every prayer they knew to pray, went through years of counseling, and even tried marriage as a solution, but still they are drawn to members of the same sex. Their refrain has been, "See, they *can't* change! They *are* born that way!"

Not surprisingly, we have played a significant role in the polarization of our culture over this matter of same-sex attraction.

Can we take a step back and look at this thing theologically? And let's simply say that no matter what the malady of our souls, healing comes in different ways. Yes, I counsel people with sexual brokenness, but I help people with a variety of issues. One lady's life was debilitated by a daunting depression. She'd been to secular therapists but found little or no help. But as we followed the leading of the Holy Spirit and prayed through some significant wounds of shame, the depression lifted after only two sessions! Praise God! I must be a miracle worker, right? Hmm . . .

During that same time period, however, I counseled a different lady battling depression. We met rather regularly for more than three years. Yes, her life improved, but it was one agonizing step after another on the path of restoration, a journey through which the Lord taught her to lean fully upon him for grace and strength.

So is there healing for depression? Without question. But in this season between the gardens there are no easy prayer formulas that net predictable results. The benefits of the kingdom are found "already and not yet" in their fullness.

Can we set aside our ideological agendas long enough to consider how this applies to healing for sexual brokenness? Can God heal the wounds of sexual abuse? Absolutely. In this "already-and-not-yet" phase of the kingdom, I've seen it happen instantaneously with one simple prayer at the altar of a church. However, just as instantaneous physical healings are not the norm, nor are healings of sexual abuse. Personally I have counseled hundreds of victims. On occasion, God takes us right to the root of the matter and brings immediate healing. More often, however, it comes by degrees after many sessions. And there are times when healing comes to the memory of abuse, but a person continues to struggle with the effects for years to come.

Sexual addiction? Much the same. Instantaneous healings are very rare in my experience. Usually it is a matter of progression, sometimes at a painstakingly slow pace as in Doug's case. A former counselee who had spent many years as a male prostitute described to me the degree of healing he had experienced over the years, but stated that some friends in his accountability group had been stuck in the same place for many years. There is no fast-track therapeutic model for most.

So can we quit wielding testimonies of ex-gays and ex-ex-gays in our battle over homosexuality? It is a Scapegoat issue. Some have found remarkable healing and are exclusively attracted to the opposite sex. Some have tried every means known to us and have found little to no change in attractions. A greater ability to resist temptation? Yes. A complete absence of struggle? Nope. But in this kingdom of the "already and not yet," they can live, as one author puts it, "Between a rock and a grace place."[10]

Grace for Endurance

As the next chapter will develop more fully, addiction to porn is running rampant in our culture. Those who come to me for counseling are usually at a point of desperation. A job has been lost or their marriage is on the edge of a cliff. Despite Internet filtering software to monitor activity, rigid involvement in accountability groups, prayer, and Bible study, there seems to be one defeat after another. Is the gospel powerless? Or have they simply not tried hard enough? What gives?!

I absolutely believe there is power in the gospel to set us free. But free from what? Sometimes sexual addicts or others with various forms of sexual brokenness have battled for so long that they simply want free from the temptation altogether. That is rarely the case. No matter what the monkey, sexual or otherwise, we will never be totally free of temptation and struggle. Even Jesus, the pioneer and author of our faith, suffered when tempted (see Hebrews 2:18). But I have seen many, many people find enough healing to live in victory over the temptation. That is what the Scriptures truly promise.

Once again, Terry Wardle enlightens us from the experience of wrestling with his own monkeys. In Paul's description of the "thorn in the flesh" in 2 Corinthians 12:7, Wardle found what he termed "sacramental brokenness."[11] A sacrament, of course, is something in this created world through which God meets us. From my own tradition, the best example is the Lord's Table, where we meet Jesus in the breaking of the bread and the taking of the cup. But the pain and suffering of our individual issues of brokenness can also become the portal through which we experience the divine. We don't like it. We kick against it. But as the psalmist assured us, "The LORD is near to the brokenhearted, and saves the crushed in spirit" (Ps. 34:18).

We want God to rescue us from pain. Rescue. Like the fairy-tale knight in shining armor, slaying the dragon and embracing the maid. Yeah, rescue. But that's not the way it plays out in this "already-and-not-yet" time between the gardens. Consider Paul's use of the word *rescue* in 2 Timothy 3:10–11:

> Now you have observed my teaching, my conduct, my aim in life, my faith, my patience, my love, my steadfastness, my perse-cutions, and my suffering the things that happened to me in Antioch, Iconium, and Lystra. What persecutions I endured! Yet the Lord rescued me from all of them.

So glad God rescued him, aren't you? Do you remember the story of Lystra? Hmm . . . yeah, that's where the crowd dragged him outside the city gate, stoned him to a bloody pulp, and left him for dead. That's not really how most of us use the word *rescue*! God's grace spared his life so he could continue to live out his mission, but he quite obviously did not rescue him from pain.

The message of restoration and grace assures us that God's restoration will be complete, but probably not until the next life. God can heal our brokenness in his way and in his timing so that we can live above the temptations of this life. Believe it. And his grace will certainly be sufficient for whatever thorn our flesh endures.

Count on it. He will rescue us. But keep in mind Paul's use of the word *rescue*, not Disney's.

Those who do not suffer from sexual brokenness have little clue what this struggle looks like. Some men fight every single day to keep their eyes from staring down a coworker's cleavage or from viewing women as objects to undress with their minds. It is a constant battle that they pray themselves through every day. To some of you that seems weak and crude, but there are others of you who will know exactly what I'm talking about.

Social media sites have fanned the flames of fantasy and emotional adultery. Those who have gone too far in flirtatious interactions with old heartthrobs or needy coworkers can find the battle to extricate themselves practically maddening. They may go to sleep in bed with the one who wears their wedding band, but each night a war is fought in their minds as they try to keep from fantasizing about the other person who has stolen their heart.

Most have no hint of the agony that haunts some marriages. Addicts who have seemingly done irreparable damage to their loved one. Husbands who have fed their minds with porn, bringing their unrealistic expectations into the bedroom, and placing enormous pressure on wives who feel unable to compete with their Photoshopped rivals. Victims of abuse who are repulsed by sexual touch and carry a truckload of shame for not being sexually responsive to their spouses. And ones married to the sexually averse as they oscillate between anger and confusion, not knowing why their advances are continually rebuffed. There's a whole lot of sorrow out there precisely because, as stated before, our genitals are the closest outward connection to the deepest part of our being. The battles of obsession and the barbs of rejection reach down to our core.

All of creation has been ravaged by sin, and Paul made clear that all of creation is groaning until the restoration is complete. Not only that, "but we ourselves, who have the first fruits of the Spirit, groan inwardly while we wait for adoption, the redemption of our bodies" (Rom. 8:23). If God's rescue mission seems less than Disney-esque, grab all of the healing grace he offers in the present and lean into him for sustaining grace to endure until we enter that next garden when the rescue of restoration is complete.

In the meantime, let us not be dismissive of anyone's pain. Despite taking steps to find healing and freedom, many will continue to struggle day after day.

Putting God in His Place

Much of the sorrow surrounding sexual brokenness is accentuated by a culture that has made sexual fulfillment an inalienable right. Men insist on sex before marriage "to make sure we are sexually compatible." Virgins are looked upon as horribly naive. And, of course, the church is viewed as incredibly inconsiderate, if not mean-spirited, for insisting marriage must be between a man and a woman.

Remember what was spelled out in chapters 2 and 5. We were not created as sexual beings and given relationships so that we might be sexually fulfilled. Quite the opposite. God's purpose for our sexuality is fourfold:

1. Reflection of the Image of God
2. Reproduction
3. Union with Another
4. Knowing Another

Also, keep in mind the perspective on sexuality found in the New Testament as discussed earlier. Celibacy is a God-honoring option and the sexual intimacy of marriage is earthbound. We live in this time between gardens, an age of open-eyed blindness, and we are called to seek first the kingdom of God and his righteousness (see Matthew 6:33). As John Oswalt has so fittingly framed it:

The Bible says that a less-than-ideal sex experience is not the cause of our problems, and an ideal one will not solve our problems. Like every other relationship in creation, sex is dynamic, sometimes highly satisfying, sometimes frustrating. But if we will let it be that and not ask more of it than it can give, we will find it offers much.[12]

All God's children got monkeys. I hope you've accepted that as fact. We all have brokenness. Will you consider the possibility that some of your brokenness is sexual in nature? Some get fooled by the fact that their struggles are heterosexual in nature. This seems especially true with men. "Aw, all guys struggle with an overactive sex drive! We are visually aroused. It's just natural." To some degree, yes. But is it possible you've crossed the line into obsession and are viewing women as objects?

And how about you ladies? Some women assume sex is a "guy thing" and, therefore, their own lack of interest is just the way it is. But do you go out of your way to be unavailable for your husband? Or do you withhold intimacy as a way to get even?

Restoration and grace were brought to our world by one who did not grasp or exploit the privileges of heaven, but emptied himself and served. May he be the one to guide you toward the wholeness that only he can provide. It could be that you will overcome by the power of his blood, and that your testimony will become a source of encouragement to others.

Most of those who come to me for counseling arrive in my office because their marriage is on the brink of disaster. Why wait until then? You can invite the Holy Spirit to begin sifting through your closet to see if there is some area of brokenness that needs to come out into his healing light. If God has been tugging at your heart page after page, consider finding time to privately pray the following:

Wonderful Savior, thank you for the forgiveness, restoration, and grace that come to us through your cross. Forgive me for submitting to sexual urges, grasping for what is not mine, or exploiting this good gift you have given us. Help me to find healing for those areas of brokenness that keep me bound in the closet. Grant me grace to endure the suffering of unmet need. Fill me with hope as I await the final restoration in your presence when all needs will once again be perfectly met. To you be the glory forever! Amen.

Discussion Questions

1. Do you have a testimony about God's healing (physical or emotional) grace that you would be willing to share with others? Was it instantaneous or gradual?
2. Did you have an "Aha!" moment while reading this chapter? What was it?
3. How did you react to the observations regarding marriage? Have you been a "hand-wringing matchmaker" for someone in your family? Does this chapter ease your mind a bit?
4. Do you think it is fair and theologically sound to draw the parallel between physical healing and emotional healing? Why or why not?
5. A contrast is drawn between Paul's use of *rescue* and that of a Disney fairy-tale movie. On a scale of one to ten (1=Paul; 10=Disney), where would you place your own expectations when you pray for God to rescue you?
6. What portion of this chapter are you least likely to forget?

CHAPTER 9

APPLICATION:
The Idolatry of Addiction and Aversion

W hat motivates someone to pick up the phone and make an appointment with a counselor like me? Pain. Like calling the fire department after a house is already engulfed in flames, a marriage is often greatly damaged and collapsing before some couples are willing to find a counselor. In some cases, separation has taken place and reconciliation seems unlikely. When it comes to sexual addiction and sexual aversion, often the offended spouse has enabled the destructive behavior until a collapse seems imminent. Regardless of how burned the structure of the marriage, however, rebuilding is often possible if both partners are willing to retool.

Thankfully, in the last twenty years much has been written about sexual addiction and aversion. Even in the past four years, advances have been made as scientists have discovered how addiction and trauma affect the brain. The possibility for recovery is improving with each passing year. What follows is certainly not an exhaustive study of these debilitating maladies, but rather a down-to-earth introduction into the dynamics of both. Let's simply begin the conversation. As this issue is discussed, maybe someone will find the courage to call the fire department before another home is entirely consumed by the flames.

The Red Shoes

Around the year 2000, I sat transfixed at a conference on sexual wholeness. There I listened to a woman tell her tale of sexual sorrows by intertwining it with her rendition of Hans Christian Andersen's grim fairy tale, "The Red Shoes." When it comes to sexual addiction and sexual aversion, sorrows certainly abound. As I summarize the story, see if you spot the parallels between the red shoes and the addiction narratives that have floated about your church.

> Once upon a time, an orphaned girl lived alone in the woods. Too poor to buy shoes, she had sewn together strips of red cloth to wear on her feet as she gathered food in the thorny woods. One day an elderly lady spotted her from her carriage and took her in as her own. Soon the girl had the finest of clothing and shiny black shoes. When she asked about her own red shoes, the lady responded that they looked ridiculous and so she had them burned with the trash. The girl was crushed.
>
> The time soon came for the girl to be confirmed at church. For the occasion, the lady took her to the shoemaker to purchase brand-new shoes. In the display case the girl spotted a pair of bright red shoes. While the lady had

insisted that only black shoes were suitable for church, the girl, making the choice from her hungry heart, pointed at the beautiful red shoes. The old woman was color blind and so gave her consent. The shoemaker winked at the girl as he snuggly wrapped them up.

The next day the church was abuzz as the girl walked in with her red shoes. Everyone stared, even the icons stared disapprovingly at the scandalous red shoes. As hymns were sung and prayers were prayed over the confirmands, the girl could think of nothing except her wonderful red shoes.

Of course the old woman was none too pleased. "Never ever wear those shoes again!" she scolded as she slammed them down upon a high shelf. But each time she could, the girl slipped by the shelf and stared longingly at the red shoes.

The following Sunday she managed to sneak the shoes off the shelf and wore them to church again! At the church entrance sat an old soldier with a red beard and his arm in a sling. He asked permission to dust off the child's shoes. As he dusted away, he also tapped the soles of the shoes and said, "Remember to stay for the dance!"

Once again the church ladies twittered with snide remarks about the girl's red shoes. The preacher peered over the rims of his glasses. The children's choir was all giggles and smirks. It mattered not. She thought of nothing for the entire service except her glorious shoes.

Later, as the girl exited, the soldier called out, "What beautiful dancing shoes!" Right then and there she did a pirouette, then a side-step, and soon she was waltzing her way down the street.

The old woman and her coachman caught her and, with great difficulty, pried the shoes off of her feet. What a sight it was with her legs kicking and the coachman losing his hat! But soon her legs were calmed and they all rode home in silence.

Once home, the scolding began. The woman again slammed the shoes down upon the high shelf. But the girl stole glances of them each chance she could.

One day the lady became quite ill and was bedridden. While she rested, the girl walked by the shelf and looked. More than look, she gazed. Then the gaze became a powerful desire. Soon she found a stool, grabbed the shoes, stole outside, and slipped them on. Immediately her feet began to twitch, so up she jumped as she began to dance. What a rush of excitement! It felt so freeing! So freeing, that is, until she wanted to dance to the left and the shoes went straight ahead.

The red shoes danced her through the fields and into the woods, where sat the wounded soldier! "Dance you shall because dance you must!" he cried.

Horrified, the girl fell to the ground and frantically pried away at the shoes, but they simply stayed glued to her feet as they continued to do their part of the dance!

Desolate dancing took her past her home where she saw a hearse with mourners. The old lady had passed. But the shoes danced on by.

Around the bend and near the edge of the village lived the town executioner. As she approached, the ax on his wall began to tremble. She called out to him for help. After he cut the straps and tried to peel away the red shoes, she begged him to simply cut off her feet! And so he did.

She spent the rest of her days humbly serving others, never again wishing for red shoes.

The Dance Shoes of Addiction

Ugh! What an ending! I know you were hoping they all lived happily ever after. If you check with your local library, you will find Andersen's original is slightly more upbeat. But addicts who have heard this rendering feel the closing scene well describes the cost of addiction.

In recent years I've noticed a trend. There are men and women in their late forties and fifties who are trying on red shoes for the first time. But rather than visit the town executioner, they have come to see me.

These are Christian people who have "done the right thing" for many years. Some have been stuck in a marriage where their sexual longings have been ignored. A few were attracted to the same sex, but married the opposite in order to honor God's pattern. But after years of bombardment with messages from a sex-crazed culture, they decide to try the shoes on for just a quick waltz around the dance floor only to find, to their horror, the shoes have begun to dance *them*. I've suggested to some that they are sexually addicted. No one seems to like how that term fits. For most of their lives, they've tried to honor God with their sexual desires and have never lapsed into addiction before. How can I call this addiction? Whether the shoe fits or not, life has certainly swirled out of control.

What exactly is sexual addiction? Marnie Ferree, citing the current guru in the field, stated that "being addicted is to have a pathological relationship with a mood-altering substance or behavior."[1] In other words, the reliance upon this behavior is diseased or unhealthy and used for the purpose of altering one's mood. As Ferree went on to point out, it is not wrong to alter our mood. We do it all the time. But as we noted earlier, a practice becomes sinful when it begins to destroy our relationship with God or with others, or when it begins to compromise our own well-being.[2]

Like the girl being danced right past her guardian's mourners, addicts often miss family functions and social events or even violate workplace rules in order to indulge. Similar to substance abuse, greater frequency or an increase in the element of risk is required to get the same buzz. A preoccupation takes over the addict as he or she spends inordinate amounts of time thinking about sex and making plans to participate. Just as the dancing evolved from beautiful to destructive, sexual addiction simply takes over control of the person so that they can no longer understand why they do what they do. Despite being faced with severe consequences, those caught in its grip seem powerless to reform.[3]

What kinds of sexual activities are found among the addicted? Mark Laaser in *Healing the Wounds of Sexual Addiction* listed the behaviors in eight categories. The first is simply sex with consenting partners. While you may be picturing clandestine rendezvous at seedy hotels, you can actually be acting out your addiction with your spouse. Just because you wear wedding bands doesn't mean your use of sexual intimacy isn't dysfunctional. Paying money for sexual encounters is the second type and can be a regular routine for addicts. A close cousin to this is cyber-sex as people hook up with partners over the Internet, sometimes by mutual consent, sometimes with credit card in hand. The fourth is less involved but far more common: an addiction to all sorts of porn that can be easily accessed online.[4]

Categories five through eight might not come to mind when you think of addiction. Exhibitionism and voyeurism both have addictive qualities and together stand as his fifth category. Laaser also cited "indecent liberties," as in groping an individual in a crowd, pool, or isolated area. Believe it or not, there are people who act out by making indecent phone calls, simply to catch a buzz off of someone's reaction. Bestiality is yet another type of addiction and is more common than you might want to imagine. And finally, Laaser observed some who are addicted to forms of sexual abuse.

Now keep in mind that having participated in any of these activities doesn't mean you are a sexual addict. Lack of control and a dependence upon them for altering one's mood are the giveaways.[5]

"Never Ever Touch Those Shoes Again!"

So why is it that someone would get caught up in such a mess? What causes someone to continue in the destructive patterns of addiction?

While each person is unique, there is usually a combination of both nature and nurture—that is, genetics and upbringing. Researchers have discovered that we all have genetic predispositions that incline us toward any number of activities. While there "is no direct path from a gene to a behavior," it does set up a grid through which we interact with the environment around us.[6] And for some, their brains are simply wired for a greater susceptibility to addiction.

But beyond biology, there are elements in our upbringing that simply nudge us a certain way. In "The Red Shoes," it is significant that the girl's first pair of shoes were made by her own hands. They helped protect her feet in a thorny world, and so she was deeply fond of them. Nothing wrong with that, right? It was not until after Confirmation Sunday that the obsession went south. At that age, with a heart hungry for significance and security, she chose the red shoes in the shoemaker's shop.

While we are children, we don't yet know how to deal with the stresses and sorrows of life. We shape shoes to help meet some of our deep insecurities and unmet needs. These coping mechanisms enable us to navigate the rough paths of life. But when we pass by the milestone of puberty and enter adulthood, those very shoes begin to take on a destructive power of their own.

The people who attend Ashes to Life and the ones who call on me for counseling usually come from horribly broken backgrounds. By comparison, my home life was embarrassingly wonderful. Perfect? Of course not. But I do know we were amazingly blessed. Mom was cast from the mold of the '30s and '40s. She firmly held the role of homemaker but also took a full-time job to help make ends meet. She has always had a quick and clever sense of humor attached to a jolly laugh. But when her face is relaxed, the corners of her mouth turn downward. Not a big deal. In fact, so what?

As a sensitive little kid, I always thought the downward curve of her lips meant she was unhappy. And as is true with most children, if things at home are out of sorts, the kids assume they're to blame. So I was forever asking, "Are you okay, Mommy?" The underlying question was, however, "Am *I* okay? Am *I* in trouble? Are you unhappy with *me*?" The red shoes that I soon pieced together were made of scraps of good behavior. I became the good little boy, trying to coax a smile of approval. There was absolutely nothing wrong with adopting that behavior to cope with the perceived stresses and insecurities of my home life. But once I crossed over into adulthood, those red shoes began to dance me over the hills, through the woods, and into the marshes. Destructive dancing. The unique person God made me to be was constantly disguised as I donned whatever persona would get people to like me.

Parents freak out when they see their toddlers rubbing their genitals. "What are you doing?! Cut it out!" But those little kids are simply putting together the scraps they can find to help them through the uncertainties of life. Psychologists call it "separation anxiety." When they feel they are too quickly separated from their moms, rubbing themselves gives them a sense of comfort and warmth. After explaining this to a kindergarten teacher, she sighed, "Ah, so that explains why kids are grabbing themselves the first two weeks of class!" There's nothing wrong with this. Kids can be taught to be discreet, but the better remedy is to provide the warmth and connection they are lacking with hugs, kisses, and attentiveness.

But passing into puberty, that behavior can begin to dance the child, especially when they discover the wonder of sexual climax. If they have any predisposition toward addiction and they are not provided with some loving guidance, those shoes can develop destructive dance moves which will take them down some harrowing trails.

Add to this some of the other factors that experts have found contribute significantly to sexual addiction. Among those who seek help for sexual addiction, abuse is highly significant. One study revealed 81 percent had been sexually abused, 97 percent emotionally, and 72 percent physically. The earlier the abuse, the greater the impact. If reports of abuse are not taken seriously, it drives the trauma further into their heart, especially when it comes to sexual abuse.[7] Patrick Carnes found that fear of abandonment is a key driver in sexual addiction. It's as if childhood separation anxiety kicks into hyper-drive.[8]

Much more could be said about how sexual negativity in the home, the siren calls of a permissive society, and the anonymity and accessibility of the Internet all add to the allure of sexual addiction. And from a biblical worldview, we also acknowledge the role played by the Evil One. Remember the old soldier with the red beard, his arm in a sling? Though disarmed through the cross of Christ, Satan can certainly have a strong influence. But he does not cause addiction. The soldier did not drag her to the dance floor. He simply tapped the soles of the shoes and suggested she stay for the dance. Satan energizes the magnetic pull of sexual addiction and provides opportunities to waltz away into the darkness.

Time and again as I counsel people caught up in sexual addiction, I am amazed at Satan's blatant attempts to derail people. Within a few days of clients finding significant healing for past abuse or distortions, they are contacted by old flings or approached by total strangers who coax and tempt them to take to the dance floor. But usually their experience of healing increases their ability to resist and they continue their journey a bit wiser and stronger.

The Trembling Ax

Wasn't there some other way to cut, pry, or strip those shoes from her feet? Such drastic measures!

The greater the grip of any addiction, the more drastic the measures for release. This is certainly true with sexual addiction. Consider for a moment why such drastic measures are needed.

First of all, addicts are accustomed to being enabled. Christian spouses are especially guilty of this. Viewing their spouse as a prodigal child, they simply view the trespasses as their "cross to bear for Jesus." One lady told me that each time her husband cheated, she just sat back, remembering the whippings that Paul endured. I quickly reminded her that Paul received the beatings for the sake of the gospel, and there was at least once when he claimed his Roman citizenship and refused to bare his back. She eventually saw the wisdom and separated from her husband. The shock of her assertiveness tapped into his fear of abandonment and brought him humbly back to God for release from addiction.

In addition to being enabled, sexual addicts are used to squirming their way out of consequences. Carnes referred to this as a superhero mind-set. When the trap is sprung and they are finally caught in their risky behavior, they have always found a way to escape. Their skills with deception, lying, and manipulation are well-honed.

One man's addiction found expression in forms of abuse, with his daughters on the receiving end. As one of them reached her thirties, she finally found the courage to bring the abuse to light. At first her family aimed all of their anger at her. Refusing to believe that the father, a leader in his local church, would stoop to such behavior, they wrote her off as crazy and delusional. But then another daughter spoke up. More evidence was presented. Outside attention began to accumulate. When there was absolutely no escape, the superhero thought of another ploy. He quickly confessed, shed some tears, rallied support, and then shifted the shame onto the daughters. "They are Christians! Look what they've done to our family! Now they need to forgive me and put this behind us!" Yuck.

You simply have to let the ax fall. Drastic measures help expose the deep wounds of abuse at the root of the behavior. The process can take much time and effort, but thankfully there are now abundant resources that take advantage of what research has gleaned regarding addiction. And those gifted in formational prayer and other Spirit-led counseling practices can position the afflicted in the healing presence of Jesus Christ.

The Hidden Shoes: Aversion

There's no lack of heartache in our broken world and few things grab our attention as does child abuse. To see bruised bottoms, head trauma, or cigarette burns on toddlers is outrageous. Far less observable is neglect. When kids lack a sense of security or never receive affirmation or affection, the trauma reverberates through their empty souls for years to come. And yet it is so much harder to recognize and quantify.

In reflecting upon her mother's neglect, one lady told me seventh grade was a turning point. As her mom dropped her off in front of the school, she told her, "Get out and don't forget your lunch this time." As she stepped from the car she noticed for the first time that other mothers were different. Kisses were blown or hugs given. Gentle reminders were topped off with, "I love you!" Until that moment, she thought her mom was typical.

If your mind hasn't blocked the memories, you can probably count the times you were abused by parents who in anger became overzealous in their punishments. But how do you number the hugs, caresses, and words of affirmation you *should have* received?

Just as abuse grabs our attention, so does adultery and addiction. We see the havoc wrought upon a marriage and we empathize with the innocent partner. Vows have been broken and trust has been trashed. A sense of outrage seizes us.

But what about aversion? Like child neglect, it doesn't grab our attention and is difficult to quantify. Not nearly as much focus has been given to this in popular print. Even the Scriptures, despite abundant denunciations of adultery, contain just one directive on the matter of withholding found in 1 Corinthians 7:5.

Nonetheless be certain of this. Just as neglect of children is as damaging as acts of abuse, so also the withholding of intimacy in a marriage is as destructive to the soul as the betrayal of trust from addiction and adultery. Both parties are harmed, actually. And is it not also a breaking of vows? Yes, we commit to "forsaking all others" but we also make a vow to "have and to hold . . . to love and to cherish till death do us part."

If the Shoe Fits . . .

As a good friend quipped, we all have the blood of Egyptian royalty flowing through our veins. Yep, we are all kings and queens of "de-Nile." We are so quick to spot the monkeys of others and yet so slow to admit our own brokenness. And just as sexual addicts are masters of deception, so also are the sexually averse.

The aim is not just avoiding sex, but holding at bay any intimacy that can lead toward the bedroom. And so excuses abound in the playbook of the averse. In fact, in the list of defensive plays, there's an entire section of religious rebuffs that can be called. But someone who is averse can find myriad other ways to keep their distance from a spouse. One friend who had been the victim of horrendous childhood sexual abuse found every way possible to avoid touching. If her husband fell asleep on the couch, she would gently cover him with a blanket and sneak off to bed to pretend to snooze. In fact, she regularly made him sleep in street clothes while in bed. Many other couples are all too familiar with the dark, cold "valley of separation" as their spouse clutches the far edge of the mattress.

Sewing Together Strips of Red Cloth

A mysterious mixture of nature and nurture no doubt lay the foundation for a lifetime of avoiding intimacy. Just as I learned as a child to lean into others for love and approval, others discovered ways to lean away from people to escape conflict and pain. Once again, these ways of coping in our innocent years are God-given modes of surviving as we develop in childhood. But once we pass through puberty, they have a crippling effect upon our souls.

Studies have uncovered other causes of intimacy avoidance that arise from the homes of our upbringing. Parents should model a warm intimacy, but sometimes a prickly and frigid alternative is the norm. When all talk of sexual matters is cast in a shaming light, the message embedded is that sex is "dirty," men are pigs, desire for sex is selfish and sinful, or that "decent Christian women" certainly don't think of such things.

But in the majority of instances where aversion exists, some form of sexual abuse or betrayal has traumatized the person. Carnes affirmed this, saying that it is often combined with other forms of abuse within the family of origin.[9] Past experiences were so distressing that the person "made a fundamental, unconscious commitment: Never combine intimacy and sexuality."[10]

For some, the euphoric state of falling in love overrides these inhibitions initially. In the early years of marriage, sexual intimacy might very well be rich and pleasurable. But when one's brain is no longer bathed in those blissful chemicals that create the euphoria of twitterpation, we return to our normal selves. The old defense mechanisms reengage. And as the castle walls go up and the iron gate slams into place, the spouse is left wondering what has gone wrong. *Have I done something to offend you? Am I not doing enough around the house? Do you no longer find me attractive?* Confusion leads to frustration. Anger and bitterness eventually follow. Often the innocent spouse's faithfulness is tested by the lure of porn or the flirtations of another. Without honest communication and some skilled intervention, the marriage will encounter a severe season of testing.

Honest communication or marriage counseling might bring to the surface accounts of past abuse. Simply knowing that the rejection stems from the traumas of the past is an enormous help for the person joined together with the sexually averse. But the problem still remains. The longing for bonding, connection, and intimacy does not go away. Even when the head knows that the stinging rejection stems from the spouse's past abuse, the heart still thirsts to know and be known in sexual intimacy. True loving intimacy, not just sex. As God has designed us, this thirst cannot be quenched when intimacy is forced by guilt and intimidation. The result invariably is either a grudging intercourse given mechanically or a ghost-like partner who mentally or emotionally detaches themselves as they dissociate to avoid past pain. Unless skilled help is found, the way forward can seem nearly hopeless.

The Path to Wholeness

So what is the loving thing to do if you are in such a marriage? Keep in mind the principle of the Box, the Path, and the Circus. Certainly this is part of the solution for moving forward in a marriage crippled by aversion. Going to the Circus, of course, is never God's will. To have an arrangement where the rejected spouse has a free pass to wallow in porn or illicit relationships is unthinkable for those who want to please God by honoring their vows.

But the Box mentality is simply a different alley leading to the same ghetto. To post the "law" of 1 Corinthians 7:5 on the headboard of the bed is not the answer. This simply brings the diseased thinking of the Box to the marriage bed. That merely takes the one you love back to those horrifying memories of abuse and betrayal, making the bedroom a potential shop of horrors. Likewise the averse spouse cannot frame the marriage with the do's and don'ts rooted in brokenness and false beliefs:

- "You can't touch me because of my past!"
- "All you ever want is sex."
- "Sex is so base. You're just like an animal."
- "Sex is dirty and shameful."

When it comes to our relationship with God, it is not about being positioned in the Box of do's and don'ts. It is a matter of direction. Are we moving toward God and greater wholeness as we become more like the Son? Similarly, in a marriage crippled by aversion, the questions are about direction and movement toward wholeness:

- Is the averse spouse willing to receive counseling?
- Is the averse spouse willing to work toward other ways of expressing intimacy?
- Is the rejected spouse willing to endure some deprivation while progress is made?
- Are both spouses willing to extend grace and forgiveness?

Never doubt the pain present in the marriage crippled by aversion. It is so easy to see the horrific pain caused by the unfaithfulness of adultery. It certainly triggers moral outrage in all of us. But what about the home where intimacy has grown cold? Behind closed doors, one little knows the sorrows of rejection as an averse spouse, out of deep brokenness, violates his or her vows "to have and to hold." Often those who are thus rejected enable the situation. Either out of respect for their partner or from a sense of shame, they feel unable to share their loss with their friends. When such marriages end in divorce, people are left wondering, "What's wrong with so-and-so that they would divorce a sweet person like that?!"

Red shoes. So attractive. How strong the pull for a hungry heart. For the averse, the longing is to be in control, well-defended, and free from violation. And yet how costly it is when those crazy shoes take on a life of their own and trample our fondest dreams.

Church Cobblers

The craft of shoemaking has long been lost. Once in a great while you can still find a cobbler shop, however. No, I'm not talking about a place for steamy, fruit-laden desserts topped with real whipped cream. (Although those shops are much too scarce as well, in my opinion.) I'm referring to a shop where your shoes can be repaired. If your worn-out soles are made of leather, a cobbler can sew on a new piece, making your comfortable old shoes feel better than new.

Sexual sorrows can wear holes in the toughest of souls. What can the church do to repair the damage and put new spring into the step of the sexually broken? Certainly there are counselors and twelve-step programs. But just as cobbler shops are hard to find, therapists and groups dealing specifically with sexual brokenness can be scarce.

Take note of what Patrick Carnes, the leader in the field of sexual addiction and aversion, had to say: "The irony of this . . . is that healthy, successful sex and a well-developed spiritual life are inextricably linked."[11] A well-developed spiritual life? Might the church have a way to contribute? Of course! With proper training, we can have a part in helping sew souls back together.

As a pastor of drug addicts and alcoholics, I am always looking for ways to improve our ministry to people in recovery. For two years we offered a twelve-step program that was infused with Scripture and embedded with some key principles of formational prayer. This particular program has enabled numerous churches in Canada to bring hope and freedom to people with addictive behaviors, but it fell flat in our setting. What I am finding at present is that in Beaver Falls the most effective means of helping people in recovery has been to connect them more fully with Jesus. In Christianese that's called *discipleship*.

In its first one hundred fifty years, the Methodist movement was a raging fire because of discipleship. The original spark found dry kindling in the grueling poverty of eighteenth-century England. Under the Spirit-empowered preaching of George Whitefield, John Wesley, and others, thousands of people from the lower classes of society placed their faith in the saving work of Jesus Christ.

What allowed the fire of this Great Awakening to spread across England and throughout the colonies for decades to come was the intentional focus on the care of souls. Wesley gathered believers into small groups known as class meetings, which will be more thoroughly discussed in chapter 12. But the nitty-gritty of soul formation took place in even smaller groups called "bands." A strange term for us today, of course, because we default to images of people on stage with instruments. Actually, the phrase "band of brothers" comes close to catching the intent of Wesley's bands— people who are staunchly committed to each other for the sake of finding victory over the besetting sins of life.

Scripture clearly proclaims that if we confess our sins to God, he will forgive us (see 1 John 1:9). James 5:16 adds a new dimension to the act of confession, however, stating that if we confess our sins to one another, we will be *healed*. There is power within a small group when people confess their sins to one another. Transparency among like-minded believers brings healing.

Wesley banded people together with three to six others of the same gender. Meeting weekly, they asked piercing questions about their inner life:

- What known sins have you committed since our last meeting?
- What temptations have you met with?
- How [were] you delivered?
- What have you thought, said, or done, of which you doubt whether it be sin or not?
- Have you nothing you desire to keep secret?[12]

Okay, I know what you are thinking: *Ain't no way I'm joining a group like that!* Yeah, I guess you'd have to be pretty desperate. But sometimes it takes an ax to free us.

But freedom can be sweet! Regarding these probing questions, Andrew Miller rightly observed: "The accountability of the band causes an initial humbling through self-disclosure, but the band's intimate friendships and healthy companionship help its members maintain lives of integrity and spiritual maturity thereafter."[13]

Because we have taught the Box, the Path, and the Circus so often that the old-timers roll their eyes, at Ashes to Life we've dubbed our version of Wesley's bands Pathway Groups. Like the bands of old, they are made up of three to five people of the same gender who are firmly committed to keeping both feet on the Path through spiritual disciplines and honest accountability. Each session ends with questions designed after John Wesley's three simple rules:

1. Do No Harm
   - Have you harmed another person this week by your actions or words?
   - Have you harmed yourself by caving into addictive behavior? (Drugs, porn/fantasy, workaholism, or whatever behavior God is working on in your life.)

2. Do Good
   - Have you spoken words of encouragement or done an act of kindness this week?

3. Stay in Love with God
   - Have you prayed for others in this group?
   - Have you completed the Bible reading?
   - Have you taken in God's grace in other ways? (e.g., attend worship, fast, help the poor, do an act of intervention.)

This means of helping addicts and alcoholics is ideally suited for people whose lives and marriages are being torn apart by sexual

addiction and/or aversion. Carnes found addicts resist accountability because of the rigid and controlling family systems in which
they were raised.[14] Such homes rarely exhibited unconditional love,
so if you misbehaved you kept your mouth shut. More than once
I've had a sexual addict confess their failure with dread fear in their
eyes as they expected me to shame them. But a band-type of group
done rightly can model both transparency and loving acceptance.
Healing comes as sins are confessed among those who truly care.

Note also what Anthony Jack of Case Western Reserve
University pointed out regarding how the sexually addicted brain
is affected. The ventral striatum is the part of the brain that receives
the reward of the addictive behavior of sexual addicts. But it also
serves other functions:

> The ventral striatum is highly sensitive to genuine empathetic
> social connection, including looking at a photograph of a family
> member, falling in love, altruistic acts, and even the simple
> feeling that someone has listened to you.[15]

Therefore, as the sexual addict withdraws from the pulse-pounding
lifestyle of porn, anonymous sex, or other practices, the symptoms
of withdrawal can be eased as he or she learns to reward that very
same part of the brain with the "genuine empathetic social connection" of a band. A small circle of caring people who will open their
hearts and lead them to a deeper relationship with God can be a
means of healing grace. They will be listened to, receive genuine
empathy, and learn from the struggles of others who are a bit
further down the Path.

Applying the dynamics of a band to aversion is problematic
from the get-go, however. They have already spent most of their
lives keeping up their guard, staying in control, and avoiding all
talk of sex. A tremendous degree of shame attends sexual aversion,
especially for men who have been conditioned to think of sexual
prowess as a badge of machismo. A small group that is closed to

outsiders, consistent, transparent, and non-judging would be a tremendous help if they would simply open the iron gate of the castle and let someone in. From what I've observed, most will resist unless they've already had the ax fall and are in the "humble servant" phase of their own red shoe story.

Dietrich Bonhoeffer once wrote, "The pursuit of purity is not about the suppression of lust, but about the reorientation of one's life to a larger goal."[16] Such a dramatic reorientation calls for a heart change only God can provide. Yes, we need an encounter with the Holy Spirit. But as Wesley so wisely discerned, we need fellow travelers who will prod us to take in God's means of grace.

Red Shoes Revisited

While reading the story of the red shoes, did you give any thought to the reaction of the church? Even the icons on the walls stared at the girl's red shoes! Uh, why? What's so inappropriate about red shoes? From where we stand, red shoes are fine for church, right? The tragic failure of this local church is that they were more concerned about the color of the shoes than they were about the soul of the girl. Where was the church when the shoes took on a devilish life of their own?

Things are not so different today. Just look at how we shoot our wounded when someone is caught in some form of sexual addiction. Stigmatizing sexual sin is so deeply ingrained that we fixate on the behavior instead of the sorrow. Just imagine a known sexual predator or exhibitionist finding an empty place in one of your pews. Would the icons in your stained glass stare as the church ladies twitter with snide remarks? Would their brokenness become a scandalous label for them to wear the rest of their lives? No wonder our people with sexual issues stay hidden, clinging to the old woolen coats moth-balled in the deep recesses of the church closet.

APPLICATION: THE IDOLATRY OF ADDICTION

Would it not please God if we instead grieved over the destruction wrought by both sexual addiction and aversion? Could we not learn to be a resource for bringing comfort and healing through Spirit-led prayer?

A pastor of a large church was caught with porn on his office computer. This being his second violation, he was forced to take a leave of absence for one year of treatment. For a brief stretch during that time he came to me for formational prayer. What few knew was that his wife was a victim of abuse and had been sexually averse nearly their entire marriage. Deeply humbled and filled with sorrow for how his addiction had stained his ministry and wounded his wife, he wrote the following lament. Read it with a heart open to the voice of the Holy Spirit. Can we learn to see with new eyes the devastation caused by the red shoes of sexual addiction and aversion?

"A Psalm of Lament" (Anonymous)

O God, who am I that you would look upon me with compassion,
And lift me into your warm embrace?
Why should I be enfolded into your bosom,
Or feel the breath of your life upon my cheek;
The whisper of your grace upon my ear?

Rather than live a life of abandon to you
I have abandoned you and your ways.
I have run after my own pleasure
until I have run far from you
and found myself in a desolate place of isolation.
I have withdrawn from you and the joys of your grace
and abandoned the comfort of the wife of my youth.
The love of God expressed through her faithfulness to me
I have disregarded and sought secret places of desolation.
And while your grace remains

I do not know if her trust can be revived.
I reap the loss which is the harvest of my sin.
O God, from the depths I cry
hear my prayer
listen to the cry of my heart
heal my hurt
and the hurt my own hurt has caused.

As you are restoring the joy of my salvation
Restore this marriage as a testimony to your grace.
May the days that lie before be years of jubilation
Finding restoration and hope that comes from you.

Yet I will praise you.
It is enough to rest in you
May the King of glory be my sufficiency
Though abandoned by all others may I hold to you
And find in you strength
To serve without response
To love without return
To show grace when hope is gone
To be ready to enfold in arms of compassion
my wounded wife
Just as you have enfolded me
when wounded and far from you.

O God, you are good
And your loyal love is everlasting.

If God so leads, consider praying the following prayer:

Gracious God, thank you for your heart of compassion.
Forgive us for being so quick to judge and so slow to under-
stand. Open our eyes to see as you see. May our church

*create safe places for deeply broken people to find healing
grace for sexual addiction and aversion. Through Christ our
Lord, amen.*

Discussion Questions

1. What did you find telling about the story of the red shoes?
2. What resources are available in your area to assist people
   caught up in sexual addiction? Are there resources for
   sexual aversion as well?
3. Was there anything in this chapter that created understanding or compassion for the sexually addicted or the
   sexually averse? What was it?
4. If you have ever been in a small group similar to Wesley's
   bands, describe it. What was helpful? What was not so
   helpful?
5. How does the story of the red shoes relate to other dysfunctional behaviors that are nonsexual?

CYCLE FOUR

The Consummation of Hope

CHAPTER 10

PRINCIPLE:
Jesus and Our
Perversity

It was Saturday night. I arrived a full half hour before the meeting began. A crowd had gathered outside the church doors. Some seemed a bit nervous, while others clearly were comfortable chatting away, cigarettes in hand, preparing for what awaited them inside. As eight o'clock approached, they crowded into the church basement, exchanging greetings and hugs as they made their way to the coffee urn. Taking up all the seats around the tables and filling the chairs along the walls, eventually there was standing room only. The bulk of them were in their late twenties and thirties, most of them men. No, I'm not describing some hip coffeehouse worship service. They had gathered with one common desire—to find God's help with their alcohol problems.

The kicker for me? At that time it was my church building!

Fourteen hours later I would be all dressed up in suit and tie peering out over the pulpit at eighteen people swallowed up in a sanctuary built for one hundred fifty. Hey, it looked nice, actually. Sunshine streamed through majestic stained glass. The choir, fully robed, was perched in the loft behind me. And the music? Magnificent. Bach blasted through the organ pipes, reverberating throughout the historic edifice.

What was wrong with this picture? *Two to three times* as many people attended that Alcoholics Anonymous meeting as were walking into worship on Sunday mornings! And our folks were generous and friendly people. For many years this tiny congregation had run a weekly soup kitchen, preparing about eighty servings for the hungry. The very fact that they opened the building at least twice weekly to twelve-step groups spoke of their desire to see God at work among them. And yet there remained this distressing disconnect.

So what's the draw on Saturday nights? A typical AA meeting looks like this: they give announcements, read statements of policy, recite a few prayers, and listen as the Twelve Steps, Twelve Traditions, and Twelve Promises of AA are read. Sound boring? It is. But they patiently wait for one thing: the speaker of the evening. They aren't polished and formally trained. Many haven't even finished college, much less seminary. But they have what the men and women are longing to hear—a story of how God delivered them from alcohol and kept their lives from falling further into a chasm of chaos. And as they nervously share their journey, others soak it in, sitting on the edge of their seats.

Some attend a church on Sundays. But most of them feel churches are clueless and can offer only cold stares of condemnation. And unfortunately, in many cases, they're not far off the mark.

Don't you feel, as I do, that the church of Jesus Christ has more to offer than simply meeting space? Don't you believe we have an answer for addicts of all sorts? Alcoholics, sexaholics, workaholics, shopaholics—surely we can offer help to such as these. The church has not only the message of reconciliation with God, but also the ministry of helping people grow into the likeness of Christ. And yet it seems there are debilitating issues that mere Bible study and worship attendance leave unchecked. Where is the power of Jesus Christ to overcome the addictions that chain them in the present? How can we help them heal the wounds that hound them from the past? Must we always refer people to twelve-step programs, therapists, and psychiatrists?

I believe we can be a valuable partner in the process of healing the deep issues that drive much of the sexual brokenness in church closets and elsewhere. But it begins by first addressing our own perversity.

Perversity in the Church?

Without a doubt. Perversity. Jesus would level that accusation against us. And really that's a pretty safe assumption in light of Matthew 17:17 where he addressed the issue with his disciples. Give the Carpenter a hammer and some nails and he could tack that citation on the front door of most of our churches: "Perversity! Enter at your own risk!"

Jesus had been on a prayer retreat. Taking Peter, James, and John with him, he climbed to the top of a high mountain. While in that time of prayer he became transfigured, his hair and clothing shining like the sun. Then Moses and Elijah appeared with him and a bright cloud enveloped them all. The three disciples fell facedown, shaking with fear. Then they all heard the voice of the Father: "This is my Son, the Beloved; with him I am well pleased; listen to him!" (Matt. 17:5).

Perhaps a glimmer of the glory remained as they descended, for Mark stated, "When the whole crowd saw him, they were immediately overcome with awe" (Mark 9:15). Soon a distraught father fell on his knees before him. "Lord, have mercy on my son, for he is an epileptic and he suffers terribly; he often falls into the fire and often into the water. And I brought him to your disciples, but they could not cure him" (Matt. 17:15–16).

That's when he said it. "You faithless and perverse generation, how much longer must I be with you? How much longer must I put up with you?" (v. 17).

"Put up with you?"! Wow. Pretty harsh. It's not as though the disciples hadn't tried. In fact, after he healed the boy, they asked Jesus, "Why could we not cast it out?" Jesus had given them authority to cast out demons and they had seen thrilling results before. But this time they hit a wall. What had gone wrong?

Their faith had been too little, replied Jesus. D. A. Carson maintained that quantity of faith wasn't the issue. Even the smallest seed of faith would have sufficed. It was the poverty of their faith that had proved ineffectual.[1] Mark's gospel adds these words: "This kind can come out only through prayer" (Mark 9:29). And so what was lacking was a quality of faith nurtured through prayer. Hmm . . .

Bicycle Generators and Solar Panels

Those of us who grew up in the days when phones had dials and TVs had rabbit ears remember the coolest of inventions for kids with bikes: the generator. Yeah, my bike once had a light powered by a D battery bolted onto my handlebars. Not very cool at all. But a bike with a generator? Whoa, baby! Push down the lever with your thumb and the wheel of the little fist-sized generator flopped down onto the tire. As soon as your wheel started turning, power began surging to the lamp on the bike. Groovy!

Okay, you had to pedal pretty darn fast to get much light out of the thing, but it was the envy of the neighborhood. You just had to pedal hard if you wanted to see where you were going. But once you arrived, you had better know the terrain because when the wheel stopped, the power went kaput. Darkness prevailed!

For a large part of my ministry experience, that was my understanding for doing God's work. If I wanted power, I'd better push the right lever and then pedal hard and steady. Once you stop pedaling, all bets are off. Satan will have a heyday. So keep the darkness at bay with furious pedaling! And likely you know what I'm talking about. Pray the glory down! Stay in the Word! For goodness sake, or maybe even for God's sake, do some fasting! Surely if we get enough people to pedal furiously, revival will in fact break out all over the place. People will get saved and healed. Our church will grow. That's just the way it works!

The problem? It *hasn't* been working. At least not to the degree I imagined. What has happened is I have burned myself out repeatedly as I've labored in the spiritual disciplines, imagining that it all depends upon me.

Now I wasn't far off the mark. Spiritual disciplines are certainly important and God, of course, answers prayer. But a slight shift in perspective was needed.

Positioning. Of all the many, many things I've learned from my mentor Terry Wardle, that one word is the most significant. *Positioning.*[2]

Bicycle generators are flat-out cool. No denying that. And it is pretty impressive to watch a kid zip by pumping her legs for all she's worth to make the light shine. Far out! But all the buzz now is about solar panels. They are totally awesome. No legs flailing away to get light. Just a matter of positioning the panel. That's it. Now certainly one must keep the panels out daily to catch whatever light the clouds will allow. And the larger the panels, the more the exposure and, hence, the more light to dispel darkness. But ultimately the wonder and amazement of the passersby is not at the strenuous effort of the positioner, but at the incredible power of the sun.

So, okay, what's this have to do with perversity in the church and our ministry of healing? Much in every way.

When I am so greatly privileged to be a channel of God's healing grace so that victims of abuse find healing for wounds that have crippled them for decades, it is obviously not about me. I didn't earn that person's healing by praying twenty hours and fasting three days. I have simply positioned myself toward God, basked in his loving embrace, gazed at the wonder of his greatness, and then positioned that person in his healing presence. Solar panel spirituality. In fact, I believe the apostle Paul pointed us to this technology when, reminding his readers of Moses's own Mount of Transfiguration experience and the liberating work of the Spirit, he said the following: "And all of us, with unveiled faces, seeing the glory of the Lord as though reflected in a mirror, are being transformed into the same image from one degree of glory to another; for this comes from the Lord, the Spirit" (2 Cor. 3:18). Transformation. Exposure to the Son transforms us. And when we position the wounded in prayer before God, the exposure transforms them as well.

For me, that is the essence of the healing in Matthew 17. Jesus and the trio of disciples didn't ascend the mountain to earn some prayer points to get recharged. They were simply positioned before the Father in such an intense fashion that a cloud of *shekinah* glory enclosed them. The open-eyed blindness of this fallen world was peeled back enough to expose them to the radiance of the Almighty. As they descended, people were wowed by the remnants of glory. Whatever demons had afflicted that young boy were likely glad to escape Jesus' shining presence!

Power Surges

During my seminary training in the early '80s, grand stories were shared by those who had experienced seasons of revival. The message seemed clear. It all started as people were led to pray. And so we prayed. Groups of students would meet informally. Once a week we would skip lunch and crowd into a classroom for urgent intercession. We had great faith that God would answer. We hungered for it. It had been a good twelve years since the glory had fallen before. Surely we were due for another outpouring.

Hmm . . . didn't happen. Maybe we didn't pray enough. Or maybe those other students who didn't give up their lunches were holding us back! Or maybe, just maybe, furious pedaling wasn't quite what was needed.

Solar panels are dependent upon the sun. And here in western Pennsylvania, we are dependent upon gaps in the clouds! Sometimes the dreary winter days far outnumber the bright ones. But nonetheless you keep the panels out, brush the snow off of them, and position them properly, so you will pick up whatever light filters through the haze. Eventually the shafts of sunlight will finally pierce through the clouds.

People continue to pray for a heavenly power surge, and rightly so. We long to see God's Holy Spirit move among us. So let's keep our panels broad and pointed heavenward, taking in every glint and gleam of Sonshine. One day, as God deems fit, the clouds will part to again reveal his glory. In the meantime, while we wait for the big beams to burst through, we can take in sufficient grace and power to cast a healing light among those willing to step out of the church closet.

Positioned in Healing Light

Positioning people is the essential means of helping them overcome the sorrows, lies, and emotional wounds which cripple their spiritual growth. *Positioning.*

That is not to say we don't utilize proven secular practices for moving people toward wholeness. The training I have received in formational prayer certainly is informed by the current insights regarding the effects of emotional trauma upon the brain. And one finds people trained in formational prayer availing themselves of training in cognitive behavioral therapy and Eye-Movement Desensitization and Reprocessing (EMDR). But positioning people in the presence of Christ is the one piece of the protocol that is having such a restorative impact for many.

Certainly the spiritual disciplines are critical for our walk with God, but it is not so much the activity as it is the positioning. When I was in bicycle generator mode, I used to intercede carefully and diligently so that people might be healed. Sometimes it was hard work. At one point I had a list of prayer requests for each day of the week. The disciplines of silence and solitude just seemed like a waste of time. But now I'm finding that the ancient practice of centering prayer, which is simply turning my solar panel toward the Son, yields much grace and power for the healing of others.

All of the spiritual disciplines and other means of grace are panels. The more you prop up and point Sonward, the more rays you take in. Just keep in mind we're not aiming for increased activity or more information. We are positioning ourselves for an interaction with God, an experience of receiving from him. Actually, you may not sense anything experientially as you are positioned. Like the surprise of getting sunburned on a cloudy day, you may not feel God's rays of grace as you put out the panels, even though transformation is still taking place. But there may come a time when you hear his voice or see something in the Spirit—like a vision.

Ouch! Yikes! I felt some pinching and wedging. Hey, cut that out! Some of you are now using a pry bar to wedge me into a pigeonhole labeled "Charismatic." Sorry. That's not a perfect fit for me. You need to look for a different hole: "Pentamethalbapterianic." Yeah, keep looking. It's rather large and fairly well-rounded. There's more folks in this pigeonhole than you might expect. And those of us from a Wesleyan tradition have found that John and Charles are in there too!

Manifestations of the Spirit

The Great Awakenings of the last three centuries often drew a lot of criticism from the established church folks. They were all for the swelling ranks of people filling the pews as long as they behaved, but the antics and actions of those coming under the power of God were simply a put-off. The revival in John Wesley's day was no exception. In his journal, he recorded what people were experiencing once under the influence of God's power:

> These are matters of fact, whereof I have been, and almost daily am, an eye or ear witness. What I have to say touching visions or dreams, is this: I know several persons in whom this great change was wrought in a dream, or during a strong representation to the eye of the mind, of Christ either on the cross, or in glory. . . . And that such a change was then wrought, appears . . . from the whole tenor of their life, till then, many ways wicked; from that time, holy, just, and good.[3]

Weary of the badgering of critics, Wesley simply invited one of them to preach at one of his meetings. I'm imagining he had a bit of a smirk as he finished penning the following:

> . . . no sooner had he begun . . . to invite all sinners to believe in Christ, than four persons sunk down close to him almost in the same moment. One of them lay without either sense or motion. A second trembled exceedingly. The third had strong convulsions all over his body, but made no noise unless by groans. The fourth, equally convulsed, called upon God with strong cries and tears. From this time, I trust, we shall all suffer God to carry on his own work in the way that pleaseth him.[4]

Through methodical use of spiritual disciplines, Wesley and his colleagues had faithfully positioned themselves in the months before that great movement of God. Then when the rays burst through the clouds and God's power surge hit, they were dancing right in the middle of heaven-sent beams of light. People were experiencing the presence of God in dramatic fashion and walking away transformed.

Formational prayer for the broken runs parallel with this, even when the spiritual atmosphere seems overcast. As God's people turn their solar panels heavenward, the power of the Son seeping through the clouds becomes focused upon a person in need. Hurting people are positioned in the light. That's when mourning can turn to dancing.

Let's face it. All of the information in the world will only make a dent for the abuse victim. Prescribing new routines and behaviors will begin to scratch the surface for a sexual addict, but not deeply enough to bring the longed-for freedom. But if positioned properly by a person whose panels are set toward the Son, God can meet the sexually broken in a powerful way and move them further down the Path.

And so as the broken bring their sorrows before God in biblical lament, they will not only spill out their pain, but they will also experience God's healing word for them. Someone bound by the lies of the Evil One will not only renounce a lie, but will be positioned to hear God himself speak the truth to their open heart. Or think of the person whose entire life has been a continual curse of compensating for abuse from the past. They will encounter God's presence in that painful memory in such a way that the poison is sucked out of the wound.

My good friend Heather has seen amazing results as she has positioned people in the presence of God. When someone with heart-wrenching sorrow comes to her, she is keenly aware of her dependence upon God to bring healing. With her wonderful self-deprecating humor, she often exclaims, "If God don't show up, I got nothin'!" But I can assure you, when her solar panels are tilted Sonward, God most definitely shows up!

Positioned and Transformed

A number of years ago I was called in to help Harold, a pastor who had gone through an emotional meltdown. Thirty-five years earlier he had started his church in a small city in Ohio. Extremely gregarious, he attended every high school basketball game, was known all over town, and was much loved. But mysteriously, he began to have chronic nosebleeds. Several visits to the doctors provided no relief. There was nothing wrong with his nose, they insisted. The culprit was stress.

Try as he might to ease the stress, the nose continued to run red. One night in the hospital they packed his nose with gauze. This, however, triggered an onslaught of emotional distress. Soon depression landed with a thud. He who had been at the center of public events was now secluded in his bedroom, overwhelmed with anxiety and despair. As he disappeared from the spotlight, his appetite also vanished. Fortunately he was able to tell his gifted staff to take over the ministry in the weeks ahead as he took some time off, but he truly had no idea if he would ever stand behind the pulpit again.

In our first session I listened to his story and explained the principle of being positioned in God's healing light. Though a godly man who loved Jesus with all of his heart and soul, he had never really experienced what Wesley described as "a strong representation to the eye of the mind of Christ." But he was willing to try.

We began with prayers of praise focused upon the glory of God and the victory of Christ through the cross. Inviting the Holy Spirit to open the eyes and ears of our hearts, we asked God to meet him in that moment. Soon I saw the tension on his face give way to bliss, so I asked him if he was seeing something. "Yes, I see myself standing by the river where I was baptized as a child."

"That must be a wonderful image. Does that bring you a feeling of peace?"

"Oh yes!" he replied. So I prompted him to ask God to enter that picture. Soon he smiled.

"So what do you see now?"

"Jesus is now standing beside me!" Even though it is often Jesus who enters into such visions, I always tell them to ask *God* to show up so that he can appear however he wants: through biblical images, streams of light, or simply a strong sense of his presence. It is through these Spirit-inspired images to the eye of the mind that God conveys his healing word, so I encouraged him to stay put by the river.

When I felt nudged by the Spirit, I had him ask God if there was a lie or a wound at the root of his depression that God might want to touch. The moment he voiced that request, his face fell. "What's going on?" I inquired.

"He's taking me down to where the river empties into a lake. When I was a little boy, I almost drowned there!"

Distress overtook his expression. His body became rigid. It looked as though he was actually struggling to get air! I urged him, "Ask God to meet you there!"

As soon as he choked out the words, his body slumped into the chair as his smile returned. Wanting to be sure he was okay, I asked what he was experiencing.

"As soon as I asked him to meet me there, I heard God's voice say, 'Somebody save the boy! I have a purpose for his life!'" Later he related that his father had actually rescued him, pulling him safely from a watery grave.

So what happened in this prayer session? Was it a calculated manipulation of images and memories? Hardly. I'm not that clever! Only God knew where to take him and what to reveal. History was not changed. In other words, I did not tell him to imagine himself swimming to safety. God simply pulled back the spiritual curtain a bit to reveal more of the picture. The truth of that event was this: he was not abandoned and alone in that life-threatening crisis. God was there! He saw his distress! And he called out from heaven for Harold's life to be spared. Having received that glimpse, Harold's perspective shifted sufficiently to bring healing to that tortured memory.

And so connect the dots with me. A few weeks before this, the gauze had been shoved up his nose, making it difficult to breathe. That suffocating sensation summoned the unresolved childhood trauma at the lake, manifesting in depression, agoraphobia, and loss of appetite. Once God's healing light brought resolution to that fear-fraught memory, the symptoms began to subside. With continued support from me and other caregivers, he was able to return to the pulpit within a few months.

This miracle has unfolded before me hundreds of times as I've helped people hidden in the church closet. It has been my honor and privilege to position victims of sexual abuse and other forms of trauma before the God of light and peace. As together we simply follow the leading of the Holy Spirit, the crippling effects of unresolved, painful memories lose their grip upon God's people. The result? Sexual compulsions become easier to manage, the luster of addictive obsessions begins to lessen, and sinful ways of coping with pain begin to be supplanted with holy habits.

A Special Irony

In his book *Sexual Anorexia,* Patrick Carnes again related the dysfunctional role the church has unwittingly played in the sexual chaos of Western culture. Though official teachings of the faithful may attempt to present a balanced view of God's good intention in creating the gift of sexual pleasure, too often what has been communicated is that sex outside of marriage is more detestable than other sinful behaviors or that sex within a marriage is a duty. Sprinkle onto this the occasional news reports of clergy sex scandals and the church has contributed much to the distortions in our society.

So what's the irony? As mentioned in the last chapter, Carnes believes that "sexual transformation and spiritual renewal cannot occur separately."[5] Did you get that? Despite the efforts and techniques of sex therapists, this renowned leader in the treatment of sexual dysfunction believes connection with God for spiritual renewal is essential in bringing about the deep transformation desperately needed by people in bondage to sexual addiction and sexual aversion. And so Carnes refers sexual addicts to twelve-step programs, which call people to reach out to a "Higher Power" to assist them.

Let that sink in a bit. The leading sexual guru says sexual addicts need a higher power. But instead of urging his clients to find a Bible-believing local church, he recommends they find a twelve-step group that probably meets in the basement of a Bible-believing local church. Is that not an indictment? Is Jesus throwing his hands up and saying, "How much longer must I put up with you?"

The sexually broken that I've counseled and the heroin addicts in my church completely agree that transformation comes more readily when one believes that Jesus is the only Higher Power. Or as one former drug dealer recently told me, "There's no high quite like knowing the Most High!"

Training

Please note that I am not calling for a hasty crusade. As chapter 12 will make clear, targeting people for healing, as tempting as that may be, is not walking in step with the Spirit of God. Once God began to use me to bring healing to victims of sexual abuse, I admit to being overzealous. Assuming that every victim I knew of would gladly open up their hearts to find healing, I got a bit too assertive. One person in particular was hurt because I rushed in to help her without first building trust and waiting for God's timing.

But I do believe that the church, if properly equipped, can become a recognized resource in helping people find freedom. Instead of only referring our walking wounded to therapists, psychiatrists, and twelve-step programs, I believe we can become a part of a team of people God uses to bring health and wholeness. But adequate training is essential. Simply reading a few books and watching a video series does not qualify one to perform delicate surgery on broken hearts. In fact, taking a person back to a memory of sexual abuse at the wrong time or in the wrong way can re-traumatize them.

Having said that, I believe many larger churches and a few vital small congregations are likely to have a staff person or a mature lay person with the right spiritual gifts and social skills to be greatly used of God. In some cases, there might even be a team of people who can be effectively equipped for this ministry. But it is certainly not for everyone.

Even though I do a lot of counseling as a pastor, I recognize that not every pastor has been called to be a counselor. Far from it. Each of us has special gifts and graces. I have made this very point to the pastors who have attended my seminars. But even if you don't have the appropriate gifts, you can at least cast a vision and make room in your church for this kind of ministry by seeing that someone is adequately trained to do this work.

So what training is adequate? Certainly there are a number of protocols that have been developed that God is using. David Seamands and Leanne Payne, two pioneers of the previous century, found means of positioning people in the healing presence of Jesus.

Other faith traditions have come up with protocols and small-group ministries that fit well within their theological framework. But in my conversations with therapists and in my work with people in the doctor of ministry program at Ashland Theological Seminary, it seems at present there is nothing quite so developed and balanced as Terry Wardle's approach with formational prayer. Wardle has gleaned insights from the field of psychology, availing himself of the latest discoveries concerning the effect of trauma upon the brain. At the same time, however, he has remained absolutely welded to good theology, finding the steps for processing trauma in the very life and ministry of Jesus. His four-day seminar does far more than convey information and pass on technique. He equips people to follow the Spirit's leading as they help others move toward greater wholeness.[6]

Repenting from Perversity

Do you have some free time on a Saturday night? Check with your AA friends to see if there is a speaker's meeting nearby. These particular meetings are open to the public. If you go one hundred times and hear one hundred different speakers, you will find an amazing similarity to the stories. About ninety-five of them will describe horrifying upbringings. Their childhood was fractured by absentee parents, divorce, physical abuse, sexual trauma, or some other kind of tragedy. But at some point they were offered a drink. It went down smoothly and felt so good! So they drank more and more until they finally realized they couldn't stop.

Is there a genetic component to alcoholism? Certainly. That's why they call it a disease. They inherited an inability to drink moderately. Therefore once they start, they just can't seem to stop. But the vast majority of the stories told on Saturday nights make it very clear. Abuse, deprivation, and tragedy tilled the soil of their soul, making them fertile ground for a life of drunken chaos.

Scientists are finding a genetic predispositioning for sexual addiction, same-sex attraction, and other conditions. I know of no promise from God to change our genes. But I do know that Jesus carried our sorrows to the cross and longs for his body, the church, to be his healing hands. If positioned before the Son, we can offer healing for the sorrows and distortions which often drive sexual brokenness.

Remember the father in Matthew 17? He was not about to give up. Pushing aside the impotent disciples of perverse faith, he fell before Jesus to seek healing for his son. Only God knows how many people have first come to the church to find healing for the deepest issues of their broken lives, but finding us to be impotent, they have pushed us aside. They haven't given up on Jesus' ability to heal them. They simply look elsewhere to find it, searching for answers from secular agencies and twelve-step programs.

May we repent of our perversity! May we become fully equipped to cooperate with the healing work of the Spirit. And may we also learn to position ourselves in the glory of God's Son so that we fall more in love with him and become channels of his healing grace for others.

If that's the desire of your heart, pray the following:

Lord Jesus Christ, thank you so much for the healing that came when we first put our faith in you. If that is all the healing we ever receive, it is more than we deserve! But like other believers, we hunger to see you more at work in our lives and in the life of our church. May we open our hearts to the sunshine of your grace and move in step with your Spirit. If you would have us be equipped to bring healing to the sexually broken, open up the way. May it never be said that people pushed us aside as impotent disciples and sought for your healing from other sources. We repent of our perverse faith and ask for more of your grace. In your wonderful name we pray, amen!

Discussion Questions

1. Describe a time when you or your local church experienced a "power surge." In other words, have you ever been part of an awakening when the Holy Spirit was frequently leading people to faith in Jesus and others were being healed?
2. What spiritual disciplines do you find the most helpful in being positioned in God's grace?
3. In what way is your local church doing a great job of being the healing hands of God? Where is it falling short?
4. Do you think the contrast between the generator and the solar panels is appropriate when thinking about spiritual disciplines? If so, why do you think it is so easy to slip into the mind-set of pedaling furiously for God's favor?
5. If your church was adequately trained to offer healing prayer for the sexually broken, do you think people would exit the closet and seek help with abuse, addiction, aversion, and same-sex attraction? If not, what would help them come forward?

CHAPTER 11

THEOLOGY:
Making the Case for Boundaries

So where have we been on our theological journey? We began, of course, with the story of creation, finding clues in the Garden of Eden regarding God's design for us as male and female. As David reflected in Psalm 139:14, we could likewise exclaim, "I am fearfully and wonderfully made!" The bonding of sexual union goes a long way toward meeting our deepest longings for connection with another.

But the story didn't end there. Temptation was presented and choices were made. Our first parents submitted to the created world and grasped for what was not yet theirs. A bite of forbidden fruit opened their eyes to their nakedness, but obscured their view of the face of God. Thus began an age of darkness where people have continued to submit to created urges and grasp for what is not theirs, leading to sexual brokenness of all sorts.

But God has not abandoned us. On a starry night with Abram, a covenant was established that launched the mission of God to restore our corrupted worldview and solidify all of its porous boundaries. The true beachhead of that effort was the birth, death, and resurrection of Jesus Christ. Under the new covenant, the kingdom has come and restoration has begun. While the full restoration of God's *shalom* awaits us in the Garden of Paradise, we even now can experience some healing for brokenness and much grace to endure suffering.

And as we will consider in this chapter, the Bible is our trustworthy guide in knowing where the boundaries are for our sexuality. Certainly people have always wanted to fudge on the lines drawn on sexual behavior. In our world of submitting and grasping, who wants to say no to their urges? If it feels good, we want to do it . . . now! G. K. Chesterton is reported to have said, "The Christian ideal has not been tried and found wanting; it has been found difficult and left untried." And we have always wanted to justify redrawing the boundaries. That is especially true regarding today's debate over the nature of homosexual intimacy, and much of what follows will engage in that debate. But please keep in mind that there are plenty of boundaries on heterosexual sex which Christians have been ignoring for decades. Okay, maybe centuries. This review of God's boundaries applies to all of us, and the Bible provides clear direction.

Debatable Values

In the late '70s I was a student at Hope College in Holland, Michigan. Like it or not, each senior was required to take a Christian ethics course. Periodically debates were held in class and each one was assigned to contend either for or against a specific topic. And so some argued for or against issues such as abortion, regardless of how they personally felt about the matter. A friend of mine and I were chosen by lot to argue in favor of premarital sex. Neither of us personally believed sex before marriage was ethical, but nonetheless were determined to win the debate. And we did!

The opposing team felt they had a slam dunk. Central to their argument was Galatians 5:

> But if you are led by the Spirit, you are not subject to the law. Now the works of the flesh are obvious: fornication, impurity, licentiousness, idolatry, sorcery, enmities, strife, jealousy, anger, quarrels, dissensions, factions, envy, drunkenness, carousing, and things like these. I am warning you, as I warned you before: those who do such things will not inherit the kingdom of God. (vv. 18–21)

With confident grins, they stated that clearly "fornication" is on the list, and those who participate are, according to this passage, outside of the kingdom of God.

To their surprise, we agreed that fornicators won't inherit the kingdom of God. But what exactly is a fornicator? The Greek word *pornea* is rather broad. And consider this list, for crying out loud. Idolatry, sorcery, drunkenness, "and things like these." Surely you can't make the case that this includes *all* sexual intimacy outside of marriage. What about two engaged students who have dated for three years and have a solid commitment to each other and to eventual marriage? You can't seriously put them on the same list as sorcerers, drunks, and bed-hopping party freaks!

Wow. Guess who won. It's not hard to believe that a roomful of single college students would be persuaded by our argument. But at the end of the debate, my friend and I stated plainly to the class that we personally did not hold to the position that had triumphed.

Regarding homosexuality, there are six main passages of Scripture that have been debated for years. The "classroom" observing this debate is increasingly made up of Christian people sympathetic with the LGBT community, and they are wanting their side of the argument to win. Unlike my college classroom, they are not wanting a victory so they can indulge in sexual pleasures. Far from it. Many of them stand by the belief that sexual intimacy should be framed by a covenant. And it is not, as many Evangelicals presume, based upon a wimpy view of Scripture. They are simply tired of seeing the gay and lesbian people they love being hurt by the church.

Persuasive for them is the much-touted conclusion that gays and lesbians are born this way. How could God deny them the fulfillment of intimate connection with a person they love? And so the Scriptures, which they highly esteem, must be lacking something. A piece of the puzzle is simply missing.

Reasonable Doubts

If you have watched one of the bazillion episodes of *Law & Order*, you probably are aware of a defense attorney's strategy in a murder trial. All he or she needs is one juror to waver. If "reasonable doubt" can be created in the minds of just one juror, the accused walks out free.

For some who are arguing the case for same-sex intimacy, the strategy seems much the same. This line of reasoning dates back at least to 1979, when Walter Wink penned "Homosexuality and the Bible" for *The Christian Century* magazine. First the seeming inconsistencies of Scripture are highlighted. *Why polygamy and concubinage among Old Testament leaders? And what of the command for a young, childless widow to be taken in by the deceased's brother so that she can bear children within that family line? Is anyone still abiding by that injunction? Semen and a woman's menstrual flow make a person unclean. Really?* After raising the doubts, Wink, along with others, appealed to Jesus' command to love God and love your neighbor, stating that some of these sexual issues, including same-sex marriage, are to be decided by us. Yep, that's right. Judge for yourselves. Just be sure your actions are dictated by love.[1]

Writing forty years later, Jennifer Wright Knust, professor of religion at Boston University, sailed with much the same tack and reaches the same shore. In her cleverly titled book *Unprotected Texts*, she does, in fact, leave no text of Scripture protected from her analysis. With strong documentation and detailed footnoting, she made her point that "looking to the Bible for straightforward answers about anything, including sex, can lead only to disappointment."[2] David's adultery, she asserted, received God's blessing rather than cursing as the eventual heir came from Bathsheba.[3] The clear warnings against adultery in Proverbs 4–7 are not really fatherly advice to sons, but cloaked warnings against marrying foreign women.[4] As for the Garden of Eden, she compared it with other ancient creation stories and concludes the story of Eden is about farming, not marriage.[5]

Again, my aim is not a point-by-point refutation, but rather to show contrasting ways of handling the Scriptures. Those seeking to rewrite Christian sexual ethics are not bad people. They are simply trying to make sense of the Scriptures in a way that is consistent and does justice to those who are attracted to the same sex.

And if you have followed the common arguments flung about in social media, you find the "reasonable doubt" approach is all the rage. *If you are going to insist upon the law in Leviticus prohibiting intercourse between two men, then you had better obey all of the laws. What about laws regarding clothing made of both cotton and wool? And the dietary laws. Are you still eating shrimp?* (Whoa! A low blow for a shrimp lover like myself!) And the one used quite often because it offers the most hermeneutical punch: *What about the law also found in Leviticus 18 and 20 that forbids intercourse with a woman during her monthly flow? Is anyone policing that one?*[6]

All of these arguments are aimed at raising reasonable doubt regarding the Bible's authority on all things sexual. If the Bible is so inconsistent, they maintain, then why apply a few scattered verses on homosexual sex to shackle two adults who love each other, want to share in a marriage covenant, and to experience the joy of raising kids? It is a persuasive argument for many.[7]

The problem, as you can likely see already, is that once you cut the ropes at the dock, there's no telling where the ship will drift. As Knust said, the "reasonable doubt" approach compromises our ability to find straightforward answers about *anything* from the Bible, sexual or otherwise.

If It Pleases the Court

The Supreme Court recently struck down the Defense of Marriage Act, which defined marriage as being between one man and one woman. And so it is not surprising that already some have been arguing for polygamy. And upon what biblical grounds can we make the case against polygamy if reasonable doubt trumps all biblical guidance? The fact of the matter is that I can make a better case from the Scriptures for polygamy than I can for same-sex marriage. Easily.

In fact, look at it from this angle. A better case can be made from the Scriptures for heterosexual marriage than for many of our key beliefs as Christians. Consider the evidence, Exhibits A through F: God's template for marriage found in the Garden of Eden; Jesus' affirmation of that template in Matthew 19; the absence of any examples of same-sex marriage; the repeated use of heterosexual marriage as an Old Testament metaphor for God's relationship with his people; the explicit statements in the New Testament regarding Jesus as the Groom awaiting the celestial marriage with his bride the church; not to mention specific teachings directed to husbands and wives . . . Whew! With metaphors, imagery, examples, and clear-cut teaching, there is far more support for heterosexual marriage than for a lot of our other beliefs.

Take, for instance, the Apostles' Creed. A few verses in the New Testament and a dubious prophecy in the Old are the basis for our belief in the virgin birth. "Conceived by the Holy Spirit" is an assertion backed by two angelic announcements, one to Mary, the other to Joseph. "The communion of saints"? Hmm . . . Hebrews 12:1 maybe? And what about the cherished doctrine of the Trinity itself? The words *Trinity* and *triune* don't even appear in the Bible. Christians debated this topic for at least three hundred years before they settled the matter.

Then there are those pesky issues that have divided entire denominations. Can we baptize infants or only those we deem believers? Should churches be governed congregationally or from a top-down episcopal approach? Are the bread and juice memory tools or means of grace? Are congregations connected with each other and required to support the connection financially or are they independent entities free to give as they choose?

You likely have strong opinions on all of these matters, as do I. For centuries the church has rightly appealed to the Scriptures to decide these issues of faith. But if we adopt the same approach to handling the Bible as is being used to make room for same-sex marriage, what do we have to stand on for answering any of these questions?

Once again, these are not evil people with an agenda to tear apart cherished beliefs. Far from it. Nor are they sexually immoral and cantankerous. Some of the ones I've dialogued with are among the friendliest and most loving kingdom folks you could want to meet. For the most part, they are driven by a sense of justice for people they have come to know—people who have been hurt by the church. But regardless of their motivation, their approach to the Scriptures takes us back to the time of the judges when everyone did what was right in their own eyes. Yep, it takes us right back to the porous boundaries of ancient times.

Instead of poking holes in the passages that address sexual boundaries, there are others who are connecting the dots, revealing the mission of God at work through history. Interpreting the Bible is more than stacking up verses that specifically address a topic and then determining their cultural and historical contexts. Some of our beliefs are based upon a kingdom context. That is, what is the larger movement of what God is doing through history and how does it apply to particular passages or matters of doctrine? This is why I have mapped out the mission of God as we've considered the theology of sexuality because, for me, the unfolding mission of God to restore our worldview is a far more powerful argument than debating the six isolated references to homosexuality in the Bible.

Anglican theologian N. T. Wright described this well in his book *Scripture and the Authority of God.* Using theater as a metaphor, Wright described the Bible as a five-act play, with each act carrying on the story of God's mission: creation, fall, Israel, Jesus, and the church. The relationship of one act with the others and how each contributes to the unfolding narrative all figure into how we interpret certain portions of the text. Therefore the early church leaders recognized that "some parts of the Scriptures were no longer relevant for their ongoing life—not, we must stress, because those parts were bad, or not God-given, or less inspired, but *because they belonged with earlier parts of the story which had now reached its climax*" (italics his).[8] This, then, leads us to the matter of the Old Testament laws.

Deciphering Legalese

Some of the reasonable doubts expressed above throw into question all of the laws in Leviticus and elsewhere simply because a few of them seem odd and many don't apply anymore. After all, didn't the death of Jesus fulfill all laws? As long as we love God and love our neighbor, it is reasoned, that should be enough. Makes things much simpler anyway, right? But consider again the mission of God after the Red Sea.

Let's face it. Moses had quite a job on his hands, shepherding more than a million malcontents and ingrates. When the going got tough, the people got going . . . back to Egypt, that is. They were so quick to wander despite the amazing miracles God had performed before their very eyes.

Remember that at this point in the mission, God was beginning some major reshaping of their worldview. Revealing himself to them through mighty wonders, he communicated that he was the transcendent and holy God who could disrupt the laws of nature on behalf of his people. They were to worship him alone, the God of their ancestors, and model themselves after his character. And an enormous tool in the reshaping process was the law in its many forms.

For centuries Bible scholars have divided the Old Testament laws into three categories: civil, ceremonial, and moral.[9] Understanding these categories and their place in the mission of God help us unravel some of these common assertions of reasonable doubt and affirm the continuing relevance of the sexual boundaries some are so quick to discount.

Civil Law

To help govern life among the people of God, civil laws were given. The principles behind these laws still stand, but the specific laws themselves may no longer apply. The example John Oswalt pointed to was a law for those who owned bulls. If your bull gored a neighbor, you were liable. But the liability increased if you knew your bull was in the habit of skewering passersby.[10]

Few of us own bulls, but my neighbor owns a pit bull. This particular Old Testament law may not exist in my neck of the woods, but the principle remains the same. As an elderly lady was walking her dog near our house, the pit bull went into attack mode, killing the dog and injuring the lady. Liability increased because the attack dog had a history of vicious actions. And so the laws regarding bulls were temporary and tied to an agrarian culture, but the underlying principle is very much with us today.

Ceremonial Law

These laws related not only to the various ceremonies, but also included purity laws that stipulated what practices would make one ceremonially unclean. They covered a wide variety of activities, could be violated accidentally, and were never punishable by death. Their main purpose? To shape the worldview of God's people.

The sacrifices and ceremonies dictated and described in this section of the law taught them the costliness of sin. Each transgression brought separation and a need for atonement. And, as we know clearly in our own age, these rituals pointed to a future time in the mission of God. They foreshadowed the coming of the One whose death would suffice as the final payment for transgressions and would bring to an end all sacrifices. These laws were a mere shadow of all that would be fulfilled in Jesus.

Similarly, the many purity laws forbade activities that would render them unclean and drew a clear distinction between them and their pagan neighbors. Touching on many aspects of common life, the laws regulated the foods that could and could not be eaten, the handling of the dead, exposure to blood, the mixture of types of fabric, certain farming practices, etc. Nothing was inherently wrong with the activities that were barred. But like object lessons for children, these restrictions taught them that they, as the people of God, were to be separate from other peoples and also that there were clear and absolute boundaries in life. God's design was to rid them of the pagan mind-set of continuity and the resultant practice of porous boundaries.[11]

As for relevance today, these laws have clearly come to an end. The sacrifices and ceremonies found their fulfillment on Golgotha. Jesus himself declared the dietary laws were no longer in effect. And so, in the unfolding of God's mission, these laws prepared his people for the One who was himself the substance of all that was symbolic and passing.

Moral Law

The Torah clearly contains moral laws, which are not conditioned by time, culture, or context. These precepts are always stated as imperatives and any infringement had to be deliberate, not accidental. Punishable by death, they were given not merely to distinguish God's people from their neighbors, but also to set forth the boundaries of the created order. The Ten Commandments were not the only laws in this category. Rather, they served somewhat as a "Top Ten" list in summarizing the law.[12] Committing adultery, for example, was not the only sexual boundary. Instead, it served as an example of one of the worst violations of God's intention for our sexuality. It set forth a firm boundary, in glaring contrast with the porous boundaries of the neighboring pagans. Given our New Testament hindsight, we now know God's intention was for marriage to mirror Christ's relationship with the church. Therefore, to make a mockery of one's covenant by hopping from one bed to another cheapens and trivializes all covenants. The God of Israel is not like the gods of mythology, hopping from partner to partner. His covenant endures!

Likewise with the commandment about bearing false witness. This law does not imply all other lying is negotiable. Instead, it serves as the epitome of falsehood. It communicates the treachery of such a lie as this—that one would speak falsely against a trusted friend, bringing unjust punishment upon them.

In the Sermon on the Mount, Jesus stated plainly that he did not come to abolish the law, but that the one who obeys the law and teaches others to obey the law will be great in his kingdom (see Matthew 5:17–19). To illustrate, he addressed four moral laws, two from the Ten Commandments. One civil law, "an eye for an eye," is simply amplified by expressing the extent to which we should love our enemies (see Matthew 5:38–42). Therefore, far from brushing laws aside and telling people to simply love, his teaching took these laws to a deeper level.

The Sexual Laws

Found within the Torah are numerous sexual laws. While the flashpoint of this discussion is the issue of homosexuality, there are certainly heterosexual concerns regarding the sexual laws in Scripture. And these concerns need to be taught and applied in relevant ways. Our cultural attitude toward teenage sex ranges somewhere between a furrowed brow and a cautious smirk. *Do these kids really know what they're doing? Well, boys will be boys!* And for the most part, sex between consenting adults pretty much gets a pass. Studies show the attitude is not much different within the church. Increasingly, boundaries are becoming more porous and concerns for scriptural parameters muted. And so the sexual laws of Leviticus have relevance for setting parameters for *all* sexual expression.

Most of the sexual laws in the Torah are found in Leviticus 18 and 20. They are introduced with the warning not to live as the Egyptians or Canaanites live. Then what follows are boundaries, many of which today we would not dream of crossing. Lines are drawn to forbid incest of any sort: with children, in-laws, aunts, uncles, etc. Bestiality is also outlawed. The warnings are laid out specifically because the neighboring nations had no boundaries in these matters and were fully practicing these varied forms of sexual expression, practices for which they were being booted out of the land. It is within this list that sex between two men is also prohibited. Then jumping over to chapter 20, one finds the punishment prescribed for the violation of each of these commands. For most the punishment was death. This, combined with the fact their violation would be deliberate instead of accidental, is a clear indication that the sexual laws were part of the moral law that still applies to today.

Understanding the three types of law goes a long way toward removing reasonable doubt from the jury. The moral laws, including those addressing sexual behavior, are transcultural and relevant for any age. The civil law that governed the community life still stands, but for the most part in principle only. The ceremonial laws were completely fulfilled in the life and death of our Messiah. Sacrifices have ceased and the worldview shaping purity practices are now obsolete.

"Your Honor, I Object!"

Not so fast! say some. *There are a number of valid objections worth considering!* Indeed there are. What follows are a few of the most common and influential.

Within the list of sexual laws is the prohibition of sex during a woman's menstrual flow. If you are going to forbid same-sex intercourse, then let's be consistent! Are Christians violating this law as well? This objection was mentioned above and has been around for quite awhile, actually.

Consistency is certainly a key. Only a few verses separate this law from the one prohibiting same-sex intercourse. But it seems likely that this particular restriction falls in the catalog of ceremonial laws, not the moral laws. First of all, it is not punishable by death as are some of the others on the list (see Leviticus 20:13, 18). The violation could conceivably be accidental—sort of an "Oops!" And it seems to be related to concerns raised in Leviticus 15 regarding the discharge of blood during a woman's period, which would be a purity concern. There it states that the woman during her flow would be ceremonially unclean for seven days and anyone having contact with her clothing or bedding would be unclean until evening. As mentioned above, ceremonial laws dead-ended at the cross.

Another common objection: *But some of the laws of the Torah seem to condone treating women as property and others seem to sanction slavery. Today we value women and abhor slavery of all sorts. We've come a long way, baby, and it's time to change our view of sexual minorities as well!*

Great point. And so, going back to the theater metaphor, if we are now in Act V, does the Author of the drama intend for these sexual laws to be written out of the script? Are the laws regarding homosexual behavior inspired portions of Scripture which, as N. T. Wright put it, are "no longer relevant"?

In his lengthy work *Slaves, Women & Homosexuals*, William Webb did some thorough spade work in this regard. As most Bible scholars will tell you, the key to discerning what portions are still relevant for today is to determine what ideas and teachings were tied to that specific time and culture and which ones were transcultural. Instead of referring to the mission of God or using the theater metaphor, Webb repeatedly referred to the "redemptive movement" of the Scriptures. For example, as one traces the development of the issue of slavery, the laws which seem so odd to us actually served to control the practice of slavery and move redemptively toward its abolition. The Pentateuch has laws, for example, which control the severity of punishment of slaves; provides for Sabbath observance and days off for festivals; and in the case of Hebrew slaves, provides for their release every seven years and in the year of Jubilee, sending them off with provisions no less. The New Testament takes it even further. Paul wrote of slavery, but he urged masters to treat slaves with kindness, even pleading with Philemon to treat his runaway slave as a brother in Christ by setting him free. These laws and admonitions provided a stark movement away from the harsh and inhumane practices of pagan cultures.[13]

In similar fashion, as one follows the development of the role and value of women in Scripture, one finds a growing contrast with surrounding cultures of the ancient Near East and the later Greco-Roman world. Jesus limited the grounds for divorce to adultery, which was unheard of among non-Israelites. And while

Paul's instructions to wives and husbands today seem the height of patriarchy, his directives to husbands were a radical departure from the abusive norms of ancient times. The redemptive movement of Scripture was always in the direction of elevating the value and status of women.[14]

But when it comes to sexual boundaries there is no similar "redemptive movement." If anything, the laws become more restrictive.[15] Jesus, as we well know, made adultery of the heart as errant as the actual act. The letters of Paul only affirm the sexual boundaries of the Old Testament, including homosexual practice, for which he used the term *arsenokoitais*. The only other place that particular Greek word appears in ancient literature prior to Paul was in the Greek translation of Leviticus 18 and 20. This makes it very clear Paul believed the sexual laws of Leviticus still apply today, including those regarding same-sex intercourse.[16]

Those who find the "three types of law" explanation lacking punch often lump the civil, ceremonial, and moral law together. *The Old Testament is about law and the New Testament is about love. After all, both Jesus and Paul said loving God and neighbor fulfills the law.* Oswalt responded by reminding us of the Sermon on the Mount:

> It is suggested that the choice is between loveless standards and a loving lack of standards. That is not so. The choice the New Testament puts forth so forcefully is: obedience to God's standards for the right reason, i.e., love; or obedience for the wrong reason, i.e., self-righteousness. The New Testament does not abrogate the standards of the Old Testament by its teachings on love. Rather, it forever shuts the door on a person's patting himself on the back for a rigid observance of certain commands when his heart is empty and cold.[17]

And finally, the objection that has been sung by Lady Gaga and drummed into our heads by the media: *They are born that way.* And so, it is reasoned, *if an orientation is genetically hard-wired, how can it be wrong? The writers of Scripture simply knew nothing of a homosexual orientation. But today science trumps Scripture.*

Psychologist Mark Yarhouse made the point that "nothing-but-isms" have polarized our cultural landscape. Some have insisted same-sex attraction is "nothing but" genetics and so gays and lesbians can't change. Others have urged upon us that a homosexual orientation is "nothing but" nurture and upbringing, and therefore they *can* change. However decades of research have not vindicated either side.[18] This is reflected in the American Psychological Association's official literature. Their 2008 statement available on their website states the following:

> Although much research has examined the possible genetic, hormonal, developmental, social, and cultural influences on sexual orientation, no findings have emerged that permit scientists to conclude that sexual orientation is determined by any particular factor or factors. Many think that nature and nurture both play complex roles.[19]

Douglas Abbott of the University of Nebraska summarized as follows: "Homosexuality is a complex psycho-social-biological phenomenon with possible genetic, environmental, and freewill influences."[20] And so we've been torn apart by forcefully spoken blanket statements from two different camps. And those folks have been persuasive. Let's face it, nuanced, complex, middle-of-the-road answers don't win many arguments.

Genetic predispositioning, however, isn't the same as predetermination. There is a measure of fluidity to sexual attraction and some gays and lesbians have found it possible to change by degrees. As we discussed earlier, some have not.[21] But to say that God has created people to be attracted to the same sex is not validated by science nor even hinted at in Scripture.

And so, risking redundancy, let me say once again that the debate over homosexuality has brought about this tug-of-war over the Bible, but there is a lot more at stake than letting people of the same sex get married with the church's blessing. Much more. The church in general has been very hypocritical when it has come to how we handle *all* forms of sexual sin. Consistency is key. *Consistency.*

Pastor on Trial

Ashes to Life, our weird and wonderful church, was at one time a church of twenty-five people, mostly elderly, and known as Otterbein United Methodist Church. Shortly before I became their pastor, a fire destroyed their building, forcing them into a season of soul-searching as they worshipped with another United Methodist congregation. Finally, as they saw a ministry to people in recovery beginning to open up, they voted to reinvent themselves: a new name, a new style of worship, ministry in small groups, and an outward focus. The change was radical and the road a bit bumpy. But God was at work!

With time, recovery people began to outnumber the Otterbein folks. One of the new men had lost everything to his addiction. At one time a successful lawyer, Robert was eventually disbarred for drug-related reasons. But working his recovery and giving his heart to Jesus brought about a dramatic change. In fact, he began to toy with the idea of becoming a pastor, and so I began training him to be a small-group leader. About that time he fell in love and his girlfriend also started attending services. At one point it looked as though they might move in together, so I warned him that he would have to give up small-group leadership. The move never happened and he soon began playing guitar in our worship band.

However the day finally came when he turned in his small-group materials and announced he and his girl were getting an apartment together. Bummer. Not God's plan. So I made plain that not only would he need to step down from small-group leadership, he would also have to pull out of the worship band. He hadn't counted on that. Nor had anyone else in our fairly new church!

Our worship leader was absolutely on board. He and I had discussed standards for the worship band long before, but he had not communicated well with band members. Knowing the teenage bass player would take it hard, I made a point of telling him myself. That didn't go so well. "I am shocked," he declared. "I can't believe it. I see nothing wrong with them living together. This is totally wrong!"

Reaction among the older crowd was pretty hot as well. No, you might not have expected that. But they had grown to love Robert and Sue, were excited about their newfound faith, and upset that this young couple just might quit the church. And so, as sometimes happens, a special meeting was called by the Pastor Parish Relations Committee and all those with complaints showed up to express their anger.

Now at this point the principle of the Box, Path, and Circus was pretty well ingrained in their thinking. So soon they launched in. *How can you, as a pastor of a recovery church, be so judgmental! You've gone back to the Box! These people are on the Path. They're not perfect, but neither are you! Not only that, you're being hypocritically inconsistent. There are people who live together who serve on the Trustees Board and you've never ousted them!*

So then I had to lay out the principles behind my actions. While it is true that we are all at different places on the Path and still in need of perfection, James 3:1 and 1 Timothy 3 both hold spiritual leaders to a higher standard. So we welcome people just as they are, love on them, and invite them to serve in our church in limited roles. But when it comes to spiritual leadership, we will use good judgment to determine if people are actually in a growing relationship with Jesus and actively working on their monkeys. We don't peer into their closets, looking for dirt, but if they are openly involved in activities that are inconsistent with Christian principles, then we will draw lines. Not only will this include couples who live together, but also those who relapse back into drugs or who frequent bars.

Their first objection was my definition of spiritual leadership. *Is playing a guitar any different than serving as a trustee?* Actually, I believe it is. Meeting once a month on a weeknight to discuss plumbing and electrical matters is a long way from standing up front every week to lead us in worship, especially in our rock-star culture where everyone in a band is placed on a pedestal.

The complaints continued. I had one more ace to play, but I truly hated to lay it on the table. Seeing no other option, I painted a different scenario: *Imagine a gay couple begins to attend church. I want you to know I am going to welcome them, hug them, and love on them just as I do anyone else. If they want to serve as ushers or help serve a meal, that will be great. But what if one of them asks to play in the band?*

As I expected, the objections were quickly spewed into the discussion. *Gays? We can't have them in the band. That's just not right!*

Well, I'm sure you know how that played out. I made plain to them that all sin is equally sinful, and anyone who openly lives a life inconsistent with Christian teaching cannot serve in spiritual leadership in our church. That's where I as the pastor draw the lines.

We lost a few people after that meeting. To my surprise, they were from the old Otterbein crowd. Robert and Sue continued to attend, however, even after they eventually broke up.

Closing Arguments

Lest I fall into the very same well-worn rut that I warned us about in chapter 1, let me remind us that issues related to homosexuality are the Scapegoat in our culture. The Elephant that needs to be chained up is sexual immorality in general. Quite frankly, I believe God has used the issue of homosexuality to force the church to develop a theology of sexuality—a task long overdue.[22] So while much of this chapter has hopped around the Bible texts pertaining to same-sex matters, we very much need to know where the boundaries are on *all* sexual behavior. You will find nothing in Leviticus or anywhere else in the laws or teachings of the Bible that runs contrary to the model for sexuality and marriage found in the Garden of Eden. Despite the examples of polygamy, adultery, incest, and prostitution found throughout the Scriptures, God's design was for sexual intimacy to be monogamous, heterosexual, and covenantal. I believe most of us can agree that in this regard, "all have sinned and fall short of the glory of God" (Rom. 3:23). If not all, then in our culture at least most.

In *The Concept of Sin,* German theologian Josef Pieper reminded us that the Greek word for sin (*hamartia*) means "to miss the mark." The theological use of the word was just one small patch on a much larger quilt. If a doctor misdiagnosed an ailment, the Greeks would use *hamartia* to describe his error. A faulty design for an aqueduct? Same word. If one missed a target in archery practice, again, it was *hamartia*. And so what is the target we miss when we sin? Pieper maintained that it is the Garden of Eden.[23] All actions that fall short of the garden are equally sinful. But it seems the further we get from God's design in the garden, the more destructive it becomes.

We live in a day when people in the church need to hear a clear and certain message about the boundaries of sexual expression. And if we are ever going to tone down the deafening din surrounding the Scapegoat issue, our culture needs to see the church live out those boundaries with consistency and grace. May it be that in the years ahead, people will see the church not as a hypocritical curmudgeon condemning gays and lesbians, but as a place to find healing for all forms of sexual brokenness and to access much grace to walk the painful path of obedience.

To that end, if the Spirit so leads, engage your heart in the following prayer:

Lord God Almighty, Maker of heaven and earth, Designer of our bodies, truest model of love, please forgive me for any way in which I have contributed to the polarization of our church and culture over the scapegoat issue of homosexuality. Forgive me for judgmentalism and hypocrisy. And please forgive my own trespassing of your laws and design for sexuality and marriage. I commit myself to your view of the world and your design for my sexuality. May I have strength to live by your standards. May I learn how to be an instrument of healing for others. And may I show much grace toward those who view things differently on sexual issues. To you be all honor and glory forever! Amen.

Discussion Questions

1. Have you seen the "reasonable doubt" argument used in other biblical issues besides sexual ones?
2. It has been stated that the sexual laws apply to *all* sexual sin, not just homosexual behavior. What heterosexual sins are people glossing over? How are they rationalizing their behavior? Which ones seem especially entrenched among Christians?
3. What might be a good way to transmit this information to your children and teens?
4. Does your church have a consistent policy and practice concerning which lifestyle issues keep one from leadership and service? If not, what seems to be the general practice? Is consistency evident? If not, what are the inconsistencies?

CHAPTER 12

APPLICATION:
Same-Sex Attraction and Other Variations

So far it's been quite a year. As I write this, it is 2015 and there have been many significant changes in American culture when it comes to sexuality. It began in February with the release of the movie *Fifty Shades of Grey*, based upon the runaway best-selling novel about a sadomasochistic love relationship. But that was just a speed bump, really. An enormous shift began taking place in our culture over gender issues. Florists, bakers, and even pizza makers are now being harassed and sued for not wanting to provide services for same-sex weddings. Olympic hero Bruce Jenner shook the headlines and drew accolades as he morphed his body and changed his name to Caitlyn. And in what will certainly have an equal impact upon our culture as did the *Roe v. Wade* decision of years ago, the

Supreme Court ruled that states cannot ban same-sex marriage. In essence, they have redefined marriage to include two people of the same sex. It was a watershed moment. With "tolerance" as their war cry and the rainbow as their battle standard, extremists have been riding the momentum, even calling for the ouster of conservative chaplains from the military.[1]

And so in writing this chapter, I am quite aware that the term "variations" may bring to mind an entirely different set of people than it did before 2015. By this I simply mean variations from God's original design in the Garden of Eden: a relationship that is heterosexual, monogamous, and covenantal.

So at issue is how the church is to welcome and minister to those who feel wired differently than what we see in Adam and Eve. They may have already married someone beyond the boundaries of Scripture or made significant changes to their anatomy. How do we gain a hearing with them?

Confessions

May I confess a sin to you? In the early years of my ministry I crushed the life out of some young Christians who had a growing excitement about life with Jesus.

This is really going to date me, but I grew up at a time in American Christendom when smoking was one of the big sins that could mar your testimony. It was a big deal. I never preached on it or taught it, but I will admit to keeping a few people out of positions of leadership and service simply because they used tobacco. *Hey, your body's a temple of the Holy Spirit! What kind of message are you sending our kids?*

Someone convinced me that if a pastor was going to encourage people to quit smoking, the local church ought to provide some kind of program to help them stop. Wonderful idea! Or so I thought.

Soon I discovered the local branch of the American Cancer Society was offering training with their Freshstart Program. Tremendous! I'm guessing that I was one of very few people to take such a course who had never actually smoked a cigarette.

With all of the best intentions, I mounted the pulpit the next Sunday and proclaimed the good news: "We are now offering a program for those of you who would like to quit smoking. I've just received training and I am willing to help you break the habit."

I will never forget the look of a young couple sitting toward the front. The wife beamed as she poked an elbow into her husband's side. He, however, began to slump down into the pew. Not long after that someone rightly pointed out, "Pastor, it seems like you are on some kind of antismoking crusade." Ugh. Not my intention, but clearly guilty as charged. I was allowing the Box mentality to thrive in our little congregation. Instead of describing life with Christ as the Path of gradual transformation under God's leadership, I'd made smoking one of the sides of the Box. "Hey, if you smoke, you are clearly doing a don't and simply aren't in the Box."

God has forgiven me. Hopefully you will too.

Nearly twenty years have passed and I think I've changed my ways. Ashes to Life is a different kind of church. Probably half of our people smoke. No longer is it the "big sin" as it was in the past. Sorry for bragging, but we have one of the nicest smoking areas of any church in town. That's a fact. Beautiful butt dispensers attached firmly to the building, nice park bench—it's great. Oh, a few people have quit smoking in the last few years, but not because I've launched a program. They were simply traveling the Path and one day felt the Lord tell them, "It's time."

Well, if you've decided to forgive me for my sin against smokers, let's talk about our sins against sexual minorities. As we discussed in chapter 1, Andrew Marin believes that gays and lesbians are more likely to have been deeply wounded by a local church than they are to have been sexually abused.[2] And it is certainly safe to assume the same is true for the transgendered or those involved in BDSM. Perhaps in some cases the sin is blatant. Or else we've simply fallen into the mind-set of bludgeoning the Scapegoat. But I'm inclined to believe that for many, it is indirect or unintended. After all, we easily notice those who are quite different, and we automatically want to revert to the Box mind-set and get them to change so that they will fit in with us.

And so when a gay or lesbian couple begins to attend, our wheels start turning. *How can we help them change?* Or the transgendered shows up and asks for the restroom. "Uh . . ." Eventually there will be a man or a woman who quietly confides his or her addiction to *Fifty Shades of Grey* types of activities. *Holy smokes! We've got to launch a program of some sort!* Not so fast . . .

The Most Among the Least

When we serve the "least," we meet him who is the Most. Yeah, I know, the "least" listed by Jesus in the parable were the hungry, thirsty, stranger, unclothed, sick, and imprisoned. But quite clearly he stated that it is among the least that we will find him. In that final judgment, the king in the parable said, "Truly I tell you, just as you did it to one of the least of these who are members of my family, you did it to me" (Matt. 25:40).

Labeling anyone "least" borders on being rude. I get that. However, it's really about how we value people, isn't it? We attach value to people all of the time, consciously or unconsciously. There are certainly people who fall into the "least-valued" category in your town, aren't there? And I'm guessing for many of us, sexual minorities fall into that group. In Jesus' day it was not only the impoverished people who were politely avoided, but also the alienated and imprisoned who were conveniently forgotten, regardless of their net worth. In fact, rich tax collectors were certainly on the list of the least—probably near the bottom.

If you grew up singing that Zacchaeus was a wee little man, you know the hatred Jewish people had for the traitorous tax collectors of their day. Not only did these outcasts collect revenue for the oppressive Romans, they lined their money bags by charging extra. Hey, if you are going to be a despised pariah, you might as well be a rich one! But as was apparent with the wee little man, money can't buy you love. One day friendless Zacchaeus went out on a limb and met Jesus. He jumped at the chance to host Jesus in his home and responded willingly and abundantly with his repentance (see Luke 19:1–10).

Matthew the tax collector responded similarly when Jesus chose him to be one of the Twelve. Throwing a dinner for Jesus, all his tax-collecting buddies crowded in at the table as well. And so the accusation of the day was, "Hey, this Jesus can't be a prophet. Look at the company he keeps! One of his closest friends is a tax collector, of all things. And he even dines with them."

Did Jesus ever speak about their sin? Of course he did. In fact, with the exception of hypocrisy, he addressed greed and the god of mammon more than any other sin. And yet the tax collectors were drawn to him. This is plain in the Gospel of Luke. More than the other three Gospels, Luke highlights Jesus' association with the poor and his rebukes to the rich. Luke 14 makes this as clear as the afternoon sunshine. Following a lavish banquet, Jesus urged his host to next time invite the poor, crippled, lame, and blind. A parable follows this admonition about a feast in the kingdom where the rich discarded their invitations and so the poor were then brought to the table. Right on the heels of the parable is a call to discipleship that ends with, "So therefore, none of you can become my disciple if you do not give up all your possessions" (Luke 14:33). But the very next chapter—the one containing the much-loved parables of the lost sheep, coin, and son—begins with this: "Now all the tax collectors and sinners were coming near to listen to him" (Luke 15:1). My point? His love for them was so evident, the tax collectors were willing to hear him talk about the sin of greed. Jesus had gained access to their hearts with his incredible credibility. It was credibility won with love.

The church generally lacks street cred. While our culture is currently highlighting and valuing the lives and lifestyles of gays, lesbians, and the transgendered, the church has often been caught in the act of devaluing them. We've at times treated them as the needy to politely avoid or the alienated to easily and conveniently forget. In some cases where sexual minorities have walked through our doors, they've been warmly greeted and handed a church bulletin, only to be approached in the foyer with recovery programs or healing protocols to "fix" them. At this point, however, fewer and fewer want to be fixed. Like my zealous attempt to help the struggling smoker, the very approach of trying to fix them devalues them.

Our bickering over homosexuality merely mirrors the division in the culture at large. It is also obvious to many that heterosexual brokenness abounds in the pews. Credibility will gradually grow as we pull the plank from our own eyes and show forth the love of Christ. The crazy thing about the kingdom is that as we learn to love, serve, and embrace the least, we find ourselves face-to-face with the Most. God will show up. And it will be in that moment when these very ones we learn to serve will become open to hearing from Jesus about their sin.

Remember Gary? He was the guy who in chapter 4 gave the finger to a few zealous witnesses as he yelled, "F - - - you! I go to Ashes to Life!" For a season, Gary was in a discipleship group. I posed a question to the group: "How can we engage with the drug dealers, drug users, and homeless people on the street so that we can pray with them and tell them about Jesus?"

Without hesitation, Gary suggested, "Give them cigarettes! Newport menthols."

"Huh?"

"Yeah. Newport menthols. All I know is that when I step out of Jay's News with a new pack, people just start coming to me, trying to bum off of me!"

And so, yes, we used church money to buy Newport menthols—took the money out of the Outreach line in the budget, in fact. Sure enough, we didn't have to chase people down and thrust a pamphlet into their hands. They simply came to us, gratefully received our gift, lit up, took a deep drag, and said, "Yeah sure, you can pray for me. Right now I am really having trouble with . . ."

God showed up. He used our smoking disciple to give us a way to reach people in the street. Oh, and by the way, a few years later God began to nudge Gary. He's now down to less than a pack of Newport menthols a day.

Refusing to Be the Holy Spirit

A few years ago, a large evangelical church in Ohio called me in to consult with their staff. God was beginning to draw gay and lesbian couples into their fellowship. Not knowing quite how to handle the situation, they simply loved and accepted them, inviting them to meet Jesus and grow in their walk with him. The lead pastor especially took the lead. (Sounds like his job description anyway!) He visited in their homes and even attended some of their social events—meetings that other pastors wouldn't have been caught dead in.

Then one day one of the ladies approached him. "Hey pastor, I was reading the Bible this week and I noticed what it says about the relationship I have with my partner!" A course correction began to happen on the Path. And what-da-ya know, the Holy Spirit, whose role it is to convince us of sin, had shown up and done his job (see John 16:8). Wow.

My role as consultant was rather simple that day. They were already doing a lot right. The key, of course, is not treating the behavior of same-sex attraction any differently than other forms of sexual sin. Consistency. After all, we've all got monkeys. The obvious example for most churches is couples that live together. The moment you treat one group differently than the other, you are out of bounds scripturally. And people will notice.

Andrew Marin provided wonderful guidance for churches in his book *Love Is an Orientation*. Sexual minorities are people like everyone else. Marin reminded us that they want to be loved and accepted as people of value even if you don't agree with their choices. They wonder if you will always look at them simply as gay or transgendered, if you will include them in all the usual activities, and if you will worry about them hitting on you. And they are anxious about when the other shoe will finally drop. When will they be asked to leave? There can be an enormous fear of rejection.[3]

The same is true with other sexual minorities. Those addicted to BDSM have an enormous fear of disclosing what they do. One of my counselees, as I mentioned earlier, simply tried to find someone to encourage her and pray her through on the road to recovery. The rejection was awkward and potent. As for the transgendered, they often sense revulsion. And imagine if you battled an erotic attraction to children or adolescents. Even if you had never acted on those feelings, you would be terrified to even hint at your underlying issues.

In his wonderful book *Forty Days to a Closer Walk with God*, J. David Muyskens related an Eastern legend that proposes a continuation of the story of the tree-climbing tax collector:

> In his retirement he makes a practice of going for an early morning walk every day. He never tells his wife where he goes on

these walks. One day her curiosity gets the better of her. Without his knowing, she follows and watches where he goes. She watches him go to the tree where he first met Jesus. He waters the tree's roots. He pulls up weeds that grow next to the tree. He affectionately strokes the tree. . . . After returning home his wife reveals that she followed and watched his actions at the tree. She asks him if he did that every morning. "Yes," he said, "that is where I met the One whom my soul loves."[4]

At the present time sexual minorities feel as though they are the least valued in the eyes of the church. When we serve and love the least, we meet the Most. It simply follows that as we become more fully the body of Christ for the least, they will meet the Most as well. Oh that one day there will be those who will wash the windows of your church building, weed the flowerbed, or simply enjoy a cigarette in your smoking area while breathing the words, "This is where I met the One whom my soul loves."

Reliance on the Spirit

Now hold on a bit! you might be thinking. *In chapter 6 you stated that a prophetic word of rebuke begins the healing for those in the fog of fantasy and adultery. Isn't that the same with these variations? Instead of coaxing them toward the light, shouldn't they be called out to clean the closet themselves?* So glad you asked. And certainly the principle remains. Truth begins the healing. But at this time in our highly polarized society, timing is everything. Even in the case of King David and his finger-pointing prophet Nathan, the timing came at God's initiative.

We are to speak the truth in love (see Ephesians 4:15). Truth spoken without love lands with a judgmental thud. Love without any truth simply enables people to remain in their brokenness. Certainly Jesus exemplified that balance among the tax collectors.

lance between truth and love when it comes to
lls for great reliance on the leading of the Spirit.
ion that sexual minorities already know how
al feels about their behavior. Truth can come
later. In the meantime, the Holy Spirit pours out the love of God into
our hearts so that it can splash out onto others. And he alone knows
the best timing for the truth. Once he convinces people of their
sin, then they are more open to learning the truth. And the most
pertinent truth to apply is that regarding our identity in Christ,
which most of us began to grasp as a part of the discipling process.
Likewise, providing clear teaching on our identity in Christ is a key
role for the local church in the discipling of sexual minorities. To
illustrate, let me introduce you to a monkey of my own.

Mistaken Identity

For a number of months a client had been receiving counseling
from me for same-sex attraction. At no point in his life had he ever
been attracted to girls. Never. And like the rest of us, he did not
consciously choose one day which sex he wanted to be attracted
to. Secular therapists had urged him to simply identify himself as
gay and move on with his life. But he wanted to learn from my
perspective.

At one point I enlisted the help of a friend who shared the same
struggle. Using an office speaker phone, we conducted a conference
call so my friend could share his story. Like my counselee, he had
never been attracted to girls. He described it this way: "Remember
as a little boy going through the 'girls are yucky' stage? It was like
I got stuck. While in sixth grade my buddies began to go gaga over
girls, I never did. In fact, I simply longed more and more for men."

A light went on. But here's the kicker: The "lightbulb" appeared
above the heads of both my counselee *and me!* For the first time in
my life, I saw my own brokenness so very clearly. And here it is: I

APPLICATION: SAME-SEX ATTRACTION

never went through the "girls are yucky" stage! Incredible. Just as some men will tell you that they never remember a time when they weren't drawn to other men, I could never remember a time when I wasn't drawn to women. Never. Beginning with my toddler years, I had crushes on girls. I can name a different girl for each grade in school, including kindergarten. But because my brokenness was heterosexual in nature, it just didn't stand out like it did for my friend and counselee. So now you know. I'm not normal!

The cause of my brokenness? Like so many things, it was doubtless a combination of nature and nurture. Likely the bonding with my mother was impeded in some way. Pediatricians of that era were not recommending breastfeeding, so the bond which oxytocin forms with such feeding just wasn't there. But not all babies of my generation were puppy-love toddlers, so likely there was some genetic predispositioning that set it up. Whatever the case, the truth of the matter is that my actions and my identity are not to be shaped by my attractions. As a married man, I am not to flirt or pursue every woman who catches my eye. God does not want me to embrace my inner polygamist. Seek healing to keep it under control? Certainly. But allowing it to goad me beyond God's boundaries? Nope.

Several times now I've had friends or former counselees tell me that they have tried everything they know to change and have finally resigned themselves to the conclusion that they are gay. "This is who I am," has been the punctuation at the end of those conversations.

And this has been the way of reasoning among those in the movement to redefine not only marriage, but to reshape our conception of what is "normal" in sexual expression. "This is what I feel, this is what I'm drawn to, this is how I am attracted, and so this is who I am." Of course, hackles are raised and accusations of hatred hurled if we draw this out to the logical conclusion. If what I feel, what I'm drawn to, and how I am attracted includes children,

animals, or multiple partners, does that define who I am? And is
that okay?

You already know the often-heard reply. Loving acts are not
loving if they harm someone. So as long as you are not harming
anyone, what you do in your bedroom is your own business. As
was explained in the previous chapter, some from the Christian
community fall right in line with this reasoning. *The law of the
Old Testament has been boiled down to one word: "love." If a
man feels like he is a woman trapped inside of a man's body, then
the script for him to follow is to embrace those feelings, make the
changes, find the love of his life, and practice their love within the
bounds of a sacred covenant. As long as they love God and are not
hurting anyone, leave them alone.* This reasoning resonates with a
growing majority in our country. But is it truly the way to understand identity and sexual expression? This is where a local church
can begin to shed some light in the closet as we disciple those God
leads our way.

Recovering Lost Identity

Unlike any other of Paul's letters, Romans was written to a church
he had never actually visited. There was no list of questions for him
to answer, and so he was free to lay out a theological foundation by
tracing the mission of God in the world. His aim? To bring greater
harmony to this local church which, like so many others of that day,
was divided between Jews and Gentiles.

A survey of the first five chapters goes something like this.
Chapter 1 paints the picture of God's revelation to pagan people.
Through the things that have been made, God's attributes can be
perceived. In other words, as Joe and Janet Pagan held hands and
watched the sun setting on the Mediterranean, they could have
rightly concluded, "There is a wonderful and mighty Creator who
has engineered all that I see!" But Paul made clear they suppressed

Rewriting the Script

In his excellent book *Homosexuality and the Christian,* Mark Yarhouse urged Christians to develop a new script when it comes to our sexual struggles. Though the book is focused on the Scapegoat issue of homosexuality, the process he laid out applies to many of the Elephant issues as well.

The "gay script" that society offers sounds like this: *okay, so you are attracted to the same sex. Not to worry. Just own it. This is who you are. This is how God has made you. To be true to yourself, you need to slowly and carefully come out to your friends and family and identify as gay. As you are openly true to yourself, those who really love you will eventually accept you. You have a right to be happy, to be married, and to have kids.*

To help us develop our own script, Yarhouse spoke of a "three-tier distinction." The first tier is same-sex attraction. Given the fluidity of sexuality, there are some who for a season may have found themselves attracted to the same sex. This might have been during puberty or later in life. Yarhouse maintained this occurs in varying degrees and presents itself to about 6 percent of men and 4.5 percent of women. The second tier is homosexual orientation. Of the 6 percent and 4.5 percent, about 2 percent of men and 1 percent of women have found that they have been exclusively attracted to the same sex all of their lives. For them it seems indelible. The third tier comes from our culture's gay script: gay identity. As Yarhouse framed it, this can be a conscious choice for the individual. Given one's attractions, they can choose to identify themselves as gay or lesbian and follow the script laid out by society.[5]

However, this is where the local church can provide an alternate script. By walking through the three tiers with someone, we can make plain that there is some plasticity to sexual attraction and that what they are feeling might possibly change on its own. If that attraction does not change, then the person may be on that second

Yarhouse's Three Tiers of Distinction

First Tier: 6% of men; 2% of women.
Second Tier: 2% of men; 1 % of women
Third Tier: Those who identify as gay based on attractions
    (Percentage unknown).

tier of orientation. But at that point they have a choice of whether or not to move on to the third tier of gay identity. They can wrap their identity around their sexual attractions, or they can base their identity upon their biological gender, recognizing that attraction to the same sex is one piece of evidence of how the fall has affected our sin-infected world. They are a person of great worth who is attracted to the same sex, but who follows Jesus Christ as Lord. And he is very present to walk with them through their sorrows and temptations.[6]

Again, let me be clear. This applies to many other forms of sexual brokenness as well. A man you know may feel more sexually aroused when dressed as a woman or might even long for a sex change. A lady in your church may feel pulled toward sexual experiences that include treating a man like a slave and inflicting mild torture. The sexual addict may be drawn to multiple partners. But regardless of the attractions or longings, those feelings may be on the first tier where they are fluid and fleeting. Possibly they are more permanent, leaving them on the second tier. But discipleship for them can include learning to lean into their identity in Christ, seeking qualified help for their temptations, and developing a vital relationship with our Savior who has been tempted in every way that we have been and gladly extends grace for our journey.

So what does your church closet look like? Do you think anyone in your congregation has these issues? Feel like launching a ministry, poking your flashlight into the closet, and calling them out? Before you do that, we'd better consider the role love plays in drawing them from the closet corners.

Sandpaper Love

Remember the old movie *What about Bob?* It has become a family favorite in our house. Bob Wiley is the epitome of dysfunction. Played by Bill Murray, Bob is a multi-phobic, manipulative, obsessively compulsive narcissist who has left a trail of frazzled therapists in his wake. His emotions are all over the place and he is so starved for relationships that he actually travels with his pet goldfish, Gill, just for company.

Dr. Leo Marvin, however, is the epitome of "respectable" dysfunction and arrogance. Though at the peak of his career as a psychologist, he is so relationally paralyzed and emotionally stuck that his son despises him. He even resorts to using puppets to talk with his daughter!

This perfect storm of clashing personalities unleashes at the Marvins' remote vacation home. Bob leaves no boundaries unviolated as he tracks down his new therapist's hideaway and is quickly adopted by Dr. Marvin's emotionally starved wife and kids. The magic of this flick is the transformation of the main characters. As Bob revels in the love and acceptance of Mrs. Marvin and the kids, his quirks begin to melt away and he eventually aspires to become, of all things, a psychologist. Dr. Marvin, on the other hand, ends up an institutional nutcase.

The takeaway of this film? It is the amazing power of loving community for those who are willing to receive it. This side of Hollywood, a loving family can't actually transform a narcissist into a caregiver. But the loving acceptance found in a Spirit-led community can sand off some of our rough edges.

John Wesley, the founder of Methodism, stumbled upon this truth as he established a small-group ministry for his converts. Labeled "class meetings," they were far from being academic. In fact, study of the Scriptures was not really the goal. The main issue at each weekly gathering was relationships, especially one's relationship with God. These small groups were co-ed and not quite as intense as the "bands" discussed in chapter 9. The key question was simply, "How is it with your soul?" And the class leader was charged with caring for his class members by visiting them regularly and praying for their souls. So critical were these gatherings to the life of the Methodist movement that Wesley stated: "These are the very sinews of our Society; and whatever weakens, or tends to weaken, our regard for these, or our exactness in attending them, strikes at the very root of our community."[7]

From the beginning of our crazy church Ashes to Life, we have brought people into "cell groups." Though they are not modeled strictly after Wesley's weekly meetings, the key objective has been to develop caring relationships within our local church. Some of the people in recovery have said our church has become the closest thing they've known to a family. One man, formerly known as "Johnny Marijuany," hungered so much to belong he had tears in his eyes as he became a member. Cell groups have been a key for transformation in his life as we've all learned to love each other. In fact, we've watched as "sandpaper love" has smoothed out some of the weirdness in all of us.

Building off of the work of A. H. Maslow, John Powell years ago described for us the five levels of communication: Cliché; Facts about Others; My Ideas and Judgments; My Feelings; and

Peak Communication. Powell maintained that while every level is important, sandpaper love doesn't connect with our rough edges until we get down to the levels of Feelings and Peak Communication. At those two levels mutual empathy is possible as souls resonate like well-harmonized music.[8] But let's face it. Most Sunday school classes and study groups never dip below the three more superficial levels. In a group fashioned after Wesley's model, however, we find tremendous potential for the Holy Spirit to bring change to everyone involved. History has certainly borne this out.

Sexual minorities are just like the rest of us. They want love and acceptance—a place to belong. They may tentatively share their ideas and judgments to see if the group is safe and accepting. If others are risking the sharing of feelings, they might join in. But opening up to a vulnerable sharing of the soul may well take time. So give them all the time they need. Create spaces where they can be welcomed as family. Allow them to experience the sanctifying love of God. As they hear from you how God is working on your monkeys, maybe they will become more open to the truth about their own.

Comfort Zones

If you attend a church of eighty or more people, you can be sure there is someone in the closet dealing with one of these issues. So consider the principles we've covered in this book as you create a welcoming environment. If church life is seen as a Path with fellow travelers instead of as a Box where one must fit in, they might move toward the light slanting in from the doorway crack. If they hear of others owning up to their own monkeys and not attaching special shame to matters of sexuality, they might actually peek through that crack. Will they be welcomed into a small circle of friends who share openly and vulnerably? Ah, then their hand just might reach for the doorknob. If they get a sense that slowly pushing the door open may bring compassionate and qualified help within a biblical framework, they just might find the courage to step further into the light. Can they trust you to keep them safe from their accusers and to put your life on the line for them?

But why would I want to reach out to them? you might ask. *I just don't feel comfortable around same-sex couples, especially if they show each other affection. And people going through a sex change? That just weirds me out!*

When Ashes to Life got started, there were about twenty-five folks who felt very comfortable being in ministry with people like them. In other words, if you were over fifty, dressed nicely, and liked hymns, you would fit right in. But then we made significant changes and people in recovery began to attend. It was a bit jarring for us at first. One man came drunk, wore his ball cap the entire service, and tried to pick a fight with another newcomer. People with mental illness and a variety of disorders also showed up. Homeless people who hadn't showered. In fact, one hot summer day a man walked in during the prayer time with no shirt on. Weird. (*Hey buddy, no shirt, no shoes, no worship service!*)

One of the original twenty-five is a bit OCD. Dirt, grime, and armpit slime just about send her off the rails. But because she saw the power of God at work among us, she began to pour out God's love on everyone who stumbles through our doors. The drunk who picked a fight during the closing song? She stepped into the middle of the fracas and wrapped her arms around him. Fight was over—love won. And since that day she has embraced everyone God has brought through our doors. No small miracle for her, really. Some folks simply don't have the resources or presence of mind to get squeaky clean.

But we see that very same love overcoming barriers in the book of Acts, don't we? Consider Paul's time in Athens as found in Acts 17. Upon observing the rampant idolatry of that city, he was deeply distressed. And that only makes sense. He had been a Pharisee of Pharisees. If those critics of Jesus freaked out about healing someone on the Sabbath, imagine how they'd feel about outright idolatry. But Paul, whose passion was to win people to Jesus Christ, did not rail about the practice of idolatry. No boycotts or protests ensued. Instead, as Chad Thompson pointed out, his sermon on Mars Hill began by complimenting the Athenians for being so religious. From there he opened the door by referring to an altar with the inscription "To an unknown god" (Acts 17:23). And so despite being hindered by his distress and repulsion, he extended the grace of God through his preaching.[9]

If your church is lacking in sexual minorities who make you uncomfortable, certainly they exist in your town or city. I can guarantee that most of them are interested in spiritual things; they just don't think you have anything to offer. What would Jesus have us do? Find a way to connect! They may be sitting at the local Starbucks or mowing their grass down the street from you. Could be they are sitting in your park or walking the streets. You don't have to hand out Newport menthols. Actually, flowers might be just as effective.

Consider the example of a mother to the prostitutes of Baltimore. A two-block stretch of town known as The Block has been the home to sexual sin at least as far back as the 1940s. Once the site for burlesque shows, it now boasts strip clubs, sex shops, and Larry Flynt's Hustler Club.[10] Walking the streets of this strip is a woman of God whom we will call Rachel. She has an agreement with the local grocery stores to receive the flowers that are dumpster bound. Handing bouquets to prostitutes, strippers, and even bouncers, she often gives them a mother's hug and prays for them. As a result, some girls have left The Block and returned home to their real moms. The Block is her parish. The people of the street are meeting Jesus. No doubt Rachel finds him there as well.

I Met Jesus

I first noticed him at a distance and wasn't quite sure. *Is this a man or a woman?* With the long curly hair, baggy gym shorts, and loose T-shirt, it wasn't so easy to tell.

We were both attending Pastoral Care Ministry School at Wheaton College, learning principles for inner healing. The next time I saw him was at breakfast in the cafeteria. We were both sitting alone, so I picked up my tray and asked to eat with him. He willingly shared both his table and his life's story, relating a remarkable intervention of God.

Jim grew up in a small Midwestern town. As an eighth-grader, he began reading the Gospel of John and found himself drawn into the text. He remembered placing his personal faith in Jesus Christ. And yet even as God was becoming very real for him, frustration and anxiety began to build as he couldn't reconcile the differences between his faith and his sexual confusion. He felt isolated. There was no one in his small hometown to whom he could bare his soul. The shame and guilt multiplied.

Jim's workaholic father was never at home. His best friends in childhood were all girls. Other guys his age rejected him. Until he reached junior high, he had not found one man he wanted anything to do with. A basketball coach did reach out to him, but soon moved out of town. All of these factors, he believed, led to his gender confusion.

"If *one* man had reached out and affirmed me, it would have made all the difference," he stated.

At the point in his life when he decided to seek help, he approached four different pastors. The first one scolded him. The next began rebuking and preaching at him. Pastor number three immediately tried to cast a demon out of him. The fourth one showed compassion and concern, but was very busy and did not know where to begin to help him.

Over the years he also sought the help of nearly twenty different counselors. On their advice, he began living as a woman every chance he could get. In his eleventh year of marriage, he finally decided to begin hormone therapy. His wife had faithfully stood by him, but when he finally made plans to legally change his name to Susan, she left.

Then the miracles began to happen. Upon contacting his attorney to confirm the name change, he was informed the judge was on vacation and wouldn't return until Monday. As Jim hung up the phone, he prayed, "If this isn't okay with you, God, then you do something about it." Monday the lawyer called, stating the judge had had a heart attack, postponing the name change indefinitely. While the incident caused Jim to pause, he really wasn't convinced God had anything to do with it.

A few days later, however, he was browsing the Internet, looking for information on transsexualism. Then he found a ministry web page and was struck by their motto: "You are not alone anymore." No one had ever told him before that it wasn't his problem alone. God was with him! It was then that he decided to attend the Pastoral Care Ministry School.

Jim and I stayed in touch for awhile. He viewed the conference in Wheaton as a definite turning point for him. Upon arrival he had been ambivalent. He had refused to wear the name tag for two days because it bore his masculine name. But on day three he found himself totally surrendering his sexuality over to Christ, and as he described it, "God broke through!" Upon returning home, he walked away from two years of hormone therapy and canceled plans for a sex-change operation.

God broke through to me as well . . . at that breakfast table.

Jim asked why I was at the conference. When I said it was part of my doctoral research and that I wanted to eventually equip churches to minister to people with sexual brokenness, he nearly shrieked: "God bless you! God is going to really use you."

It seemed prophetic. Jesus was speaking to me through him. And why should we be surprised? Jesus said that when we serve "the least of these my brothers," we are actually serving him. Breakfast with the one who seemed the least put me face-to-face with him who is the Most.

In a highly polarized and overly sensitive culture strait-jacketed by political correctness, love will carry more decibels than proclamations of truth. The Holy Spirit, however, is quite capable of convincing us all of our monkeys and taking us further down the Path. As this happens, sexual minorities will eventually be open to hearing what the Scriptures have to say about their truest identity and the way to live it out. In the meantime, perhaps the Spirit would have you keep close to your heart the following prayer:

Gracious God, how we need your wisdom! Help us to value others as you value them and to rightly balance truth with love. May we be moved with compassion to open our arms to "the least" that we might all experience more of the Most. To you be the honor and glory forever! Amen.

Discussion Questions

1. What was the most eye-opening insight in this chapter for you?
2. How is the story of the anti-smoking crusade a fitting parallel? In what ways does it *not* fit?
3. Just as Paul was distressed and repulsed by idolatry, is there anything that distresses you about sexual minorities? How might be the best way to deal with that repulsion so that, like Paul, we might reach people for Christ?
4. Does your church have anything similar to John Wesley's class meeting where people can be transparent? If not, how can you create such an atmosphere?

5. As Andrew Marin stated, people from the LGBT community fear they will not be fully accepted and included in the life of the church. Are there any obvious ways your church can communicate love and acceptance?

6. In the final story, Jim said if one man had reached out to him, it would have made all the difference. Are there young people in your congregation who might feel similarly? How can friendship and mentoring be provided?

EPILOGUE:

"When Will This Ever End?"

One evening the phone rang. It was late enough in the day that every pastor's reaction would be, "Uh, this can't be good." Sure enough, Clara was on the phone wailing, trying to choke out her words. I could barely understand. "Pastor Mark, please come!"

After calling Bertie, another lady in the church, we met outside of Clara's apartment building, then rang her room for her to open the locked lobby door.

Clara had been attending our church for more than a year and was pressing hard into God for her addictive problems. At a certain point she started to come for counseling for her issues with alcohol, but before long we were plumbing the depths of some horrific memories of sexual abuse. It had begun as a child with incest, but it seemed as though throughout her life perpetrators were simply led to her. She was always in the wrong place at the wrong time. Her second husband had courted her so that he could sexually dominate her and prey upon her two children. At one point even a police officer had forced himself upon her.

Despite amazing moments of healing and progress, another crisis had now hit her with blunt force. A call had come from Texas concerning her grandson. He had been spending a lot of time at a neighbor's house, earning money by doing yard work and other chores. But the man eventually took him on a trip to the woods, beat him, raped him, shot him, and left him for dead.

Bertie and I wrapped our arms around Clara and prayed for the presence of Jesus to descend upon her as we simply let her sorrow pour out. This latest violation tapped into all the remaining rage for the injustices committed against her. Finally she blurted out, "When will this ever end?! It just keeps on happening. First my mother was abused, then me, then my kids, and now my grandson! Oh, God!"

A few months later Clara moved to Texas to help stabilize the family system. But her question still rings in my ears. "When will this ever end?!" When will sexual abuse of little boys and girls become less frequent? When will sex trafficking subside? When will porn and adulterous trysts be on the decline? And more to the point, when will the church disentangle itself from this rampant evil and begin to offer healing to the broken?

Yes, this is the final chapter. There could be any number of reasons you have pressed onward through each unit of principles, theology, and applications. Perhaps your own pain and brokenness have turned the pages for you. Or likely you love someone whose life has been wrecked because of the grasping after or submission to the pleasures of sexual idolatry. But let me challenge you! Will you be a part of the solution? Will you allow God to use your gifts and abilities?

"When will this ever end?" It never will. Not this side of the Garden of Paradise. But it *can* get better. Perhaps even now God is raising up a new generation of Christians who will say, "Enough is enough!"

The Mess We're In

Some are heralding a new day of justice for sexual minorities. North America has taken giant strides in abolishing slavery, and in creating greater equality and opportunity for minorities and women. And now, it is reasoned, we've evolved further by normalizing same-sex relationships.

Please don't misunderstand. I am genuinely thankful that gays, lesbians, and others will likely endure less bullying and discrimination. That is absolutely an advancement. But I certainly do not believe gay marriage is progress. Far from it. Actually we are regressing, moving further from God's design for marriage and sexuality. The pagan worldview is quickly becoming the dominant lens for people in Western culture. Boundaries in general are becoming more porous, but this seems especially true with sexual ethics. Increasingly people bow before the altar of Baal as sexual fulfillment becomes the object of worship. But this enormous shift in worldview didn't begin with the legalization of gay marriage. Far from it.

The Sexual Revolution of the '60s was a perfect storm. With the end of World War II, a new generation of parents spawned the Baby Boom. Having just exited the military, many brought with them a rigid and authoritarian style of parenting. This swing of the pendulum toward discipline without a corresponding increase in nurture provided an incubator for rebellion in many families. At a time when traditional values were being challenged in every segment of society, sexual mores were further muddled as John A. T. Robinson's book *Honest to God* and other proponents of situational ethics shook our theological foundations.[1] Add to this the development of the birth control pill, which now meant the stripping away of a natural inhibition for sexual expression. As the decades rolled onward, the church floundered miserably when addressing issues of sexuality and also failed to issue a clear and

certain message regarding the rapidly growing trend in divorce. As
Albert Mohler stated in his recent book *We Cannot Be Silent:*

> Heterosexuals did a very good job of undermining marriage
> before the culture forces began advocating for the normaliza-
> tion of same-sex relationships and the legalization of same-sex
> marriage. The marriage crisis is a moral crisis that did not start
> with same-sex marriage, nor will it end there. . . . Once marriage
> can mean anything other than a heterosexual union, it can and
> must eventually mean everything . . .[2]

So how are we as God's people to respond to this free fall of sexual
morality? How can we do our part in bringing this mess to an end?

Confronting Dysfunction

Remember the parable of the Tifflebaums? They were the family
of chapter 1 whose home life was out of kilter because of the dad's
drinking problem. The kids adopted dysfunctional roles because
Tiffany, the mom, was too busy enabling Lex's drunkenness.
Eventually Teddy, the middle child, acted out with rebellion and
received all of the ire and angst of the family. A counselor was
called to sort through the mess and pointed out that Lex was the
Elephant in the room no one had permission to talk about, while
Teddy was merely the Scapegoat.

Taking the parable forward a bit, what will it take for the
Tifflebaum family to change? Someone will have to face their
dysfunction and take the lead. Likely it will have to be Tiffany.
Allowing the pain of the present to motivate her, she will need to
confront the Elephant, demand change, and set the house in order.
Sounds simple enough—unless you are Tiffany! Changing from
enabler to enforcer is a huge shift! Huge! And so with the ongoing
help of her counselor and healthy support from some friends, she
will have to demand that her husband, Lex, go to rehab and enter a

recovery program. Additionally, she will need to step up to the plate for her kids. Taking the nurturing role away from the oldest sibling, Biff, she will need to call Marsha out of her shell and lavish some love on wayward Teddy.

Never does such a transition go smoothly. Tiffany herself will now become the object of anger as she shakes up the entire family system. Others will want to go back to their old roles, especially Lex. There will be pressure put upon her to do what she's always done: to enable and to let things slide. In fact, without God's help, the family will either break up or die the death of a thousand cuts.

Truly the church in North America is a dysfunctional mess. We've spent years squabbling over the Scapegoat issue of homosexuality while by and large ignoring or enabling the Elephant of sexual idolatry. Like Tiffany, the effort to change the family system will be enormous and could very well make the leaders of such a movement the target of much anger. To call the church to account for its sexual idolatry and to steer the focus away from the Scapegoat issue of homosexuality will shake up the system. But like the Tifflebaum home, enabling the Elephant is strangling the church. Denominations and local churches are, in fact, breaking up or dying the death of a thousand cuts.

But before we get ahead of ourselves, what truly is the starting point?

You

Tiffany's challenge begins with Tiffany's own monkeys. There is always deep brokenness, which drives enabling behavior. So while she is attempting to bring health to her family system, she needs to find some healing to deal with her own issues.

Before we can work on the specks in the eyes of others, we need to yank the altar of Baal out of our own. Sorry, but I continue to maintain that most of us have some degree of sexual brokenness or sexual idolatry to own. It could be that only our spouses know of our struggle. Whether the idolatrous practices take place in the bedroom, at the computer desk, or merely in our minds, each of us has to allow the Wonderful Counselor access to our hearts. No, it's not an easy journey. But the best change agents in a cultural mess like ours are wounded healers and weeping prophets—those who have experienced the pain of transformation and are acquainted with the sorrows of sexual brokenness.

Four and a half years ago a homeless heroin addict began attending our evening worship service. She had lost everything to her addiction: partners, children, jobs, and about thirty pounds. At the end of the service she was making a hasty exit, but I intercepted her just outside the door. After the usual pastorly chit chat, I asked where she was going in such a hurry. She was off to a Narcotics Anonymous meeting. So in order to have a longer conversation, I offered a ride.

"Oh, it doesn't matter. I'll just walk."

Pressing further, I asked, "Where is it?"

"It's at the church at the top of the Eleventh Street hill."

"What? You're kidding!"

Now this is no ordinary hill. More than a half-mile long, it is so seriously steep that my worship leader's S-10 pickup can't climb it on a rainy day unless laden with a heavy load in the back—his wheels just spin!

"You *walk up that hill* for an NA meeting?"

"Sure! I would have walked up that hill for a bag of heroin, so I should be willing to climb it to stay clean!" Incredible.

Yes, the destructive force of her addiction certainly added some motivation to climb the hill. But would to God every Christian struggled against sexual sin with that same sense of determination!

And is that not the will of God for us? If you know the Scriptures, your answer is "Yes!" I dare you to read these verses with a willing heart:

Finally, brothers and sisters, we ask and urge you in the Lord Jesus that, as you learned from us how you ought to live and to please God (as, in fact, you are doing), you should do so more and more. For you know what instructions we gave you through the Lord Jesus. For this is the will of God, your sanctification: that you abstain from fornication; that each one of you know how to control your own body in holiness and honor, not with lustful passion, like the Gentiles who do not know God; that no one wrong or exploit a brother or sister in this matter, because the Lord is an avenger in all these things, just as we have already told you beforehand and solemnly warned you. For God did not call us to impurity but in holiness. Therefore whoever rejects this rejects not human authority but God, who also gives his Holy Spirit to you. (1 Thess. 4:1–8)

Pretty plain, isn't it? "For this is the will of God . . ." Living holy and pure lives is God's will. And Paul felt compelled by Jesus himself to urge these readers to bring their sexual lives under the reign of God. It is not simply a matter of making a resolution to toe the line. Being sanctified means being set apart for God. That includes setting apart our bodies as God's, using them only as God desires.

And sanctification is a continual process of transformation. Greater wholeness frees us to walk in greater holiness. And so Paul affirmed their current level of obedience while at the same time urged them to please God in this area of sexuality "more and more." He specifically stated we are not to "wrong or exploit a brother or sister in this matter," which would include all of the sexual sins of a grasping nature. But I am sure he would expand the list to encompass such sins as soaking our minds in porn, withholding intimacy from our spouses, or simply allowing our imaginations to camp out in a voyeuristic fantasy land.

So enough of the protests, boycotts, and pulpit-pounding over Scapegoat issues! Let us lead by example. As this book has hopefully made very clear, moving toward sexual wholeness is a steep uphill climb for many. Finding healing for abuse can seem terrifying. Detoxing from adultery requires an emotionally taxing, Spirit-led rehab. Overcoming sexual addiction calls forth enormous effort and a support team of loving brothers and sisters. And most of you will never know how extremely difficult it is for some to overcome sexual aversion or to live above the pull of same-sex attraction. But how hypocritical it is to point others toward the Eleventh Street hill if we aren't willing to take the journey ourselves! How dare we cry out against brothers and sisters who are attracted to the same sex, demanding they remain single and celibate, when we ourselves have not submitted our own sexual brokenness to the Lord Jesus Christ!

Your Local Church

As a pastor, I stifle a groan each time someone approaches me about launching a ministry. Most pastors are already overtaxed, so some of us reflexively wonder what each new initiative is going to require of us. Who will do the recruiting? How will this be funded? Will we be left with the job of propping up a program once the initial enthusiasm wanes?

In this regard, I try to keep this verse as my filter for such requests: "Jesus said to them, 'Very truly, I tell you, the Son can do nothing on his own, but only what he sees the Father doing; for whatever the Father does, the Son does likewise'" (John 5:19). The context, once again, is a sparring match with religious leaders. He had just healed the man by the pool of Bethesda and the leaders were ticked. Not only had Jesus "worked" on the Sabbath, but he had also told the man to pick up his mat and carry it.

Now think this through with me. As Jesus walked into that poolside infirmary, the place was filled with invalids. As he was watching to see what the Father was doing, he spotted this one man.

Walking right past the many others, Jesus approached only this one man. Why him? If you've read the story, you know he didn't quite have a stellar faith in God. In fact, Jesus had to ask him if he really wanted to be healed in the first place. Probably not the guy you and I would have picked for a reclamation project. But for some reason, Jesus could see the Father at work in him.

Even though I try to keep this principle as my filter before starting a ministry, sometimes I get it wrong. At times I think I see the Father at work and end up jumping in too soon.

Take Beaver Falls, for example. There is one main road that travels the length of our tiny city. On the north end you can find an adult bookstore and a gentlemen's club. Just across the river on the south end you find the same thing, an adult bookstore and a gentlemen's club. For a town of about nine thousand, that's pretty weird, right? Upon arriving in Beaver Falls, I thought, *Surely there are sexual addicts galore in this area. Certainly the Father is at work here.* So I decided to start a small-group ministry for sexual addicts. A mailing was sent to all of the area churches and I placed an ad in the county paper. The result? Only one phone call. It was from a retired psychology professor from the local college who thanked me for the effort. "It is surely needed," he commented. "But I doubt anyone will take you up on it." He was right.

I've seen similar results as others, driven by well-meaning compassion, have started recovery groups for victims of sexual abuse or for those with unwanted same-sex attraction. It can be difficult to get such an endeavor off the ground, let alone maintain momentum, especially if your church is small.

From my perspective, the first step is training. If you or someone in your church has suitable gifts for a prayer ministry to the broken, consider getting the proper tools. Often God calls the deeply wounded to become channels of healing for others, so a good candidate might be someone who has found some healing for their own sexual issues. Look into formational prayer as a form of care which can help people find some inner healing. There are certainly other types of prayer ministry that God is using, but formational prayer is a balanced, biblical, and Spirit-empowered approach that will likely sync with your ministry regardless of your theological bent.

Once someone is trained and begins to gain experience in positioning people in the presence of Jesus for transformation, watch for evidence of the Father at work. For example, if two or three victims of sexual abuse begin to come for prayer, perhaps you will have momentum for a support group. If a crisis erupts around the issue of sexual addiction, maybe God will use that as a catalyst for a ministry in that area. And what is the Father doing among the other churches in your area? Are there already people pooling their efforts to address sex trafficking?

But whether you see evidence of the Father at work or not, you can always begin by addressing issues of sexuality. Bring the conversation to the table. Church leaders need to get over this centuries-old inhibition about speaking of sexuality inside of church buildings. We simply have to ask God to untie our tongues so that we can talk about sexuality with grace and balance.

Now I know from personal experience there is a special form of denial unique to pastors. It might even be a disease. It goes something like this: "Hey, I preached on that subject last February, so they already know that material." Let's face it. You can't preach or teach a series on sexuality or any other topic and expect that your church folks have mastered the content, have fully repented, and are now walking in lockstep with the Savior. It just doesn't work that way.

And a special sermon series is not the best approach anyway. We need to find ways to weave the subject into our messages all year long. Use stories of sexual problems to illustrate your sermons and teaching sessions. Refer often to books on the subject. And if appropriate, speak of your own progress in overcoming sexual issues. One pastor I know of began to share from the pulpit how God was helping him to overcome a porn addiction. Instead of people running for the doors, word got around that at his church it was okay to not be okay. Folks began to fill his pews. But no matter how God leads you to weave the subject into your material, you will at least be modeling how sexuality can be a part of normal conversation in very casual ways. Will people complain? Count on it. But you will be surprised who the whiners are.

During my doctoral studies, I began weaving the subject into my messages. A teenager, of all people, filed an official complaint. Elderly men and women, however, came up to me with smiles, saying, "Thank God someone is finally preaching about this!" To my surprise, one of my most vocal critics used to ride with the Hell's Angels. Seriously! "Church is no place to be talking about that kind of stuff!" he growled. Wow. (No, he didn't threaten bodily harm! He just looked disgusted.) I suspect that those who squawk the loudest have some deep inner pain that has been tweaked. And that's okay. Healing won't come for them or anyone else by relegating all talk of sexual matters to the church closet. We need to bring the talk out where people walk.

If you don't take the lead in your congregation, who will? An uphill climb? You bet. Nit-picking critics? No doubt. But the Father may well direct your steps to someone who's been paralyzed for decades by sexual issues—someone who may not have stellar faith and might even seem as though they don't *want* to be healed. But you can also be sure of this: there is tremendous joy watching someone pick up their mat and walk!

Your Denomination

Sometimes I am just too serious. As a recovering workaholic, I have been multitasking myself to death. It used to be that any book on my shelf had to have something to do with my work. Fiction was simply a waste of time. But as God has tamed that particular monkey in my life, I have found that reading a good novel is a tremendous way for me to relax. In the last five years I've actually read a shelfful.

Someone who reads my blog posts recommended an author. "If sexuality and the church are of such interest to you, try the Starbridge series by Susan Howatch." What an incredible tip.

In the space of six lengthy novels, Howatch developed a cast of characters, most of whom are leaders in the Church of England during the twentieth century and all of whom have sexual struggles, obsessions, or missteps. They span the theological spectrum: a mystic monk, a charismatic priest, a very conservative evangelical bishop, and a liberal cleric. But by the sixth novel, Howatch masterfully illustrated how God had used them all for the sake of the kingdom. In fact, the mystic monk managed to facilitate a marvelous reconciliation between the cranky conservative and a fast and loose liberal. It is a fascinating portrayal of the sexual brokenness of God's people and how he uses all traditions within the church as channels of his grace.

At a time when my own denomination seems headed toward a split, I've mused over the matter of our oneness in Christ. Is Howatch's portrayal of the bride of Christ in England mere wishful thinking? Can we remain within the same ecclesial structure, continue to learn from each other, and allow the Spirit to balance out our seemingly contradictory passions and concerns for the good of the kingdom? Or is this ideal to be forever catalogued among the works of fiction?

Interestingly enough, I had a conversation recently with a local Anglican who is also a fan of the Howatch series. Her congregation was among those who split off from the Episcopal Church over the ordination of gay clergy. Because there have been rumblings in my own denomination about division, I asked what she'd observed from her corner of the kingdom. Unfortunately, once the split took place, the liberals within the Episcopal Church drove their tribe way off to the left, and the conservatives among the Anglicans raced for the right. As one example, she has found tremendous resistance toward the ordination of women among the Anglicans.

I've already identified myself as "Pentamethalbapterianic." But that's simply how I've allowed God's grace to stretch me. My DNA is quite a bit evangelical with a strand or two from the holiness tradition. On the list of core values for Evangelicals, *fidelity to the Scriptures* is near the top. *Unity in the midst of diversity* is also on the list, but toward the bottom. Stray too far from the Scriptures and we by nature start looking for the exit signs. Those from the Social Justice camp, however, seem to prioritize their list quite differently. *Unity in the midst of diversity* probably ranks in the top three, so all talk of division seems quite heretical to them. That is why they have stayed wedded to us Evangelicals even though they strongly oppose where we have drawn the lines on some issues.

Having read broadly, engaged in dialogue, observed other branches of the church, and stewed on the matter, I have little hope that my own denomination will avoid fracturing. The evangelical churches are growing, especially in Africa. Most of us will not compromise on what we believe the Bible says about the nature of homosexuality. The Social Justice folks among us are equally resolute about maintaining unity in the midst of our diversity and are going to extreme lengths to make sure same-sex marriages are sanctioned. You can bang heads only so long before something starts to crack open.

Whether or not splits can be avoided, my contention has been that it is never too late to begin doing the right thing. The right thing is to join forces and attack the Elephant. In an ideal world, our Social Justice brothers and sisters could lead the charge on some of these issues. If they channeled as much righteous indignation upon the Elephant as they have on defending the Scapegoat, we could see some amazing shifts in how the church brings healing to

abuse victims, rescues the captives of sex trafficking, and cries for
justice against a mammon-fueled porn industry.

So, too, with us Evangelicals. Richard Foster called us the
"Word-Centered" tradition of the church. How does one even
begin to quantify the amount of time, energy, ink, paper, and cyber
space that have been expended to spar with foes regarding same-
sex marriage and related matters? What might God do if we instead
spent ourselves in developing a detailed and practical theology
of sexuality that addresses all sexual issues and urges all of us to
embrace the uphill climb of healing? And as for our passion for
sharing the Word of God with others, could we set aside our revulsion and begin to reach out to sex offenders, sex addicts, and those
who promote the porn industry?[3]

As for the rest of the body, the Charismatics among us have
much to teach us about Spirit-empowered healing ministry for
those who have been crippled by abuse and neglect. Perhaps those
from the Holiness tradition could shine a light on how to live holy
lives in this sin-infected world without developing the mind-set of
the Box. And those steeped in the traditions of the mystics could
most certainly share how the use of ancient prayer practices could
be used to bring strength, healing, and wellness to those scarred by
sexual sin.

Our Culture

Whether or not denominations continue to fissure and fracture,
the question still remains concerning our role within the culture.
Opinions differ regarding the church's responsibility. Are we to be
actively engaged in transforming cultural structures and instilling
Christian values? Or is our focus primarily upon transforming indi-
viduals? Your answers to those questions may determine how you
apply the message of this book to the community in which you live.

Regardless of how you feel about those questions, we are certainly called to be salt and light. But how effective can we be if, as Jesus warned us, the salt has lost its saltiness? Yes, for the chemists among us, we know that salt cannot become other than salt. Technically it cannot lose its saltiness. But in Jesus' day salt could lose its taste if enough dust and dirt got mixed in with it. And that is truly our problem. With our lack of sexual holiness and our in-your-face combativeness over Scapegoat issues, we've lost our distinctiveness.

And so, as I've already stated, the church generally lacks street cred. Our bickering over this one issue of homosexuality merely mirrors the division in the culture at large. They perceive we hate the sinner about as much as we hate the sin. It is also obvious to many that heterosexual brokenness abounds in the pews. Seeing the hypocrisy, some are quick to cry out, "Injustice!"

Instead of mirroring our culture, we must model unity in the midst of our diversity by joining hands in compassionate ministry to the abused, addicted, and averse, while at the same time holding in tension our unresolved differences. But is that even possible at this point?

Back in the '80s Dr. Bob Lyon, one of my seminary professors, asked his classes, "Who is the most powerful person in Calcutta, India?" The answer was *not* a military officer, a government official, or a crime boss. It was Mother Teresa. No one dared lay a hand on her. Her power came through selfless acts of love.

As you may remember, in 1994 she spoke at the National Prayer Breakfast in our nation's capital. Because of the bipartisan atmosphere, speakers of the past avoided the controversial. Not so the Calcutta sister. She preached a scorching pro-life message on abortion. Noting the obvious displeasure of the Clintons, a reporter asked the president what he thought of her talk. His reply? "How can anyone argue with a life so well-lived?"

Through her years of selfless and grace-filled service among the poorest of the poor, the nun had earned enough street cred to declare a prophetic word to the most powerful people in the world. That same credibility, in fact, later led to cooperation with the Clintons themselves. The nun and the first lady joined hands to establish an adoption house in Washington DC.

In *The Good Book,* author Peter Gomes foresaw continued strife and division over this one issue of homosexuality. Slavery, he stated, was decided not by biblical exegesis, but by gunpowder and cannonballs.[4] Really? Slug it out and winner takes all? Is that our only option? I believe there is a better way. Truth and love held in a proper balance is the way of the gospel. Okay, I hear you. *Liberals and conservatives combining efforts to corral the Elephant while agreeing to disagree about Scapegoat issues? Is that even possible?* Yeah, I know. Crazy. About as crazy as a nun and a pro-choice politician working together.

To win the ear of our culture on sexual issues, we will have to demonstrate in sacrificial measure our love for the least of these. Blithely repeating ad nauseam that we love the sinner but hate the sin now elicits mockery and derision from the unchurched. We have failed miserably to demonstrate such love. A defensive or combative posture will only make things worse if not balanced with extravagant acts of love and service to the last, the least, and the lost.

How does this begin? Perhaps by stepping across the divide and initiating friendships. Which divide? Wherever you see the Father working. Close to a dozen times I have initiated contact with progressives from the Social Justice camp. Whether it was inviting them for coffee, attending one of their events, or connecting with them to dialogue, they have welcomed me warmly. Rarely have they returned the favor, but I have always sensed God was pleased with such attempts on my part.

And consider the divide between your church and the sexual minorities in your community. Certainly the Father is at work among them as well. I especially encourage you to develop a friendship with someone who struggles with same-sex attraction. But make sure they don't become a project for you to fix or an ideological foe to sucker-punch. I have a number of colleagues and friends who struggle with same-sex attraction. Some believe that is how they were born, others do not. Refusing to make that an issue, I simply seek to understand and to be understood. Hey, I could use a friend as well!

"When Will This Ever End?"

Clara is not alone in asking this question. In fact, I have heard the same cry practically word for word from people with every form of sexual brokenness: those addicted to sex, porn, fantasy, and adultery; those attracted to the same sex; those who are drawn to children and fetishes. Many of these dear people who have looked me in the face and posed this question have actually found some freedom. The behavior has finally been reined in, but to some degree they still feel the pull of desire, especially when under stress or experiencing loneliness. It is frustrating for them. When, indeed, will this ever end?

In this time between the gardens, in this world of open-eyed blindness, we will never be entirely free from brokenness. Paul promised in Romans 8 that we will, in fact, go through suffering as we await the redemption of our bodies. All of creation, he stated, groans with us until the gate to the Garden of Paradise swings open to the bride.

But a beachhead has been formed. The kingdom is advancing. The One who was sent to proclaim good news to the poor and release to the captives leads his church forward. As his body in this time of the "already and not yet," we will share in his sufferings. But God also promises that any suffering we endure will work together for the good of those who love him (see Romans 8:28). Besides that, the glory to come far outweighs the sorrows of this earth.

Until the day the Lord returns, churches will still have closets. But if you continue to assert that all God's children got monkeys, closet dwellers will feel less like they are worse sinners than anyone else. If you communicate with blatant redundancy that life with Christ is about a transforming Path instead of a legalistic Box, those crouching in darkness will feel more like they belong. And if you will join those who want to repent of our common perversity of faith and learn to offer healing prayer for all who struggle, they just might come out into the light and feel the Father's embrace. Are you ready to open your arms?

One last time, I invite you to pray a prayer:

> *Lord Jesus Christ, Head of the church, continue to cleanse your bride. We have spots, wrinkles, and blemishes! We have enabled the sexual idolatry of the majority while mistreating the minority. Increasingly our culture mocks us. Continue to make us holy. Guide us in balancing truth with love. Enable us to be your healing hands to a desperately broken world.*
>
> *And as for my part, I repent of my own idolatry and place my feet upon the transforming Path. As I sanctify and set apart my sexuality to be used as you desire, bring healing grace into my life. And may I be privileged to have a part in bringing healing to others, empowering our church for ministry, and in bringing peace to the church. In your dear name I pray, amen!*

Discussion Questions

1. How did this chapter leave you feeling? Hopeful? Despairing? Explain why.
2. The parable of the Tifflebaums resurfaces in this chapter. What did you find helpful about how the parable is applied?

3. Four arenas are identified where, with God's enabling, we can begin to bring about change. Which of these four do you think is the most difficult? Why?

4. Considering this guidance for the local church, what can be applied in your church? Is there someone who could be trained in some form of prayer ministry for the sexually broken? Where else might the Father be working?

5. How could you begin to weave the subject of sexuality into the conversations in your church? What would be appropriate or inappropriate ways to do so? And how would you handle any friction that might arise?

6. Do you personally know of someone who is a sexual minority? How could you begin to develop a relationship with this person?

7. What other churches in your area might be willing to hold in tension disagreement over the Scapegoat while cooperating to corral the Elephant?

RESOURCES

Sexuality

Comiskey, Andrew. *Strength in Weakness: Healing Sexual and Relational Brokenness*. Downers Grove, IL: InterVarsity Press, 2003.

Hollinger, Dennis P. *The Meaning of Sex: Christian Ethics and the Moral Life*. Grand Rapids, MI: Baker Publishing Group, 2009.

West, Christopher. *Theology of the Body for Beginners: A Basic Introduction to Pope John Paul II's Sexual Revolution*. West Chester, PA: Ascension Press, 2009.

Sexual Abuse

Allender, Dan. *The Wounded Heart: Hope for Victims of Childhood Sexual Abuse*. Colorado Springs: NavPress, 2008.

Hunter, Mic. *Abused Boys: The Neglected Victims of Sexual Abuse*. New York: Fawcett, 1991.

Langberg, Diane Mandt. *On the Threshold of Hope*. Carol Stream, IL: Tyndale House Publishers, 1999.

Yantzi, Mark. *Sexual Offending and Restoration*. Waterloo, ON: Herald Press, 1998.

Sexual Addiction

Carnes, Patrick. *Don't Call It Love: Recovery from Sexual Addiction*. New York: Bantam Books, 1991.

———. *Out of the Shadows*. Minneapolis: CompCare Publications, 1983.

————. *Recovery Zone: Making Changes That Last. Vol. 1.*
Carefree, AZ: Gentle Path Press, 2009.

Ferree, Marnie C. *No Stones: Women Redeemed from Sexual
Shame.* Fairfax, VA: Xulon, 2002.

Laaser, Mark R. *Healing the Wounds of Sexual Addiction.* Grand
Rapids, MI: Zondervan, 2004.

Homosexuality

Cohen, Richard. *Coming Out Straight: Understanding and Healing
Homosexuality.* Winchester, VA: Oakhill Press, 2000.

Grenz, Stanley J. *Welcoming but Not Affirming: An Evangelical
Response to Homosexuality.* Louisville: Westminster John
Knox Press, 1998.

Jones, Stanton L., and Mark A. Yarhouse. *Ex-Gays?: A
Longitudinal Study of Religiously Mediated Change in Sexual
Orientation.* Downers Grove, IL: IVP Academic, 2007.

Marin, Andrew. *Love Is an Orientation: Elevating the Conversation
with the Gay Community.* Downers Grove, IL: IVP Books,
2009.

Via, Dan O., and Robert A. J. Gagnon. *Homosexuality and the
Bible: Two Views.* Minneapolis: Fortress Press, 2003.

Yarhouse, Mark A. *Homosexuality and the Christian: A Guide for
Parents, Pastors, and Friends.* Minneapolis: Bethany House
Publishers, 2010.

NOTES

Introduction

1. Diana Russell, *The Secret Trauma: Incest in the Lives of Girls and Women* (New York: Basic Books, 1986), 112.

Chapter 1 Principle: The Elephant and the Scapegoat

1. David Kinnaman and Gabe Lyons, *unChristian: What a New Generation Really Thinks about Christianity . . . and Why It Matters* (Grand Rapids, MI: Baker Books, 2007), 92.
2. Robert Kuyper, *Crisis in Ministry: A Wesleyan Response to the Gay Rights Movement* (Anderson, IN: Bristol House, Ltd., 1999), 190f.
3. Dennis Hollinger, *The Meaning of Sex: Christian Ethics and the Moral Life* (Grand Rapids, MI: Baker Academic, 2009), 44–46.
4. Andrew Marin, *Love Is an Orientation: Elevating the Conversation with the Gay Community* (Downers Grove, IL: InterVarsity Press, 2009), 46.

Chapter 2 Theology: Creation and God's Good Design

1. James Newton Poling, *The Abuse of Power: A Theological Problem* (Nashville, TN: Abingdon Press, 1991), 11–12, 193.
2. Maxine Hancock and Karen Mains, *Child Sexual Abuse: A Hope for Healing* (Wheaton, IL: Harold Shaw Publishers, 1987), 10.
3. James V. Heidinger II, citing a study by Faith in Public Life in *Good News*, April 2009.
4. Dan B. Allender, *Sabbath: The Ancient Practices* (Nashville, TN: Thomas Nelson, Inc., 2009), 69.

5. John Oswalt, *What You Should Know about Homosexuality*, ed. Charles W. Keyser (Grand Rapids, MI: Zondervan Publishing House, 1979), 43.
6. Ken Blue, *Authority to Heal* (Downers Grove, IL: InterVarsity Press, 1987), 140.
7. William H. Masters, Virginia E. Johnson, and Robert C. Kolodny, *Human Sexuality*, 3rd Edition (Glenview, IL: Scott, Foresman and Company, 1988).
8. Gary Chapman, *The Five Love Languages: How to Express Heartfelt Commitment to Your Mate* (Chicago, IL: Northfield Publishing, 1992), 30.
9. Masters, Johnson, and Kolodny, *Human Sexuality*, 651.

Chapter 3 Application: The Violation of Abuse

1. The nature of this chapter is simply to create awareness. To that end, the information is a bit general. For more information, refer to the list of resources.
2. Mic Hunter, *Abused Boys: The Neglected Victims of Sexual Abuse* (New York: Fawcett Columbine, 1990), 8–22.
3. Dan Allender, *The Wounded Heart: Hope for Adult Victims of Childhood Sexual Abuse* (Colorado Springs, CO: NavPress, 1995), 24.
4. Hunter, *Abused Boys*, 45–49.
5. Written May 7, 2009 at 3:30 a.m. and dedicated to Rev. Darrell L. Greenawalt.

Chapter 4 Principle: The Box, the Path, and the Circus

1. The Box and Path are adaptations of concepts developed by Paul Hiebert, professor of missions and anthropology. For more information, see "The Category 'Christian' in the Mission Task," *International Review of Mission* 72, no. 287 (1983): 421–27.

Chapter 5 Theology: The Fall and Open-Eyed Blindness

1. Leanne Payne, *The Healing Presence: Curing the Soul through Union with Christ* (Grand Rapids, MI: Baker Books, 1995), 59–67.
2. Christopher West, *Theology of the Body for Beginners: A Basic Introduction to Pope John Paul II's Sexual Revolution* (West Chester, PA: Ascension Press, 2009), 37.
3. John Oswalt, "The Old Testament and Homosexuality," *What You Should Know about Homosexuality,* ed. Charles W. Keysor (Grand Rapids, MI: Zondervan Publishing House, 1979), 30.
4. Donald J. Wold, *Out of Order: Homosexuality in the Bible and the Ancient Near East* (Grand Rapids, MI: Baker Books, 1998), 8, 10.
5. Oswalt, *What You Should Know about Homosexuality,* 26
6. Ibid., 37
7. John Money, *Lovemaps: Clinical Concepts of Sexual/Erotic Health and Pathology, Paraphilia, and Gender Transposition in Childhood, Adolescence, and Maturity* (New York: Irvington Publishers, 1993), Loc. 63, 69. Money does not use the term "imprinting" but speaks of developing a "lovemap." While he affirms the impact of one's first sexual experience, he believes the development begins in earnest between five and eight years old.
8. Dennis P. Hollinger, *The Meaning of Sex: Christian Ethics and the Moral Life* (Grand Rapids, MI: Baker Publishing Group, 2009), 64–65.
9. Ibid., 66.

Chapter 6 Application: The Idolatry of Fantasy and Adultery

1. Donald M. Joy, *Rebonding: Preventing and Restoring Damaged Relationships* (Nappanee, IN: Evangel Publishing House, 1986), 22.
2. Ibid., 45.

3. Larry Crabb, *Inside Out* (Colorado Springs, CO: NavPress, 2007), 58, 95.

4. Ravi Zacharias, *Can Man Live Without God?* (Dallas, TX: Word Publishing, 1994), 136.

Chapter 7 Principle: All God's Children Got Monkeys

1. William Barclay, *The Daily Study Bible Series: The Gospel of John, Vol. 2* rev. ed. (Philadelphia, PA: Westminster Press, 1975), 292.

2. Terry Wardle, *Healing Care, Healing Prayer: Helping the Broken Find Wholeness in Christ* (Orange, CA: New Leaf Books, 2001), 137.

3. Philip Yancey, *What's So Amazing About Grace?* (Grand Rapids, MI: Zondervan, 1997), 11–12.

Chapter 8 Theology: Restoration and Grace

1. Don Piper, *90 Minutes in Heaven: A True Story of Death and Life* (Grand Rapids, MI: Fleming H. Revell, 2004).

2. Information on these seven-day intensive retreats can be found at http://hcminternational.org/grow/come-away-with-me -retreat.

3. J. A. Motyer, *The Message of Philippians,* in The Bible Speaks Today Series, eds. J. A. Motyer and John R. W. Stott (Downers Grove, IL: InterVarsity Press, 1984), 108.

4. Martin Luther, "A Mighty Fortress Is Our God," ca. 1529; trans. Frederick H. Hedge, 1853.

5. D. A. Carson, "Matthew" in *Expositor's Bible Commentary Vol. 8,* ed. Frank E. Gaebelein (Grand Rapids, MI: Zondervan, 1984), 412.

6. John Oswalt, *What You Should Know about Homosexuality,* ed. Charles W. Keyser (Grand Rapids, MI: Baker Books, 1995), 41.

7. *More Letters of Herbert Hensley Henson* as quoted in *Glittering Images* by Susan Howatch (New York: Fawcett Columbine, 1987), 91.

8. For an excellent treatment of a theology of healing, see Ken Blue's *Authority to Heal* (Downers Grove, IL: InterVarsity Press, 1987).

9. Terry Wardle, from a teaching at the Advanced Seminar sponsored by Healing Care Ministries, hosted by Ashland Theological Seminary, September 2008.
10. Carol Kent, *Between a Rock and a Grace Place: Divine Surprises in the Tight Spots of Life* (Grand Rapids, MI: Zondervan, 2010).
11. Wardle, Advanced Seminar, Ashland Theological Seminary, September 2008.
12. Oswalt, *What You Should Know about Homosexuality*, 42.

Chapter 9 Application: The Idolatry of Addiction and Aversion

1. Marnie Ferree, *No Stones: Women Redeemed from Sexual Addiction* (Downers Grove, IL: IVP Books, 2010), 43.
2. Ibid.
3. Patrick Carnes, *Don't Call It Love: Recovery from Sexual Addiction* (New York: Bantam Books, 1992), 12.
4. Mark Laaser, *Healing the Wounds of Sexual Addiction* (Grand Rapids, MI: Zondervan, 2004), 36–39.
5. Ibid., 40–44.
6. Douglas A. Abbott, "Behavioral Genetics and Homosexuality," *Journal of Human Sexuality* 2 (2010): 92.
7. Carnes, *Don't Call It Love*, 109.
8. Ibid., 76.
9. Patrick Carnes, *Sexual Anorexia: Overcoming Sexual Self-Hatred* (Center City, MN: Hazelden, 1997), Loc. 190.
10. Ibid., Loc. 662.
11. Ibid., Loc. 376.
12. Kevin M. Watson, *Pursing Social Holiness: The Band Meeting in Wesley's Thought and Popular Methodist Practice* (New York: Oxford University Press, 2014), 64.
13. Andrew B. Miller, unpublished paper on the history of Wesleyan bands, 2013.
14. Patrick Carnes, *Facing the Shadow: Starting Sexual and Relationship Recovery* (Carefree, AZ: Gentle Path Press, 2005), 152.

15. Anthony Jack, taken from his foreword to *Your Brain on Porn: Internet Pornography and the Emerging Science of Addiction* by Gary Wilson (Commonwealth Publishing, 2014), Loc. 102.
16. Dietrich Bonhoeffer, as quoted in *Surfing for God: Discovering the Divine Desire Beneath Sexual Struggle* by Michael John Cusick (Nashville, TN: Thomas Nelson, 2012), Loc. 164.

Chapter 10 Principle: Jesus and Our Perversity

1. D. A. Carson, "Matthew" in *Expositor's Bible Commentary Vol. 8*, ed. Frank E. Gaebelein (Grand Rapids, MI: Zondervan, 1984), 392.
2. Terry Wardle, *Untamed Christian, Unleashed Church: The Extravagance of the Holy Spirit in Life and Ministry* (Abilene, TX: Leafwood Publishers, 2010), 62.
3. *The Works of the Reverend John Wesley, A.M. Vol 3.* (New York, NY: J. Emory & B. Waugh, J. Collord, Printer, 1831), 134. Journal entry dated May 20, 1739.
4. Ibid., 144. Journal entry dated July 3, 1739.
5. Patrick Carnes, *Sexual Anorexia: Overcoming Sexual Self-Hatred* (Center City, MN: Hazelden, 1997), Loc. 518.
6. For a schedule of training events, visit hcminternational.org.

Chapter 11 Theology: Making the Case for Boundaries

1. Walter Wink, *Homosexuality and the Bible*. Revised version in booklet form, 1996, 13. A reprint of an article that first appeared in *The Christian Century* in 1979.
2. Jennifer Wright Knust, *Unprotected Texts: The Bible's Surprising Contradictions about Sex and Desire* (New York: HarperCollins, 2011), 244.
3. Ibid., 24.
4. Ibid., 181.
5. Ibid., 53.
6. Wink, *Homosexuality and the Bible,* 4.

7. This is, admittedly, a simplified summary of arguments. Impassioned and well-argued cases have been made that this book simply is not designed to unpack. For more thorough treatments of the varied arguments, please take note of the works by Oswalt, Wright, and Webb for thorough explanations of how to handle the passages addressing homosexuality. Yarhouse's *Homosexuality and the Christian* provides an overview of scientific research in palatable terms.

8. N. T. Wright, *Scripture and the Authority of God: How to Read the Bible Today* (New York: HarperCollins Publishers, 2011), 53.

9. As an example, see Article VI of the Doctrinal Standards as found in *The Book of Discipline of the United Methodist Church*.

10. John Oswalt, *What You Should Know about Homosexuality*, ed. Charles W. Keyser (Grand Rapids, MI: Zondervan Publishing House, 1979), 56.

11. Ibid., 59.

12. Ibid., 45.

13. William J. Webb, *Slaves, Women & Homosexuals: Exploring the Hermeneutics of Cultural Analysis* (Downers Grove, IL: InterVarsity Press, 2001), 74–75.

14. Ibid., 77–79.

15. Ibid., 250.

16. Richard Hays, *Homosexuality in the Church: Both Sides of the Debate*, ed. Jeffrey S. Siker (Louisville, KY: Westminster John Knox Press, 1994), 7.

17. Oswalt, *What You Should Know about Homosexuality*, 23.

18. Mark Yarhouse, *Homosexuality and the Christian: A Guide for Parents, Pastors, and Friends* (Minneapolis, MN: Bethany House Publishers, 2010), 60.

19. *Answers to Your Questions about Sexual Orientation and Homosexuality*, https://www.apa.org/topics/lgbt/orientation.pdf.

20. Douglas A. Abbott, "Behavioral Genetics and Homosexuality," *The Journal of Human Sexuality* 2 (2010): 67.

21. For a thorough study regarding the efficacy of treatment for same-sex attraction, see *Ex-Gays: A Longitudinal Study of*

Religiously Mediated Change in Sexual Orientation by Stanton L. Jones and Mark A. Yarhouse (Downers Grove, IL: InterVarsity Press, 2007).

22. Two excellent resources are available and listed in the Resource List: *The Meaning of Sex* by Dennis Hollinger is written from the view of a Christian ethicist. *Theology of the Body* by Christopher West provides the Roman Catholic perspective and has tremendous group resources.

23. Josef Pieper, *The Concept of Sin*, trans. Edward T. Oaks (South Bend, IN: St. Augustine's Press, 2001), 37.

Chapter 12 Application: Same-Sex Attraction and Other Variations

1. Billy Hallowell, "'Get the Hell Out': Activist's Frank Call for Military Chaplains Who Don't Support Gay Marriage and Homosexuality." http://www.theblaze.com/stories/2015/07/07 /activist-calls-for-military-chaplains-who-vocally-oppose -homosexuality-in-the-armed-forces-to-quit-or-be-terminated/.

2. Andrew Marin, *Love Is an Orientation: Elevating the Conversation with the Gay Community* (Downers Grove, IL: InterVarsity Press, 2009), 46.

3. Ibid., 31–32.

4. J. David Muyskens, *Forty Days to a Closer Walk with God: The Practice of Centering Prayer* (Nashville, TN: Upper Room Books, 2006), 26.

5. Mark Yarhouse, *Homosexuality and the Christian: A Guide for Parents, Pastors, and Friends* (Minneapolis, MN: Bethany House, 2010), 42.

6. Ibid., 51.

7. John Wesley, "A Plain Account of Christian Perfection as Believed and Taught by the Reverend Mr. John Wesley, from the Year 1725, to the Year 1777," in *John and Charles Wesley: Selected Prayers, Hymns, Journal Notes, Sermons, Letters and Treatises*, ed. Frank Whaling (New York: Paulist Press, 1981), 365.

8. John Powell, *Why Am I Afraid to Tell You Who I Am?: Insights on Self-awareness, Personal Growth and Interpersonal Communication* (Chicago, IL: Argus Communications, 1969), 54ff.
9. Chad Thompson, *Loving Homosexuals as Jesus Would: A Fresh Christian Approach* (Grand Rapids, MI: Brazos Press, 2004), 44.
10. https://en.wikipedia.org/wiki/The_Block,_Baltimore.

Epilogue "When Will This Ever End"

1. This concept is aptly illustrated in Susan Howatch's fiction, especially her book *Scandalous Risks* (New York: Fawcett Crest, 1990).
2. R. Albert Mohler, Jr., *We Cannot Be Silent: Speaking Truth to a Culture Redefining Sex, Marriage, and the Very Meaning of Right and Wrong* (Nashville, TN: Thomas Nelson, 2015), 31.
3. Richard Foster, *Streams of Living Water: Essential Practices from the Six Great Traditions of Christian Faith* (New York: HarperCollins Publishing, 1998), 185.
4. Peter Gomes, *The Good Book: Reading the Bible with Mind and Heart* (New York: Avon Books, 1996), 96.

ABOUT THE AUTHOR

Mark Ongley has more than twenty-five years of pastoral ministry experience. He currently serves part-time as pastor of Ashes to Life in Beaver Falls, Pennsylvania—a United Methodist congregation reaching out to people in recovery. In 2001, he received a DMin degree in formational counseling from Ashland Seminary with a special focus upon sexual issues. He has helped many people find healing and greater wholeness in the area of sexuality. Since 2006, he has been part of a team of counselors for the "Come Away with Me" retreats sponsored by HCM International. Through Restored Image Ministries he offers counseling, seminars, and a monthly blog, which can be found at restoredimage.org. His wife, Lauri, and their two daughters bring him joy and remind him not to take himself too seriously.